THE FAR-OFF HILLS

RITA ANTON

THE FAR-OFF HILLS

DOUBLEDAY & COMPANY, INC.
GARDEN CITY, NEW YORK

This book is dedicated to the Presentation Sisters out
of Ireland, whose loving friendship made my sojourn
in the far-off hills of Kodaikanal most enjoyable and
happy.

"Spirit of the Land," by John Moffitt, from JOURNEY TO GORAKHPUR, by
John Moffitt. Copyright © 1972 by John Moffitt. Reprinted by permission of
Holt, Rinehart and Winston, Publishers.

ISBN: 0-385-14366-4
Library of Congress Catalog Card Number 78-60282
Copyright © 1979 by Rita Anton
Printed in the United States of America

CONTENTS

The Catholic Church
Woodstock Road
Oxford
11/30/78

My dearest Rita,

In the days of St. Thomas More, forewords in books were less in favor; authors preferred an open letter from a friend. This Tudor custom seems to meet the present situation, for our long friendship, treasured by me, was fostered by a mutual love for India. I told you, first, of the plight of the outcaste Christian children of Madras, and of the funds raised in my country to improve their lot. Friends in Britain were generous, but nothing that we could attempt did as much for the outcaste Christian children as I achieved, Rita, by telling you!

As a mother of five, you had the edge, with Al and the children to help you, in rounding up friends. Contributions increased, but, more important, your zeal went far further, indeed—all the way to India. I had been to India for a month to carry our funds to Father Nevett and to see the outcaste children for myself. Mine was love at first sight; your visit, Rita, lasted much longer and has proved more fruitful not only in giving alms but by rewarding our efforts with a book.

As the grandfather by proxy of a thriving infant, I long to read The Far-off Hills. *The publisher kindly offered to send me a Xerox copy, but I am happy to wait. After all, I knew you when India was but a name, when the outcastes were just a cause, when Father Albert Nevett was little more than an earnest missionary. I met you since your return from the subcontinent, heard your lectures, gathered your impressions, read the letters of the children raised from the gutter through your zeal. Yes, you showed me your snaps and slides, and I left your home in Oak Park saddened that I had achieved so little and you so much.*

Rita, the credit is yours and the joy is mine, but we share, together, a nasty secret: that we owe all to the generosity of quiet and anonymous friends. Father Albert Nevett is a common bond, for he gave his name and administered the trust and inspired us both. You also share with me an overwhelming and enduring affection for Brigadier Patrick and Mrs. Mary Preston, both in love with India, who carried the whole burden in the early years. After these three names, the Atlantic comes between us and I mourn in private so many friends and generous supporters now dead.

You and I mourn Al, on your side of the ocean, but your figures should jump from the hundreds to the thousands as new readers catch the love of India and of the outcaste Christian children through the enthusiasm that inspired your book.

Sincerely in Christ,
Bernard Basset, S.J.

SPIRIT OF THE LAND

Out of the unaging earth,
Out of a dark, soft, immemorial
Womb—not the thick paddies only,
Not the slim herons, not the buffalo
And the calm milch cow,
The lifted palm and sturdy deodar;
Not the thatched hut, the naked boy
On the road's edge, the grain winnowed
And piled on the road; not the flowing
Woman, the jolly hawker, the clasped hands
Of brothers joined in artless affection,
The spare, orange-clad monk striding alone;
Not the close bazaars, the cozy
Lamps dotting the twilight,
The straining coolie, the round brass pot
Poised on the lithe peasant woman's
Head; not the soiled white saris
Stretched in the sun to dry;
Not all these only, but above and beyond
And through all these, the veiled
Shape, the infinite Mother brooding,
The much affronted, the reviled, the secretly
Serene—long-suffering and forgiving:
She, rising out of this earth,
Above and beyond them all—it is she,
Mysterious and benign,
Whose presence, as you thread the crowded lanes,
Stills you, holds you,
Cheers you like a healing wind.

John Moffitt, *Journey to Gorakhpur*

CHAPTER 1
Endings and Beginnings

The north woods are Octobering. A fog blanket hovers protectingly over the low marshes. Thin frost wraps the tangle of fallen leaves and logs and begins its work in the edges of the cabin windows. The last birds sound preoccupied, as if with logistics of both food and flight, and the sun, too, has fled south. But the cabin is warm. Over the fireplace (unusable because an efficient son-in-law has already sealed the top of the chimney against squirrels and chipmunks), The Largest Muskie in the World bares his teeth in eternal defiance. Years before, when Al and this behemoth engaged in epic battle on a remote Canadian lake, he had been conquered not once but twice. The muskie, in losing, had placed a permanent bend in Al's best rod during the forty-minute battle; Al got even by having him mounted and cosmetically improved for generations of grandchildren yet unborn.

I recall the small struggle Al and I had over Muskie's central position in the place of honor among our modest possessions. Al wanted him hung over the bed in our room. I demurred. He finally bore The Largest Muskie in the World to his office, where it was installed over his desk and served as silent propaganda to the prowess and genius of the occupant, and made possible an oral history that improved with the telling. Eventually we bought the cabin in the north woods and gave Muskie a fitting abode. Our first trip there was enriched with his silent disapproval, having been forcibly conveyed, wrapped in beach towels, in the back seat of the car. He was unpacked first and ceremoniously installed by means of several large nails and eye hooks in the logs over the fireplace whence he accepts homage amid the smoke that often arises there in mute adoration.

It is now nine months since Al went home to God. It happened on his birthday, December 19. The grandchildren and children had all gathered for a weekend at home to help Pop celebrate the great event. If, as Tolstoy says, all unhappy families are different in their sorrows, all happy families are the same. Our thirty-six years together had been laced with great joy and content. The five children had brought in their hands the means and end of our life together; we spent it nest building, educating, laughing, sharing, weeping and loving around a rosary of years. There had been, in time, the glint of satin, lace and silver as the two eldest girls married and our eldest son found a lovely wife. The circle of birthdays and anniversaries grew a bit wider; the table extended and filled the dining room.

On that last birthday, I arose early and announced that I was taking the three youngest grandchildren, from Clinton, down to Michigan Avenue to see Water Tower Place. They were delighted. Children around six or seven adore seeing things with Grandma. We rode up and down the glass elevator, inventoried the F. A. O. Schwartz toy store in preparation for Christmas, listened to the carols, which now sounded miraculously fresh though they had been playing since Halloween, and we had a somewhat distracted lunch at the Ritz Carlton. Home again, I noted that Al was watching TV (football) in the living room and thought it would be wise to take the kids up for a brief rest. We went up to my bed, where they removed shoes and I found a place beside them and began reading *The Little Prince*.

Tragedy entered swiftly and inexorably. Laurie came running upstairs to shout that something was wrong with Daddy. One ran to the phone for the Fire Department, another ran for the priest. I remember a frantic and silent battle on the living-room couch, where I tried mouth-to-mouth resuscitation and continued it until a strange man pulled me away and said he would take over. A large fireman pushed me into a chair in the dining room and stood over me to prevent my return. My prayers were jerky and shrill. I have no doubt that they were heard. It's just that the answer was no.

The next three months are a curious blank. I know that my answer to grief was what it has always been: work, and more work. I had a job that took much of that, and the household, the grief-stricken family, the eternal paperwork and arrangements, all were a merciful release for the pent-up emotion. I recall awakening in the night many times during that period and finding my face and pillow wet. Many times still I imagine that I hear his step in the house.

And thus my world, and my life, had been neatly sliced into two parts: the thirty-six years of life with Al, and the unknown number still left to live without him. I have never, for an instant, doubted that Al is with God, whom he loved and served all of his life. The children and I were plunged into purgatory. None of the famous Kübler-Ross attitudes toward death seemed authentic in my case. I was not bitter, or angry at God, or bewildered. I was numbed—the feeling I imagine a sharp blow on the head would induce.

The best advice (and there is much gratuitous advice offered to the new widow) seems to be this: do nothing for at least one year. This advice, of course, implied not a lack of work, for work is the salvation of the widow, but an admonition to refrain from changing life-style in any significant way until grief has done its necessary work. So the house in Oak Park and the cabin in the northern Wisconsin woods remain as they were: ours. I did sell Al's car and stored my own old Ford away for Bill, now away at college. I bought (used) a little Datsun that looks like a streamlined pumpkin and kindly cut my fuel bill neatly in half. And I remodeled the kitchen, where I had prepared meals for thirty years with never enough counter space or convenience. As a hedge against inflation, and the certain knowledge that this would add much to the value of the house, it seemed a wise thing to do. I went alone to family parties and learned to speak of Al with a grin on my face, rather than spread the agony. And life, it seemed, went on in a strangely crippled way, like a mockery of what it had been before.

Eventually, of course, it is wise to try for an evening of entertainment outside the dim glow of the TV screen. I decided to see *Pippin*, a much-touted musical then cavorting at the Shubert. Thirty-six years of purchasing tickets for all events led me to the phone on the night of the experiment, and when I discovered I could have a single if I came down before the performance and picked it up, I coordinated myself into white tie and black velvet and drove downtown to the box office two hours before show time. The single seat was $14.50, first balcony, center. It seemed extravagant, but in the general aura of a give-the-cat-the-canary-ism, I bought it and strolled over to the Palmer House to complete the interim wait. Don the

Beachcomber was drawing the usual crowd of youngsters in long gowns and new corsages and preshave escorts in suit coats two sizes too small. I sipped white wine in the Polynesian dark, meditating on the fact that as far as the habitués of the Beachcomber were concerned, my presence was, if not invisible, inadvisable.

Fortified with sugarless gum, I negotiated the stairs at the Shubert and found my perch in the aviary. The show was a bang-bang loud ballet with coarse and suspiciously unlaundered costumes, and while not conspicuously blasphemous enough to insure immortality, ill conceived and stillborn enough to bore on a colossal scale. Pippin is called upon, as the final scene is played, to respond to a question about his miniature psyche. The interlocutor (a black chorus man who keeps popping up throughout the proceedings) asks him how he feels. "Trapped," squeaks Pippin. I knew the feeling. The entire audience seemed to share it. Some had paid $17.50 to be trapped for the evening.

The experiment was a success. The parking garage cost $4.25. The wine was $3.80, plus the tip, and a quarter to the lady who sold me a paper towel in the washroom. This, with the $14.50 ticket, to say nothing of the gum and the gas to get me there and home, comes to roughly $25.00. A small amount, one might say, to learn finally that there is something more desirable in life than what the world calls entertainment.

But here, in this chilly cabin, where November has begun to find its way through the bare trees and is nearly visible over the gray waters of Garth Lake, I have reached a time of rebirth. The second part of my life is before me, a tiny infant just born in nine months of silent work and pain. It is new, wrapped in a soft blanket, and only God knows whom it will resemble. Perhaps no one who ever lived before this time. It is my plan for the rest of my life. Perhaps it will be spent on the other side of the earth. In southern India.

*　　*　　*

There is, in the Western Ghats of southern India, high up, at 7,500 feet, a lovely little town called Kodaikanal. I saw it first in 1971, when I visited there with Father Albert Nevett, S.J., a missionary with whom I had worked for a number of years securing sponsors for his plan to educate outcaste children. Kodai was a kind of resting spot in the journey around India, where we could get our clothing washed and our minds rested from the continual round of planes, trains, rickshaws and carts that made up our travel for some seven weeks. We approached Kodai by bus, hanging from the conveniently placed brass bar on the seat directly in front because it's the only way to steady oneself during that perilous climb into the mountains. Lumbering past teak forests, coffee plantations, little bustees where villagers squatted in huts and waved us on, up, up into monkeyland, where strange birds and beasts roamed in towering forests, past Shembaganur, the Jesuit seminary where Father Nevett had spent many years of study and prayer, and finally into Kodaikanal, at the top of the run.

I had stayed at the Carlton Hotel in 1971. A matchstick old dragon that stretched over a couple of hillocks, the Carlton offered a room with a fireplace, a boy to build a fire each afternoon, decently cooked meals leaning heavily on fish and vegetables in a dining room where the turbaned waiters outnumbered the diners. The main part of the town edged up to a lake of just the right dimensions, and the entire area was one of peace, beauty, exotic flowering shrubs, waterfalls, and a populace neatly divided between American Protestant missionaries and natives who seemed much stronger and more energetic than those of the plains. Father Nevett stayed with the Jesuits, who had a house called La Providence there, and walked with me over every square inch of the territory, recounting the local history and legend of the place.

As a young seminarian, some forty years before, he had often come to Kodaikanal from Shembaganur, one thousand feet below. One of the stunts of those days was the all-day picnic, when the seminarians would pack up food, frying pans and water jugs and, tucking their white habits into their belts, climb twelve miles to the hills beyond Kodai, cook their lunch, rest, talk and dream together, and then scramble down to Shembag again at dusk. So he knew the place well. He introduced me to the nuns at Holy Cross Orphanage, where he was educating some children, showed me how to get to La Salette, the incredibly lovely little church where I heard Mass sung by the entire congregation in Tamil, kneeling on a wood-plank floor. It was there I encountered an embarrassment. When Mass was over, I stumbled on my numbed legs to the vestibule and waited there for the congregation to emerge. Fifteen minutes passed, and I was the only one outside. Finally I tiptoed in again.

"What are they waiting for?" I asked a lady with a baby near the back of the church. "Will there be benediction?"

"No, madam," she whispered, smiling. "They are making their thanksgiving after Communion."

Kodai, I hope, is still much the same today. I don't think it's the place James Hilton had in mind when he wrote *Lost Horizon*, but it will do. I will return there now, as a kind of experiment, to see if I can find a life there for half the year in each of my second set.

Longevity rates in my family run high. My grandmother died at ninety-six. Mother, at eighty-three, is still comparatively healthy. And I, at fifty-seven, probably have another thirty or thirty-five years ahead of me. The little store of possessions Al and I had left after our major investment in children will have to stretch over those years somehow. I know I will have to change my life drastically so that this can be. My tiny income from the job that paid me more in satisfaction and achievement than in wages cannot now sustain me. In Kodai I can live a simple and comfortable life for six months of the year on about two hundred dollars per month. And I will be able to save enough to return home to Oak Park for the other six months. It will make possible a life where prayer, service, writing and thought may be easier, and still keep me in touch with the most precious people on earth to me, my children and grandchildren. I'm going to try.

So I wrap up the lamps in the cabin with plastic bags, empty the refrigerator and defrost it. I pack all the breakable food containers and put moth balls in the mattresses. I clean the cabin one last time for the season and sweep the gathering leaves from the doorway. I lock the door and say good-bye until next May. It will hibernate for the winter, like the bears in the woods. Deer will come and nibble on the young shoots left in the garden, and snow will rise to the window ledges. I will remember it from far away in the Western Ghats of southern India, where flowers will bloom and birds will sing while snow covers this quiet little cabin.

CHAPTER 2

What to Do till the Passport Comes

The journey was planned for early February, to allow time for the proper celebration of Christmas and to permit an interval of time in which to prepare the house, find a replacement for my job, and make the necessary arrangements in India via the slow mails.

Christmas, which had always been the peak of our year, was now approached by the family with an air of vague apprehension. Al was not going to be sitting near the large tree on Christmas Eve, handing out presents to the assembled family and warming the house and the holiday with his great laugh, or pasting red and green bows from opened packages on the dogs' fur. No one could quite conjure up Christmas without him. Changing the pattern seemed not only prudent but imperative. I announced a Christmas journey to Orlando to give the grandchildren a few days of Disney World, and we spent several weeks pondering details.

Laurie was pregnant and didn't want to travel. She elected to come to Oak Park with Ed and her two youngest, and keep house there and visit friends while relinquishing her two eldest, Sean and Dan, to me for the trip. Ann and Paul would drive to Florida with their sons, Peter and Mark, while Laura, not a notable success at long-distance car rides, would fly with me. Barbara, my twenty-six-year-old daughter, made the fifth in our plane party. Two days after Christmas, we flew down to the land of sun and oranges and settled in a motel to await the driving contingent. By midnight, Ann and Paul's LTD snuggled up to the motel, and we were all united in three adjoining rooms.

Next morning, we drove to Disney World in a snake of cars that stretched, it seemed, back to Chicago. But nothing could dim the sunny day, or the excitement of the children as we approached wonderland and hooked up with the welcoming committee via the car radio.

I don't know how social historians will rank him, but Walt Disney was surely one of America's greatest sons. If noble men are distinguished by the degree of happiness they spread about during a lifetime, Disney qualifies in the top rank. I have not seen his establishment in California, but the first impression at Orlando is that of a vast, unqualified joy. Every age group can be seen strolling down Main Street, poking about the Victorian shops, purchasing and *wearing* silly hats. Elderly dowagers clutch balloons with fierce concentration, while their life partners, in old golf togs, chase grandchildren down lanes leading to their own childhood dreams. And everywhere, from the signposts to the buildings themselves, from the benches to the trash cans, an unmistakable quality is obvious. Each item used in Disneyworld is the very best of its kind. Leaded glass, bronze chandeliers, wrought iron and enduring stone and mosaic proclaim the permanence of this fantasy. This is no wandering circus that will disappear in some morning mist. Disney World is here to stay, and will, perhaps sad to say, outlive the orange groves.

The kids loved it. The first day, we tried to stay together, savoring as a family the Small World, the Hall of Presidents, the cable-car ride and a bright bunch of lollipop adventures. By eight in the evening we threw in the sponge and retired to showers and bed rest. The following day, Ann got us all up at six—to the fairland by seven —and this time we split into compatible groups with complex plans for hourly rendezvous and meals for which advance reservations were made. It worked out fine. I skipped off with Dan, and we boarded the paddle boat for a leisurely glimpse of Tom Sawyer's world. We cable-carred over to Tomorrow Land and peered at the improbable world to come. We ate tacos and watched a man blow Mickey Mice in glass, and bought some. And we met back at the Hospitality House in time for the parade.

Christmas is perhaps the only holiday that permits Disney World to pull out all the stops. The parade was a marvel. Bands played better than any Fourth of July, and I glanced around with deep pride in a loving family. I noted a handsome young man about twenty feet down the veranda, wearing a brown leather jacket. He resembled my son Sarge, I thought, and was mentally chiding myself for softening of the brain when I looked more carefully. It *was* Sarge. He had awakened at 3 A.M., and unable to go back to sleep, had driven to the airport and boarded the first available flight to Orlando to join us. It was a terrific treat. After the parade, he took Sean and Dan off for a day they will always remember. We spent a total of twenty-five hours in this paradise, and topped it off with an enormous phosphate of fireworks, one of the best of a lifetime. It was a good Christmas.

But, home again, once the tree was down and the ornaments and decorations packed away, many items called for attention. My job as administrator at the Center for Pastoral Ministry had to be filled by a new person as yet unidentified, and a job description had to be written for her guidance. It turned out to be a mini-book of thirty pages.

The Center for Pastoral Ministry is a continuing-education facility for those engaged in ministry in the Archdiocese of Chicago. There are mainly priests, but in response to the emerging Vatican II Church, many women religious and lay people are also part of the scene. The Reverend James Roache is the founding father and director. In the past eight years, he has gathered a staff of people who are remarkably versatile and talented. Father Frank Kane is in charge of pastoral training, in addition to his duties as associate pastor at St. Nicholas of Tolentine. He also oversees the tape library, a growing collection of cassette tapes of the Center's programs, which are lent out to those interested in increasing their knowledge of a wide range of topics from Scripture through Moral Theology. Father Wayne Prist is in charge of television production, as well as creating and directing the Summer Scripture Seminar, one of the best of its kind in America. Now in its fourth season, this year the SSS would include in its program two weeks of study in Israel. With his gifted associate, Dr. Dolores Nicosia, Father Prist has gathered an appreciative audience of Scripture scholars from all over America, many of whom come every summer to participate. Father Prist is also associate pastor of St. John Berchman's. Father MacDonald also conducts a seminar on moral theology each summer, in addition to his parish work.

Father Roache, in addition to his task of directing CPM, was also Cardinal Cody's communications secretary, associate pastor at Holy Name Cathedral and chaplain at the Rehabilitation Center of Wesley Memorial Hospital. So the success of CPM is clearly based on the truism that if you want something done well, ask a busy man to do it. Certainly these gifted priests have learned the skills of time organization and allotment. Their performance demonstrates the canny wisdom that selected and decreed that they work together. But nothing except grace and the Holy Spirit can account for the joyful and wholehearted gift they make of their lives. The Center is a great place, where beautiful things happen, and where the welcome mat is a permanent fixture.

So I wrote a manual, labeled everything in the storeroom, tried to anticipate shortages in supplies by reordering, and wrote endless notes. The day of departure drew near and finally came, crowned by a lovely luncheon at the Arts Club (Father Prist had prudently become a member) and tender farewells all around.

My evenings were occupied with packing, measuring, weighing and repacking. I knew I would need clothing for both heat and cold, that I would need supplies for writing, a typewriter, kitchen stuff for the rented house, bedding, towels, some books, and, of course, a valid passport and updated medical record.

January of 1978 was one of the worst months in eighty years of bad climate. It flew by. The little Datsun performed well on dry streets but proved to be a three-season car in Chicago. Winters are just too much for it. I resigned myself to being stuck on three-inch rises in driveways and to relying on the impersonal muscle of strangers daily to get me to and from work. It was with a rueful sigh of relief that I had the salt washed off the Datsun's handsome coral skin and a coat of hot wax applied, and then drove it into the garage for a well-deserved three-month sleep.

The income tax, property tax and odious bills were a painful bundle of thistles still awaiting my touch to weave them into a rug of paid receipts. The household was tightened up, and Barb was treated to a gratuitous series of lectures on a wide range of topics, from the sump pump in the basement, to which plumber to call for emergencies. I wrote a book-size manual for the maintenance of the house, and another for the Nevett Fund. Father Nevett, sitting atop a snowbank in Darjeeling, sent requests for hearing-aid batteries, camera batteries and lenses, and other small things, which I was happy to send but which had to be found and purchased, wrapped and shipped to India. The phone at home rang constantly as more friends got wind of what was referred to as "your interesting experiment." I developed a short talk, which outlined the plan, described

Kodai, gave a brief history of India and of the Nevett Fund and asked for prayers.

It is perhaps not surprising that I caught a beaut of a cold, and the doctor refused to inoculate me for typhoid or cholera till it was better. The final shot was administered three days before departure, which insured that I carried a very sore arm all the way to India.

At length, as they say in the books, all was in readiness. My purse was stuffed, my bags had been inventoried so often I knew the contents of each by heart. All five of them. A week before departure I took three of them to the O'Hare Pan Am cargo office and made a large sign of the cross over them, praying to meet them again in Madras. I said good-bye to so many so often, I began to think of myself as the Goodbye Girl.

CHAPTER 3

Getting There Is Half the Fun

Though normally appreciative and even eager for the subtle, ever-changing face of reality, I require very little novelty from plane trips. I prefer them to be boring and monotonous. Life itself supplies enough variety and surprise; I never board a plane hoping to find adventure. It if wearies me beyond telling, I consider the flight a huge success. This one falls in the Academy Award class. My nether regions, confined in an aisle seat of the 747, numbed and inactive from February 9 until the wee hours of February 11, are only now beginning to return to life. A kind Providence awarded me an aisle seat that was also an isle seat, since no one was placed next to me, though the plane was overcrowded by 747 standards, due to the snowstorm that had closed down Kennedy Airport the day before. I can recall 747 flights to Europe on which one could play baseball in the tourist section and endanger no passengers. During this flight, I read Agatha Christie's *Curtain* and did not guess the identity of the killer until she revealed it. I also watched two Korean businessmen work throughout an entire night on mysterious papers that seemed to be the themes of some class in higher math, using Korean characters for the formulas. Calm, buddha-like, and infinitely attentive to this task, the two black heads remained bowed over sheaves of paper that they restored to attaché cases only as we approached London. A large group of tourists across the aisle chirped softly in Spanish, and blessed each landing and takeoff with huge signs of the cross. I appreciated those prayers but could only smile and nod. A very handsome couple from the group, deciding I was *simpático*, passed a photo across to me, showing a crowd of beautiful young Mexicans standing on wrought-iron stairs in a tastefully decorated Mexican room. There seemed to be eleven or twelve people, reaching all the way to the top of the staircase. It was a beautiful sight, and I was about to conclude that it was some club or organization when the man said proudly, "My home—my family—twelve children." I longed, privately, for someone from the Birth Control League to see that photograph and then to look across and see that beautiful couple, still young enough to travel, holding hands at each takeoff, secure in the love of God and the secret of what life was all about.

At London I changed position long enough to make the dash to the duty-free store and buy some scotch and wine for my Indian friends and pay more for them than at home. But when we at length arrived at Delhi, at 2 A.M., I was very happy to have that large Cutty Sark as a gift to Father Joe Willmes who met my plane and spent the next four hours with me, dealing with the mysteries of Indian air travel. He is the brother of Father Robert Willmes, S.J., a dear and cherished friend, who is one of the directors of Jesuit Missions in Chicago. I thanked God for my foresight, though it had pried this good Jesuit from bed in the middle of the night to meet my plane. He gave no sign of the inconvenience of a lost night of sleep and graciously carried my luggage around Delhi Airport, finding all the clues of the game amusing and even interesting, though it surely was a strain on his charity. As we chatted of Chicago and brother Robert, and sipped Indian coffee that was every bit as bad as I had remembered it, I had a chance to breathe again the air of India and to see through the airport windows the dusty, irretrievable shabbiness that I remembered so well.

Nothing in Indian officialdom had changed, I noted with grim amusement. It still took three or four men to do a simple job that would have provided scant challenge for a fourteen-year-old kid. Customs and passport checks finished, higher negotiations with the bearer completed (one had to pay his superior, not him, the two-rupee fee, which was discussed in Hindi by the two for a full five minutes), I retaliated by privately slipping the bearer another two rupees, the equivalent of about a quarter, which seemed to agonize his delicate conscience strangely. He furtively pocketed the princely gift and ran from me.

But having set foot again on Indian soil was for me a tremendous thrill. In spite of every reasonable impulse that prefers efficiency, comfort, cleanliness and understanding, I am hopelessly in love with this country. Probably something in the genes. An old man told me once that I had been a Tibetan in a former life. He's wrong. I must have been a Tamilian. I can't explain it, even to myself. All I know is, having landed in the most exasperating and maddening land on earth, I found myself young, filled with vigor, eager for the challenge the next five minutes would surely provide, and loving it.

This new ardor was somewhat dimmed by the discovery that Mother India had found a new way to rip off the unsuspecting traveler to her shores. International regulations now permit air travelers to carry (by whatever means: derrick, block and tackle) two pieces of luggage, which can weigh as much as seventy-seven pounds each, provided they do not exceed the combined dimensions of 107 inches total. Mine were marvels of exactitude. They measured in inches the exact figure, and weighed in at about 110 pounds combined. In America, Pan Am accepted them as baggage without turning a hair. It remained for Delhi to suddenly change the game plan and charge me a whacking $19.50 to put them on their plane to Madras. I was stunned but not surprised. If one realizes that this practice, carried on for a period of time, could easily build a new and badly needed airport, one glimpses the rationale behind this robbery. There is no way the traveler can decide to send back half of his luggage to America. He's going to need his stuff to survive. He pays through the nose and begins his Indian stay without the smile of welcome one so longs to find after a long journey. His purse, not his heart, is lightened.

Father Willmes, a gentleman to the core, saw me off at 6:30 A.M. without yawning once. Someday I hope to be able to repay his thoroughly Christian and Jesuit kindness.

The flight to Madras was standard Indian fare. The plane had been built long ago, and not cleaned since, but was graced by a movie-star-type Indian male steward and several young goddesses in saris, who served juice, excellent scrambled eggs, coffee and anise seeds. The passengers were mostly male, wearing the dhoti (a long sheet tied around the waist) with western suit coats, and all carrying attaché cases. I was the only American on board, and came in for a lot of attention from the assembly, who pilgrimaged past my aisle seat to get a look at that strange breed, the American lady tourist. I tried to give satisfaction but have no way of knowing whether or not I was up to standard. One of the goddesses came to me after breakfast and bent down with her hand cupped for privacy. "Was the coffee any good?" she asked.

I assured her it was excellent. It was. The remainder of the flight evolved into a small struggle to discourage the first fly I had seen since last August, which was also making the journey to Madras.

Outside the left window I was thrilled to see the Indian dawn.

CHAPTER 4

Madras

Madras was a most welcome sight. Having left winter behind in New York and having passed through a very brisk spring in Delhi, I stepped from the plane into the full bloom of summer. The brief struggle with hand luggage was forgotten as I began the game of dealing with porters again and trying to identify which ramp my bags were likely to arrive on. Porter #43 got my baggage checks and waited for the bags while I looked over the welcoming committee to see if I could identify which of the fifty young men there might be Brother Aloysius. It took only seconds. Since I was the only white lady on board, Brother found me. He brought me notes from Father Varaprasadam and Brother Paranjothi, and together we began a high-level conference on how to find my three bags, which had been shipped ahead to Madras on February 1. Pan Am had assured me they would take four days to reach Madras, so it seemed reasonable to assume they would be in the station cargo room, as this was February 11. Brother Aloysius and I began the rites of passage known only to India. We inquired the exact location of the cargo room of Indian Airlines. It was down the road. Ascending two flights of stairs, we entered a room where some men at a desk were discussing last night's fête. We succeeded in getting their attention long enough for one of them to search through a large ledger for my claim number. Long minutes passed. Finally he said, "Madam, your luggage is not here. Probably it has come on Air India. You just go over there and ask them. If not, phone us in the afternoon around 4 P.M., because another flight is in later today, and they could be on that one."

Brother Aloysius and I began searching for Air India's cargo room, and at length we found it to be innocent of my luggage. We thought the bags might be in customs in the station, so we trekked back there. This time a little man in brown clothing and bare feet, who looked official, led me through a labyrinth of corridors, up some stairs into another small, hot room where a party of young men were discussing last night's fête. This time I did not wait for the punch line but began my recital to the most imposing fellow present. He referred me to the man next to him and resumed his funny story. The second man again asked me all that I had just related, in his hearing, to the first man. I produced my receipt with the magic numbers on it, and asked if my bags might be there. He assured me they were not, and suggested we try both Indian Airlines and Air India. Brother Aloysius and I exchanged potent glances. We decided to return to our waiting cab and go on to the hotel, where I could continue my campaign in air-conditioned comfort, by phone. I did not realize at that time that, in India, no business is ever successfully conducted by phone.

Outside the airport, a slim young man in a white cassock came toward us. It was Kanikairaj, whose ordination I planned to attend in April. He had been waiting at the airport to greet me since eight-thirty. It was now ten-thirty but he gave no sign of irritation or impatience. We explained the dilemma in the cab en route to the Connemara, and he made all the traditional and polite inquiries about the family at home.

At the Connemara, a comfortable old-fashioned hotel where I had always stayed while in Madras, the service and promise of cool air made registration assume a festive air. In the lobby to greet me was Winifride Douglas, friend of Ann Marten of Chicago, who had been delegated by Ann to book a room for me there. From the moment we met, I knew I had found that rare and priceless jewel, a true friend. She was slender and cool in her simple cotton dress and sandals, and her graying hair was cropped in a very becoming bob. Blue eyes that crinkled into smiles proclaimed the compassion and charity that signaled the dedicated soul. She is English—London-born—and has been in India twenty-six years. We found the room very comfortable, the air conditioning working, the hot water flowing, and a general air of cozy comfort after our harrowing morning. I ordered some tea and sandwiches, and the four of us sat awhile and got acquainted. I told Winnie of the lost luggage, and she immediately went to the phone and in very proper British made a few phone calls. These drew a blank, but apparently whetted her appetite for the hunt. This kind of tracing is obviously a great game in India. Everyone with any spirit or spunk gets into it with rolled-up sleeves and a heart of courage for the ordeal. Winnie made some notes of phone numbers for me to try later, and we began to talk of her work in India.

Some twenty-six years ago, the Archbishop of Madras, desirous of opening a Catholic center that would be run by lay people, wrote to Winnie and invited her to come as the first administrator and founder of his center. She came, and six months later Lore Termehr also answered the call, from Germany. The two of them have been a very important part of Catholic life in Madras ever since. The Archbishop apparently was a man who thought big (heeding the advice I heard the priests at the Center state: "Make no small plans"). For the Catholic Center, which I visited the following day, is no cozy little storefront. It occupies the better part of a city block in Madras and resembles City Hall. One corner of it houses a very large bank, and the offices of many important businesses rent space there. The revenue derived from these rentals gives the Catholic Center its funds for the work of charity and education it has accomplished since its founding.

Winnie, perhaps noting my half-closed eyes, decreed that I have a nap, and she gently but firmly conducted an exodus from my quarters, with an invitation to dinner that evening. "I'll pick you up here at 6 P.M.," she said. "Now go to bed and get some rest. You must be half dead."

I was glad to obey. I had been on planes for the past twenty-six hours, casing air cargo rooms for another three, and waiting in line with tiny slips of paper in my hand for the rest of the time since February 9. It was now February 11; I was safely in Madras, for which I most sincerely thanked God, and in the hands of one who obviously knew what she was about. I slept the sleep of air travelers who have found a bed at last.

At six o'clock Winnie knocked on the door and drew me out into her world. We caught a cab in front of the hotel and held a somewhat distracted conversation while I caught my breath and clutched at my throat, closing my eyes against the scene framed in the windshield. The Madras cab driver is half matador and half Indianapolis-

500 aspirant. The first half is quite useful, since most of his adversaries are either bulls or cows; in his skillful maneuvering of the small and ancient car is some of the bravado of the flashing red cape. The only ingredient missing is the roar of the crowd. No one notices his skill and daring (except the cowering occupant of the back seat). Encounters like this are daily routine for the locals. We flew along, on the wrong side of the road for me, gaily missing lorries, bullock carts, pedestrians, bicycle rickshaws and small children, while I, finally determined not to notice, trained my eyes on Winnie and told her of my immediate plans. When I mentioned I had to leave for Madurai on Monday, she said, "You haven't confirmed that flight yet?" I had not, so she spoke to the driver in rapid Tamil, causing him to execute a wide turn, midstream, in the crowded street; we were in front of the Indian Airlines office, and all flights must be rewritten and confirmed there. I had forgotten that quaint custom. I had a confirmation on every flight before leaving America. India has her own method, however, and simply joins this patch to the large crazy quilt called "the inscrutable East." So I alighted in front of the Indian Airlines office and entered a room where a long counter was being tended by two or three Indians, and sat down to wait. Eventually a very efficient and polite young woman issued me the proper ticket for Madurai and corrected the flight times I had previously been given. It made me wish every official in India were a woman. I thanked her, and entered the Madras traffic stream again with Winnie. We found the Catholic Center, and I had time to ponder its massive size and imposing façade when we were inside and on our way to the quarters where Lore Termehr waited for us.

Lore is very well known in Madras. She combines the German intelligence and prudence with a Christ-filled spirit. The combination has been tremendously beneficial to India. Her influence and work are well known throughout the city, and her approval is sought by bishops and clergy for any plans that will promote social justice or the welfare of the people. We had a short tour of the simple living quarters, which spoke of poverty mixed with the feminine talent for homemaking. A lovely little roof terrace filled with beautiful plants and flowering shrubs provided a setting for conversation and rest high above the crowded road, and we sat there in the beautiful warm evening discussing the Indian Church and the vast amount of work still ahead. A crescent moon lit the sky, and billions of diamond stars twinkled overhead, like the eyes of angels. I felt again the great good fortune of having met a special soul gifted with the canny wisdom the Christian needs to make her selfless dreams reality.

The three of us went to dinner at the Ganga Restaurant for an excellent vegetarian meal. I am well on the way to adopting this way of eating for life. There are so many interesting ways of cooking vegetables and fruits, and meat in India is both difficult to store and limited in variety. Three months here would give me ample opportunity to get a good start on a vegetarian diet. I told them of my experiment in living. Both were very reassuring on the chances of successful adaptation. They both plan to live out their days in India. Lore even brought her old mother here, where she spent six happy years in a little villa in the hills before she died a beautiful death at eighty-six years. Her final illness was comforted by liturgy and the gentle care of the sisters. It sounded to me like a clue for my own mother, who, in her eighties, is nearly totally blind. I had some hope of bringing her to India if the experiment succeeded. The family at home had been dubious of this plan, believing that mother would soon tire of a strange environment and ask to be returned home. It would be impossible to return home more than once a year. Could mother take this life? I would try to assess that as I went along. Lore's experience certainly made it seem not only possible but desirable.

The following day was Sunday, and I went for Mass to the Church of St. Francis Xavier, where Kanikairaj was deacon. The parish had just celebrated its one hundredth birthday, and a beautiful new grotto had been built and dedicated the evening before. The compound around the church still bore flags and palm decorations, and in the sand were the footprints of the thousands who had attended the event. As I awaited the English Mass, at nine-fifteen, I had an opportunity to stand in the shaded portico and listen to the Tamil Mass in progress. Strong and melodious voices lifted in song throughout the service. St. Francis Xavier Parish is staffed by the Salesian Fathers and is two thousand strong. I took some sound movies to catch the singing, and then went to sit in the shaded waiting room near the sisters' convent. On the wall there, a poster proclaimed the Holy Childhood and offered a poem:

> Where do smiles come from?
> Sunny and pure—
> Down from the eyes of Mary, I'm sure.

Where do smiles go to
Once they've been given?
Under Mary's mantle
Way up in heaven.

Pondering the sweet unlikelihood of the poem, I was suddenly a
girl again, back in boarding school in Iowa and immersed in a world
of piety and devotion to Christ and loyal love for His mother. How
long ago it seemed! Some thirty-six years have passed; Marian devotion peaked and declined, and the world is strangely poorer.

The Mass at nine-fifteen was in English, and I knelt in the pew
(on the women's side of the church, the left) and watched in awe as
hundreds of parishioners went around the church touching the feet
of the statues in reverent petition. The little shrine of Mary was particularly favored. It looked like the May altar at school years ago. My
eyes filled with tears.

Kanikairaj was a most reverent deacon, his voice clear and precise.
He is going to be a good priest, filled with a desire to serve Christ
and His poor. It was worth coming to India for just that experience
of seeing the finished product of one of our scholarships.

After mass, Kanikairaj took me to the priests' house and introduced me to the pastor and his associates, and to the priests who
come to this busy parish on Sundays to help with masses. I was
served tea in a shaded room with a little garden outside, where many
of Kanikairaj's friends came, one by one, to meet his friend from
America. Brother Julian, a close friend, joined us on the ride back to
the Catholic Center, where Winnie and Lore took charge of my program again.

At the School for the Deaf and Blind, where I visited Sister Stella,
an old friend, who was in charge of the best workroom in Madras,
we had a fine lunch with the sisters. Sister Stella showed me her
beautiful new workroom, gift of Misereor, a German charitable organization, built a year ago. It is very spacious and has living quarters
for her needleworkers on the second floor. The work she has done in
India is phenomenal. Coming from Belgium at the age of forty, with
experience only in office work, she found herself in charge of the
deaf and dumb. She did not know how to communicate with them
and had never held a needle in her hand. Yet today she has a "family"
of deaf and dumb women who have been trained by her to do exqui-

site needlework that is much in demand by Indian ladies of fashion, who order embroidered saris. The workroom creates table linen and baby clothing, as well as ornate linen handkerchiefs. Most of the work is done to order. People bring their fabric and a design, and Sister Stella and her deaf and dumb girls do the rest. But this is far more than a successful workroom. This is a true family, where love, consideration for one another and a shared love for Christ are the keynotes of the community. Mass at this convent is one of the most touching and beautiful I have ever attended. I remember still the first time I came to India and attended Mass said by Father Nevett for this convent. The chapel is dark and cool, with the altar in the middle of a high-ceilinged room. No kneelers or pews mar the lovely simplicity of the polished floor. The rich color of bright flowers and birds seen through the high open windows are decoration enough. Sunshine streamed in that morning, I recall, as Father Nevett, tall and straight in his white Gothic chasuble, offered Mass for the women of the school. These knelt around the altar on the floor, their saris making white pools around them, with varied colored bands denoting their rank within the convent. A sister stood next to Father and made the signs with her hands that communicated the message of the gospel to the deaf worshipers, and the air of complete repose and stillness, broken only by birdsong from the trees just outside, made an experience of ineffable beauty I shall never forget.

I had arranged for Sister Stella to make a set of vestments for Kanikairaj's forthcoming ordination, as well as some clothing for myself. These things she produced. The clothing for me was exquisitely done, as usual, with hand smocking around collar and cuffs. The vestments, Sister explained, could not be done in the workroom in time, because she had been ill. She had, however, purchased a set from Bombay, bearing beautiful Indian symbols down a center panel of red velvet: the lotus, chalice, wheat and grapes, embroidered in gold thread against white silk. I was delighted with them, and knew that Kanikairaj would be too. It was to be a surprise for him. I also purchased a fragile set of table mats in linen, with Florentine cutwork around the edges. I simply could not pass them up. Perhaps they will wind up in Barbara's trousseau.

In the evening, Winnie and Lore and I went to visit Winnie's home, a two-story building surrounded by a wall, behind which bloomed a fragrant garden. I am not sure whether it was the English talent with gardens or the lush Indian climate that made it so perfect. On the stone walls, poinsettias, bougainvillea and other flowering shrubs clung, laden with pink and coral blooms. Paths had been marked, so one walked through an outdoor conservatory of species I had previously seen only in hothouse conditions. There were palms as well, a banana tree, a lime tree and a huge coconut palm with many fruits. Tucked into an ancient wall, a little shrine of Our Lady proclaimed in whose care this garden flourished.

The house was a quiet sanctuary of high rooms and shaded places for study and reflection. On the mantle was a decorated card of blue, which I recognized as the work of Ann Marten, who loves to print verses and Psalms and decorate notepaper this way. It was good to see her work in this peaceful setting. Winnie uses the place as a training center for girls involved in the lay apostolate. On the second floor, a tranquil chapel was separated from a study area by a pierced shesham-wood screen. In one corner a most unusual statue of Our Lady stands on a black marble pedestal. The tabernacle contains the Eucharist, by special permission, and before it, one can sit on low bamboo stools for prayer and meditation. All my life, I have wished for a chapel in my own home. Winnie has it; it is clearly the center of her life and work.

Winnie's small brown dog, Lassie, came slowly from a dim corner to greet us, and gave me quite a shock. She was the reincarnation of our own Lassie, the first dog Al and I had when we were first married. This Lassie was a bit taller, but that was the only discernible difference. The same warm eyes, the same alert ears, smooth coat and curled tail were there before me, after an absence of thirty years.

We visited Aikiya Alayam, the Dialogue Center built by the Jesuits and opened recently. En route, we met the priest in charge, Father Ignatius Hirudayam, S.J., a venerable, bearded Indian with a black patch over his left eye. He rode with us to Aikiya Alayam, and thus I entered the Center with its founder and director. We passed under the portico, which proclaimed its dedication to Roberto di Nobili, the great Jesuit who is known not only as the father of Tamil prose but as the originator in India of the missionary attitude called "adaptation." Passing under this portico reminded me once again of the question I had been asking in Madras: Was there any truth to the rumor that the Brahmins claimed to know the present whereabouts to the tomb of Di Nobili, long considered lost? I put the question to Father Ignatius. "Is it true that someone has come to the Archbishop with such a claim?"

Father Ignatius nodded his head. "Yes, it is," he replied.

I was quite excited. "What does the Archbishop think of it?" I asked.

"The Archbishop thinks of nothing else" was the surprising answer. This seemed curious; I noticed Winnie and Lore exchange glances. Sensing a mystery, I probed a bit further. "What about it, Father? Is there anything in it?"

A strange and troubled little silence followed. Then, sensing that I would not give up easily, Winnie related with some reluctance the story which is well known in Madras.

Some time ago a man came to the Archbishop with the information that the Hindu Brahmins of the temple in Madras had discovered an old tomb on their premises that was the burial place of Roberto di Nobili, who died in 1656. Di Nobili had come to India in 1606 as a Jesuit missionary. He was the son of an important family in Rome, nephew of the great Cardinal di Nobili, and cousin of Cardinal Francesco Sforza. He was related to two Popes, he owned property in Rome, Monte Pulciano and Vivitella, he was handsome and intelligent. Yet he chose to become a missionary priest to India and do great things there for the service of the Lord. He set out for India from Portugal in 1604, and his own account of the voyage from Portugal to Goa, written to Marquis Don Gregorio Boncompagni is worth retelling, as it is given in Father Rajamanickam's book *The First Oriental Scholar*:

We left Portugal with a favourable wind in 1604. Our fleet consisted of five large transports. Three of them were compelled by bad weather to return to Lisbon, another struck against a reef near the African coast and capsized, many lives being lost. The ship of the Viceroy on which he received us with the greatest kindness, after running many dangers, reached Mozambique.

The favorable winds which accompanied us from the time of our departure from Portugal drove us southward as far as the 8th degree of North Latitude where we were delayed by the calms of the torrid zone, so called because of the excessive heat caused by the sun's direct rays. After travelling about eight degrees in that intense heat we reached the Equator . . . but by the grace of God no one perished. We thus reached the Cape of Good Hope famous for its dreadful storms and shipwrecks. We found the sea very calm, which is very rare in those parts, for Africa forms there an angle which juts into the Austral seas where the two oceans which bathe the Eastern and Western coast of Africa meet, and are continually churned by contrary winds so that it is extremely rare to find there a serene sky. From the Cape we sailed to Mozambique, a small island which, if we count all the detours is situated 4000 leagues from Portugal and 900 from India.

When we were eight leagues from that island, we nearly lost our lives by running into a sand bank, the worst thing that can happen to a ship. The mast was broken and the rudder torn away, so that there was no hope of escape. The horror of a dark night, and the dismal lamentations of the passengers, added to the general anguish. The men began to think of their souls and according to their opportunity and means tried to make a good confession so as to secure their eternal salvation. However by God's mercy, after midnight, the rising tide rescued us from those shallows. Reaching Mozambique in September we remained there five months, so that although the voyage to the Indies takes only six months, the calms and storms we had gone through had caused us such a delay that (we came too late to catch the South West Monsoon winds which would have driven us straight to India) we were compelled to winter in Mozambique.

Though very small, that island boasts of a Portuguese fortress. It is situated on the East Coast of Africa at about fifteen degrees from the Equator. We remained there till March, 1605, when we embarked with the Viceroy on small vessels called Fuste. Ten of our Fathers boarded one of those vessels which happened to be in a bad condition and they made shipwreck a second time, but they managed in spite of great dangers to reach the coast by clinging to the wrecks. At the cost of great fatigues they made their way on foot back to Mozambique, (and embarking again) they reached Goa in September.

As for me, sailing on board the same galley as the Viceroy, after weathering another dreadful storm I finally landed at Goa on the 20th May, 1605, where I was most kindly received. I remained there a few months during which I fell ill.

He finally reached Cochin in January 1606, where he was stricken with a malignant fever. Thus came to India the Jesuit who was to become a sannyasi, speaking all the Indian languages, revered as a holy man by the Hindus of the highest caste and converting many among them. His life in India, where he lived daily with austere penances, dressed in the saffron robe and sacred thread of the Brahmin for the next fifty years, was the center of a great controversy. The Portuguese Church, which had come a little earlier, made converts from among the pearl divers and fisherfolk who were considered outcastes by men of culture and learning in India. Di Nobili knew that to win Brahmin souls for Christ it would be necessary to become one of these caste men, and this he did, despite much difficulty and bitter opposition on the part of some of his fellow priests and superiors. But he succeeded in doing what none before him had done: he attracted to the Faith the highest strata of Indian society, and won a permanent place among them.

To this day, no one has located his grave. As Vincent Cronin points out in his wonderful life of Di Nobili, A *Pearl to India*, the important thing was his life and work, not where his weary bones reposed.

But now, it seemed, the grave might be found. I was deeply interested since I first heard the rumor from Father Nevett two years before, and I was eager to know if it was true. The rumor stated that when Di Nobili died, his body had been buried near the Hindu temple at Madras, because of the great respect his life had earned among the Hindus. Later on, perhaps after several hundred years, the temple grounds were enlarged and thus came to include within the new boundaries the ancient grave of Di Nobili. Because temple ground is sacred to the Hindus, no Christian could enter there, and thus the grave had been hidden from Christian eyes for centuries. Now, it appeared, the Brahmins had come to the Archbishop with this startling news, and it was being investigated. I came to India eager to hear what had transpired since the rumor began, since no one in America seemed to have known of it.

Winnie and Lore certainly knew of the rumor but were not a bit impressed. They seemed reluctant to speak of it until Father Ignatius did so, and then it was only with the greatest hesitancy.

A certain man had come to the Archbishop with photographs he claimed had been made of documents in a Hindu temple, which indicated Di Nobili's grave was there. The Archbishop was intrigued, and the documents began to multiply rapidly, each visit revealing more of them. When a rather imposing number of them had accumulated, not photographs of actual material but photographs of "documents," many became suspicious of the situation and tried to alert the Archbishop to the possibility of fraud. These photographs were being sold to him, and the mystery man had a very great number of them. Then the drama entered a new phase, in which the mystery man produced ancient translations that "foretold" the finding of Di Nobili's grave by this same Archbishop, and which had been written, supposedly a thousand years ago, in Sanskrit.

This new development finished the matter for most of the people who knew of the situation. Winnie and Lore are convinced that it is a clever scheme to make money from the sudden interest in acculturation on the part of the Church, and that it is being milked for all it's worth. The man of mystery comes and goes frequently to the Archbishop, whence no one knows, nor do they know where he lives. He appears suddenly with more "proofs" and additional photos for sale, and disappears as suddenly. I believe that, at the present time, the Archbishop, a very holy man, is the only person who has any faith in the existence of the grave of Di Nobili on the temple grounds.

Yet, how wonderful if it were true, and the grave of this great saint of India could be found and identified by the proper scientific methods. What an opportunity for dialogue between Hindus and Christians in our own age, and what an opportunity for two great religions to meet again as they did in this holy man!

Father Ignatius took us around the grounds of Aikiya Alayam, where Hindus, Muslims, Christians and Jews are meeting to discuss and ponder not their differences but their commonly held beliefs. One can remain for a period of study, to participate in these discussions and prayers. It is a most hopeful sign for the world that such a place is now a reality at Mylapore, where the great apostle St. Thomas preached and left behind a large body of people who today call themselves "Saint Thomas Christians." The entire town of Madras seems to have sprung from this association with St. Thomas: its main road, Mount Road, leads from St. Thomas Mount, where the saint was martyred, according to the tradition that goes back almost two thousand years.

We visited the St. Thomas Cathedral, a venerable building, which contains, under the altar, a crypt where is preserved the blood-stained sand and pieces of the lance that killed St. Thomas. It is a place of great pilgrimage and has been so for centuries. Among those who wrote of it was Marco Polo, who visited the shrine when he traveled to Madras.

I am very partial to Madras. It is a warm and friendly place, and perhaps part of this affection stems from the fact that this was my first glimpse of India in 1971. I came at that time to be met by Bert Nevett, and to visit Loyola College, Sister Stella and the School for the Deaf and Blind, and Pushpanagar, from which slum many of our children of the Fund were selected and placed in schools. The first glimpse of Indian traffic had been stunning for me, and I thoroughly enjoyed the street scenes, the potters on the roadside, the trees, crows, cows and flowers. It seemed to me that I had never seen such beautiful people. The women, like birds of paradise, in the most graceful of all dresses, the sari, and bearing themselves like queens, wore fresh flowers in their hair, which they purchased from flower vendors in the roads. Even the coolie women, dressed in rags and working on the roadside, bore themselves with great grace and dignity. The men, too, were nearly all good-looking, with fine features and curling black hair. Though the city is ancient and combines features of the English Georgian style with both ancient and modern Indian architecture, and though much of it is in need of maintenance and repair, it nevertheless has a charm that won me forever. The Connemara Hotel, where I have stayed each visit, is well run and managed; the bell captain there, with the improbable name of Charles Thip Thop (pronounced Tip Top), is indeed that: a gracious, smiling man who seems determined to make the visitor welcome and comfortable. It is a great pity that he does not open a school to teach the officials of Madras his courtesy, attention to the needs of the tourist, and the art of hospitality. He could make a fortune.

On Monday morning I packed up, and Father Varaprasadam, S.J., came to the hotel to greet me. We had a fine visit together over breakfast at the hotel. Many years had passed since I last saw him, in Chicago, where he had been studying. Now he had a very important job with the Jesuits, that of furthering the work of adaptation, so that the Church in India can give expression to a truly Indian culture, rather than a European one. He is a scholar, and a man of great dignity and prayer. Quiet and considerate, he exudes a sense of competence and trustworthiness. It was he who had arranged for Brother Aloysius to come to the airport to meet me, and he had also made many arrangements for my stay in India, in spite of his own very busy schedule. Now he and Winnie accompanied me to the airport, the two of them chatting of mutual friends. I bid them good-bye with reluctance, though I knew we would meet again in April, when I returned for Kanikairaj's ordination. Winnie promised to keep on Pan Am's back and ship my luggage to me when it finally appeared.

CHAPTER 5

Madurai

The plane to Madurai was small and propeller-driven; I was cramped and paralyzed by the time we had completed the journey. It was made interesting, however, by conversation with the Muslim gentleman in the seat next to mine. We spoke of our two faiths, and he told me that as a faithful Muslim he was supposed to hate Christians, and that for this reason he was becoming skeptical. "Men should not live like that," he said. "This is a small planet and we should be able to get along together." He believes that the day will come when the entire world will be one vast community, with farming in one country, residential areas in another (where the climate is the best), industrial works situated in another country, and so on. Goods and food would be transported from their sources to the residential countries by swift transports. It's an interesting concept. We parted with mutual agreement that we are all children of the same God, and therefore brothers and sisters.

Brother Paranjothi was not at the airport to meet me, though this had been prearranged for some time. Some mix-up with the mails. When I had waited in the little station for some time, I decided to proceed by cab to St. Mary's, Madurai, where we have six students being educated on the Nevett Fund. The road to St. Mary's was rural and most beautiful. Country scenes in India have a special charm. The day was bright, and, it being early morning, not yet hot. We passed little villages where naked children played in the red clay, and crumbling Hindu shrines where painted gods and horses stared into the morning light. At last we found the gateway into St. Mary's compound and drove along the side of the newly painted church—beige trimmed with pink—to the priests' residence. There I alighted from the cab, arousing great curiosity among the gentlemen in dhotis standing nearby, and entered the doorway to inquire for help. Within minutes a young Jesuit brother was there, and hearing that I needed help, went immediately for Father Minister. He came, a tall, very handsome Indian named Father Ignatius, who listened to my tale with immobile features. Finally I said to him, "Father, do you know Father Nevett?"

"Father Nevett I know," he answered. "You I do not know."

"I am Rita Anton, and I work with Father Nevett in America," I told him, beginning to worry a bit. "We have six boys here in your school on Nevett Scholarships." At this his face changed, and he gave me a most gracious welcome. A small guest room was opened for me, while we began the struggle to contact Brother Paranjothi by phone. Brother's residence is a coffee plantation in the hills. The phone proved useless. We finally gave up. I turned my attention to the matter of continuing my journey alone to Kodaikanal, a trip of about three and one half hours by car.

Meanwhile, at my request, the six boys on Nevett Scholarships were sent for, and these came to meet me and have their photos taken. They lined up before me in very clean and freshly ironed shirts, shorts and bare feet. Like nearly every Indian I met, their eyes shone and their teeth were perfect. V. Selvarajan, M. Selvaraj, M. Arulraj, S. S. Raj Kummar, A. Arockiasamy and Kanikairaj all seemed to be doing well in school and were now preparing for examinations.

In the great open compound, games were going on, with shouts, whistles and much laughter. A group of very small boys, about six years old, I thought (later I found they were around nine), sprinted across the clay in a tight group and returned hopping like frogs. Their gym instructor called the tune. There are two thousand boys in this school.

Father Rector, Rev. James Rodrigues, came to greet me, and ordered coffee and bread to be served in my room while the question of my transport to Kodai was being solved. Renting a car proved impossible, and he told me I would be driven to Kodai in the school's car, accompanied by himself and driven by Father Arockiaraj, the headmaster. Some internal arrangements having been completed, my bags were loaded into the trunk and front seat, and the three of us departed for Kodai. I bought the gas, over their strenuous protests, knowing it was costly in India: about two dollars per gallon by American standards.

It was a delightful ride. We quickly broke the barriers of strangeness and were soon laughing like old friends. I was in the midst of relating the plot of *Close Encounters of the Third Kind* when our motor conked out. Father Arockiaraj said, "One of those spacemen must have gotten into it," and pulled to the side of the road. Fortunately, we were passing a little village at the time. The car was quickly surrounded by curious faces intent upon watching the small drama enacted daily on every road in India: the hood was up, Father Arockiaraj touching one thing, then another, and looking serious. Father James got out too, and I counted thirty faces at the windows examining my eyebrows, my dress, my feet, my bag, and giggling and nudging one another like kids everywhere.

"Where is your birthing place, madam?" one asked.

"America," I told him.

"America!" the shout went up through the group, and a small cordon of men detached themselves from the shop across the road and joined the audience. It was about 90 degrees, and the warm sun beat down on the roof, while the warm bodies effectively shut out any air. I began to feel like a chicken in the oven. Everyone was jolly, however, and it seemed churlish to ask them to move back a bit when the event was obviously causing such a welcome distraction from the village routine.

Someone ran for the mechanic, and this gentleman came and opened something in the engine that began to squirt gasoline. He closed it quickly and adjusted something else. Then he told Father Arockiaraj to try the starter. It worked. We left amid cheers and good-byes all around.

"Praise the Lord," sang Father Arockiaraj. Father James and I added our "Amen."

I continued my tale of the movie plot. Unidentified flying objects are reported in India, they told me, but no one is able to discern whether they are experiments being carried on by the government, weather balloons, or tricks of light. It sounded just like home.

Father James said the best thing for this ancient vehicle would be to proceed slowly and carefully, so as not to place undue strain on the engine. It took a delicate touch with the gears as well, to find the exact groove; Father Arockiaraj was an expert driver. We chugged past paddy, beautiful trees with numbers on them, a Boys' Village, where great work is being done for poor boys ("just like your Boys Town in Omaha"), and stopped to visit the tailor shop of Mr. Jeganathan, who has a son studying with the Jesuits and about to be ordained. We went into the dark, cool room hung with photos of Kodai and of the children of the family (there were ten) and met the two daughters at home and his wife. They served us tea, and we chatted about photography. Mr. Jeganathan brought out his camera, an ancient Canon, and opened it for me to admire. On the sewing machine nearby was white cotton fabric, and when I asked what he was making, he said, "Cassocks, madam. I make cassocks for the priests." Father James told me that he supplies all the Jesuits at Madurai. We bid the family and the portraits good-bye and continued on our way.

Now the hill began to rise, and the drop-off on our left was very steep. Ominous breaks in the foot-high wall gave testimony of the dangers there, and I could see, higher up, places where rockslides had created further hazards on the roadway. Hairpin turns became the rule, and we fed our reverend driver plantains to keep up his strength. He praised the Lord quite frequently now. The evening had come, and I knew that such a drive could be terrifying at night, particularly on such a narrow road, with only split seconds in which to veer to one side when huge trucks and buses came hurtling down the road from above.

I was suddenly reminded of the trip Al and I took to Glacier National Park, when we entered the park at sunset and drove many thousand feet up a strangely bumpy road in the pitch dark, and finally arrived at our lodge and went to bed. In the morning we awoke to find we were in the midst of snow-capped peaks, awesome in their glory. I remember the kids tumbling out in their pajamas, one by one, to sit down hard on the doorstep at the shocking beauty of their new environment. The road, we found later, was actually under construction, and we should not have been on it.

I related this tale to my two companions as we swerved and swayed around more curves, and began to see the twinkling lights of the plains far below. About three hours later, we pulled into Uttu— about six shops and one block long. We again alighted, giving the car and the reverend driver a break, and I took some flash photos of the more intriguing shops.

"Good morning, good morning," sang the ragged children. It was pitch dark. En route once again, praising the Lord and consuming plantains, we came through the gates of Sacred Heart Seminary, Shembaganur.

CHAPTER 6

Shembaganur

The name of Shembaganur has rung in my heart with a strangely familiar sound since I first heard it, in 1971. I cannot explain it, but I feel something in the word that is almost mystical. It is as though I had been there before, hundreds of years ago. Sacred Heart College, which is a Jesuit seminary, has been at Shembag about ninety years. The town is much older. When I was leaving it in 1971, passing Silver Cascade, the lovely waterfall, I asked the driver to stop the cab, and ran over to the ancient wall nearby. There I removed one of my earrings, and buried it.

"What's that in honor of?" Bert Nevett wanted to know.

"Someday I intend to come back and find it," I told him.

I even had hopes of convincing Al he should come to these hills and fish and perhaps retire, but in this I failed. Al was content to be captain of his dining-room table. He had no wish to travel anywhere except to his little cabin in the north woods. Now I passed Silver Cascade again, and glanced at the wall under which my earring was quietly rusting. It was good to return again.

In the darkened compound of the college, where the flower beds could just be glimpsed by the light of the moon, we met Father Aelred d'Silva, who was surprised and delighted to see his two Jesuit brothers and made us all very welcome. In seconds he was joined by the superior, Father John de Mello, who offered me a room in their guesthouse and supper in the refectory. We walked across an interior courtyard, surrounded by ghostly verandas where Bert Nevett had walked long ago as a student and later as a professor there, and I silently thanked God for the safe journey, now nearly completed. In the dining hall, Father de Mello saw me in the light and recognized me.

"I drove in a car with you and Father Basset," he said with a laugh of excitement. "I remember you lived in Oak Park. I visited you and had dinner in your home." I hated to admit how bad my memory is, but when he told me it had been in 1963, I didn't feel so bad. A scholastic was playing a phonograph in the hall—Beethoven —and the sound filled the whole compound. We shouted at one another over the music, relating our adventure on the road, and I had a chance to look more closely at my two hosts. Father de Mello is clean-shaven, with an open, friendly face, a great laugh and the easy manner of a man who has seen the world and found it good. Father Aelred d'Silva, with his beautiful black and gray beard, olive skin and keen eyes, looked like someone I ought to know and could not identify. I finally placed him among the portraits of the early missionaries to India. He has the same look of the man with his heart in heaven, his eager, eagle eyes totally aware of earth, and his whole spirit on the alert to serve and honor Christ through every passing moment. He is a minister indeed. He gathered me and my needs into his hands and heart from the first moment, and undertook the task of getting me settled in Kodai.

The two of them, De Mello and D'Silva, made me very comfortable in their guesthouse, which is very simple and spartan; qualities one always finds in Jesuit houses. The room was ample in size, with a bed, a table and chairs, a cupboard, washstand and mirror. Blue oilcloth covered the table. The room was innocent of any other decoration, except an enormous spider, elephantine, it appeared to me. Father de Mello thought so too. He went off to get a box to capture it in.

"I'll just give this fellow to Brother Robert for the museum," he explained.

It was nice to know that my spider was a "keeper" and would be duly mounted for the admiration of visitors to the museum.

Thus, through a strange turn of events, I had a firsthand opportunity to sleep on a Jesuit mattress, celebrated in the West as one of the austerities of Jesuit life. It consists of a thin pad of (I think) straw, fully two inches thick and laid over a woven frame with no give whatever. My mattress at home is an innerspring affair with an extraordinary number of coils per inch, and is about one foot thick. This is laid over box springs that support every cell of the body in comfort. It is known as a very firm mattress in America. I now realized that, up to the present, I had been misinterpreting "firm." But such was the purity of the air and the state of my weary bones after the ride up the ghat, I fell asleep on the straw bed immediately, and only awoke in the very early morning to the sound of strange and wonderful music. I think it was Muslim prayer. A rooster, secure in his own theology, joined in the praise of the Creator, and shortly thereafter came the song of the scholastics, calling to God in the early light. Church bells, birdsong, and strong young Jesuit voices raised in prayer: this was my introduction to the far-off hills.

Breakfast with the scholastics at Shembaganur, in their large white refectory, provided further insight into the life of the clergy in India. There were many young students there, all Indian, muffled in coats and shawls over their varied clothing, an odd mix of cassocks, dhotis and slacks, it seemed to me. It's cold in the morning at Shembag— around 45 degrees—and I was thankful that among the few things I had with me was a woolen shawl that served very well to keep me warm. The simple meal was soon disposed of, in complete silence. Long wooden tables and benches stretched down the length of the room, lit by the early sun streaming through high windows and glinting off the two large wall hangings depicting scenes in the life of St. Ignatius. I glanced around at the raised platform and podium, at the young, strong faces turned to their breakfast, apparently intent on observing custody of the eyes, and found no one interested in the fact that a guest had joined them. Father d'Silva, too, seemed wrapped in silence, having just come from Mass and morning prayer. He sat next to me, offering me plates of food and very good bread, and ate his own simple meal with great dispatch. He whispered he had work to do and would see me later, told me to wander around and see the place, and left the hall. One by one the students also melted from the room, and I finished my meal with very good coffee served in a soup bowl.

I wandered around the seminary grounds, wrapped in my wool shawl, and found again the orchid garden I remembered from 1971. Nothing was in bloom yet, but much promise was there of glory later in the season. A few coolie women clipped grasses, squatting easily and gracefully. Small thatch-roofed garden houses were there, reminding me of little Japanese teahouses, where the students could sit and study or meditate amid the flowers.

Farther on I found the cemetery, a most wonderful and tiny world of sleeping Jesuits on a high terrace overlooking the seminary. I counted the graves there—sixty of them, the early ones with French names. I noted the eldest, who had died at ninety-eight, and the youngest, who went to heaven at twenty-one. By my rude calculations and somewhat suspect arithmetic, I calculated the average age at sixty-one. Jesuits live a long time in these hills, it seems. I recalled that it was for this hoped-for length of days that they first came up to the hills. They had been dying very early in the plains, amid the terrible heat and diseases. Shembaganur had provided cool air, opportunities for brisk exercise and arduous walks (thus increasing the strength of heart and lung), and an almost total freedom from pollution. They had more than doubled their life-span with this wise move. In addition, the native beauty of these hills must have enriched the spirit and the soul of the missionaries from Europe, giving them the kind of inspiration for prayer and tranquil conditions for deep study that the world in the West seems to have lost in our time.

I was very sorry to learn that the students now seem bent on moving the seminary to the city. Surely there is time enough later to discover the city, to find what the libraries there contain and to join in the rat race mankind conducts. The West has already learned this and is frantically trying to regain the lost world of the village it gave up at the beginning of the industrial revolution. There is a land rush on in America. City people are moving out farther and farther from the filth and noise of the city, and even young families are willing to cut the umbilical cord from educational opportunities, shops and commerce, to live again in country places and try to rediscover the simple beauty they alone can provide.

I hope the Jesuits will manage to retain ownership of Shembaganur for its future priests so that the next generation of them, catching up with Western experience, will be able to return to these hills again. Perhaps by that time so many Americans will have discovered the hills that they will be very different; certainly more and more are learning of Kodaikanal, and the thin trickle will grow inevitably. But not just yet, perhaps.

I rediscovered the famous post office, where Brother Peter, at ninety-two, is still the best postmaster in India. This is not just an idle expression: he has been awarded the national prize from the Indian Government for many years now and has the carefully framed documents in his post office to prove it. A small man, with a long beard, olive skin and wonderfully wise eyes peering through old-fashioned wire spectacles, he greeted me at the doorway and led me into his sanctum with the gracious dignity of one who knows his worth. He showed me his records, kept like jewels over half a century of work, and I marveled again at the way in which a dedicated life can transform a simple service into fine art. Here before me was the kind of order and serenity one finds in Zen Buddhism. Brother Peter has found the *tao* of his work, the hidden value of taking one man's communication to another, and making its path through his hands almost liturgical. No smallest aspect of the transaction has been untouched by his art. I thought suddenly of the Postal Service of America and its costly and ruinous state.

Later that morning, Brother Thomas found me and invited me to see the wonderful museum of the Seminary College. The creation of a remarkable Jesuit, the late Father A. Anglade, who was a professor at the seminary and who not only left a treasure of archeological and anthropological studies but gathered the usual mammals as fauna specimens native to the Palni Hills: the tiger, spotted leopard, black panther, wild boar, bear, hyena, wolf dog and jackal, plus elephant tusks and grinders. In the words of the published brochure,

> Next comes various types of, thank God, milder animals like the big Sambar; the spotted barking and mouse deer; one ibex about to leap into the void; two monkeys: the Common and Ordinary Nilgiri Langurs; three small felines: the leopard, civet and wild cats; the Malabar and flying squirrels; two Iguanas; a Marten; mummy and cub pole cats (the latter with its white tipped tail being a special variety of the Palnis); the head of a hare; the Common and the Brown Mongoose. Here an otter is set to dive swiftly up-stream; a little further a Porcupine threateningly stiffens its sharp quills. There is also a Pangolin or ant-eater, not, however, of the pre-Mammal type; that strange animal that laid eggs like Reptiles but like Mammals suckled its young.

Here were also displayed seventy-nine varieties of snakes, three hundred wood specimens, fourteen skeletons of animals, a variety of bones and teeth, two hundred and nine specimens of butterflies, one hundred and eighty-nine mounted birds of these hills, and a great number of plant specimens.

Father Anglade and the students of the college over the years had unearthed an abundance of pottery of many shapes, brass bangles, iron implements, burial urns and nearly one hundred dolmens. These are not yet exactly dated, though they are believed to be prehistoric; Father Anglade believed that this area contained regular human settlements where men were buried under their own houses. "When these had afterwards to be abandoned, the original cities of the living became gradually underground cities of the dead."

Father Anglade, a wood carver of tremendous artistry and talent, created exact wood replicas of the dolmens, more than thirty of them. Dolmens are groups of stone chambers similar to those found in many parts of the world. Each chamber is a long rectangle (12 by 3 by 5 feet) made of four vertical slabs capped by a horizontal one, the whole colony being normally enclosed within a thick wall of the same height and consisting of huge dressed stones often several feet long and fitting closely together without mortar. To my untutored eyes, they resembled very much the photos I have seen of Stonehenge, but were considerably smaller. Hillmen here call the dolmens "Pandavan Kottai," or fortresses of the mythical Pandavans. "In fact," states the museum brochure, "and unless they be no more than funeral monuments, given their general structure, orientation, strategic position mostly on well-chosen hill spurs within sight of each other, the Palni Hills Dolmens might well have served as fortified outposts, or as places of refuge or store centres for the villages close by." Speculation about these primitive men still goes on. Several attempts to get carbon tests on materials found there have failed, due to the distance of adequate facilities and the great cost of such a project. Brother Robert promised to take me to the site of these structures in the jeep one day and let me rummage about for myself in these ancient digs. I determined not to let him forget it.

Perhaps as remarkable as anything else Father Anglade bequeathed to his Society is the collection of his watercolor paintings, comprising ten volumes of two thousand species of plants and flowers of the Palni Hills. I examined these precious books and marveled at the exquisite artistry and exact scientific detail of the work, which had been hand bound and left by him with careful notes. This collection alone would have been the crowning achievement of most men, but this Frenchman was clearly a genius of many talents.

It was Father Anglade, too, who laid the foundations for the famous orchid garden of Shembaganur, where some two hundred

varieties of orchids glow in exotic color in a terrace above the seminary.

The chapel, entirely his creation, was a wonder in itself. During
the 1930s, Father Anglade set himself the task of building and
adorning a chapel entirely of wood. I entered it, wondering at the
draperies that hung from the pillars around the center of the room
and those that hung like enormous and dramatic curtains above the
altar. I was struck by the wondrous design of grapes and wheat
carved and tinted in natural tones on the altarpiece, but as I came
closer to examine the workmanship, I realized for the first time that
not only the huge fringed "curtains" above the altar but every bit of
the drapery that hung all around the room was carved wood, and not
soft fabric as I had supposed. Here again, craft had become art. The
Stations of the Cross were adorned by fourteen portraits of Christ
created by an artist of tremendous ability.

I visited the kitchen and bakery, accompanied by one of the
Jesuits. In the very large kitchen a number of workers were busy over
the enormous stoves imported from Belgium many years ago.
Pointed out with great pride was a huge black machine now reduced
to a minimum function, that of whipping potatoes. Originally it had
had parts that could shred, grind and otherwise process a variety of
foods, but these parts are now lost. It, too, had had a long and
difficult journey, probably by ship, from Europe. I regretted the loss
of the other parts, knowing the joys of this kind of food preparation.
All the women of America have fallen for the new kitchen toy first
introduced by Cuisinart, which does food embroidery on a small
scale. On the lovely gold counter in my kitchen at home reposes a
similar kitchen god, The American Food Processer, which I have had
great fun with. I could appreciate Shembag's cook's joy in his huge
black mixer.

The baker led me to his bakeshop with the professional air of one
who knows his job thoroughly. He executed a marvelous dance
drama for me, in Tamil, in which he outlined in broad, artistic gestures, the making of bread. Marcel Marceau would have applauded.
This bread, incidentally, is quite famous. The nuns as far away as
Dindigul know of its excellence. The old-fashioned brick oven, into
which the risen dough is inserted on wooden paddles, reminded me
of Augusta Bakery, in Chicago, one of the few such places where
Polish rye has reached the zenith of perfection. Sara Lee's famous

computerized bakery operation, for all its efficiency and excellence, has not one baker on the payroll who can match the eloquent joy of creation of the baker of Sacred Heart Seminary.

That afternoon, after I had lunched and rested, Father Aelred came to my guest room with a plan of action all worked out in his methodical mind. I would need help at Kodai. He knew a woman who would be ideal for my servant. He, himself, would stand guarantee for her. He would also drive to Kodai himself, since he had a meeting there, find my rented house, look through it to see what I would need there, and come back and report to me. He would, if I wished, produce the proposed servant and give us both a chance to meet. I agreed readily, and a few hours later he returned with a little dark lady in a sari that was soiled and stained. She had been working in the garden, he explained, and had no time to change before the interview. She was painfully shy and had a tendency to lower her head at every question and twist her small bare toes on the floor. Father explained that hill people are very shy before strangers but that I would find her both capable and honest. Her name was Regina. She had five children, most of them raised, but she still had a small daughter at home, Philomena. Her husband, a coolie at the college, would have to be brought before me to give his consent to the arrangement. Regina would do everything necessary in the house: cooking, laundry, cleaning and marketing. I looked at the modest little figure before me, eyes still bent on her toes and smiling in confusion and embarrassment.

"Does she speak English at all?" I asked him.

"Very little, but she understands a great deal. She worked in the house of a man who speaks only English, and did very well there. I suggest you give her a trial. If she doesn't work out, we will find someone else, but she is really very capable."

"What would I pay her?" I asked him.

"Whatever you wish. She will be grateful for anything. The family is very poor. The man she worked for last was very generous. He gave her seventy rupees."

I calculated in my head as quickly as my turgid math would permit. "That's roughly seven dollars," I said to myself. "What about her child?"

"No problem. She has relatives who will look after her house and the cooking there. It's a large family and they are very close."

I decided to trust Father's judgment, though my own instincts were not overly enthusiastic. The husband was sent for, and Regina returned with him, this time very clean and wearing a fresh sari with flowers in her hair. She had a bright smile, and an abundance of teeth for such a small mouth. She looked rather pleased to present her husband, who bowed over clasped hands in namaste to me and indicated through Father that I looked all right to him. He would permit the queen of his domicile to work for me for two and one half months. It was settled. I afterward discovered that the seventy rupees was per month, not per week. Later we adjusted it upward to two hundred rupees per month.

Aelred d'Silva then brought to my room a pile of fresh bed linen, two pillows for my bed—one hard, one soft—and several woolen blankets. These were on loan to me, pending the arrival of my own stuff in the missing suitcases. He also wrapped some of the excellent seminary bread for my kitchen, and promised to provide a load of firewood. He asked Regina if she had brought all that she needed for her stay with me, and she indicated a bag only a little larger than a purse and said she had it all. We piled into the seminary car and drove into Kodai, about four miles up, and straight to Snyder "B," the house I had arranged to rent.

CHAPTER 7

Kodaikanal

I had assumed that if there is a Snyder "B," there must also be a Snyder "A." My instinct was correct. The place was a low stone duplex, nicely painted around its french windows, and set on a hill with a little terraced garden marked off by white stones along its brown clay path. A low stone wall surrounded it, with a locked gate, and there were lovely begonia bushes five feet high growing along the side of the building. Chrysanthemums and poppies greeted me. Altogether, it seemed a lovely spot. There were about five towering pine trees around the house. The Snyder "A" was unoccupied, the season not having officially begun in Kodai.

The door was opened by a dark lad named Job with a bad case of pink eye. Hovering in the background was a rather elderly man with a mole on his face, a dirty rag wrapped around his head and another around his middle. This was the gardener and "outside" man, Muthusamy. When I got to know him, I found him very obliging and a clever improviser; the first impression, as in the case of Regina, was misleading.

Job opened the door with a flourish, to reveal the wonders of the "de luxe" house. It opened on a living-and-dining-room combination, about 22 by 18, to which was added a little sun porch with windows offering a beautiful view of the hills. A stone fireplace ascended to the slanted, beamed ceiling, and a cupboard built into one wall, its glass diamond-shaped doors very dirty, enclosed a set of mismatched dishes, also dirty. A hanging bookshelf near the fireplace seemed useful, however, as did the "suite" of Swedish modern chairs and table, overhung by a lamp with three conical crystal shades. The dining room was very ample, and sported five chairs—a curious number, I thought. The floor was covered with a green rug of uncertain vintage, and a few small tables completed the room. The sun porch had a most welcome desk for my typewriter, a daybed, a baby crib and a rocking chair.

Exploring further, I found two bedrooms, both large, one furnished with a good double bed, dresser, built-in shelves and drawers and a large standing cupboard for clothes. The other was equipped with twin beds, very bad mattresses, and bedspreads with a large hole eaten through to the mattress. I asked Job about this curious hole.

"The people who were here before had a small dog, madam, and the dog has done this damage."

It seemed reasonable enough but did not explain why the spread had not been replaced. The bathroom had a toilet and shower, and a geyser for hot water I was to know on intimate terms later on. Cabinets in the wall permitted storage of bathroom articles and towels.

But it was the kitchen that really shook me to the core. It was very large, at least twice the size of mine at home, and had an island in the center with a formica top. Shelves under this island and under the sink were fitted with screen doors. There were three possibilities for cooking (presumably to permit madam to express her culinary arts as widely as possible). Near the window sat a little wood stove, circa 1900. On the counter near the only wall outlet was an electric plate (double, madam) with a frayed cord that invited all kinds of exciting adventures including electrocution, provided it worked. It was out of order. And near the door to the dining room reposed an ancient, very rusted kerosene stove. It looked lethal. A picture of a lion and its mate, cut from some magazine and framed rather hastily, added a zoological touch. I suddenly knew why a cook had been strongly recommended as essential. I would never be able to manage in that prehistoric kitchen. Regina, however, was satisfied, and thought it excellent.

Job insisted on an inventory. With a list in hand, which covered three pages, he resolutely checked off every item in each room, including the contents of the kitchen cabinets, which contained so much mouse dirt I was horrified and demanded to see Major Lal, the rental agent in charge. Job promised to let him know. "Major Lal will come tomorrow, madam," he said.

The complete inventory of Snyder "B" wore me out, and God help me, I thought, if anything is missing or destroyed during my

tenure. I tried hard to discipline my facial muscles during the
lengthy exercise, a skill at which I am not notably successful, and the
comedy went forward for about forty-five minutes. The list went as
follows:

DRAWING/DINING ROOM

Sofa set with Cushion	3
Bellows—waste paper box	2
Rosewood stool	1
Drum for Firewood	1
Center Table	1
Side Table	1
Curtain	4
Picture [print of street scene]	1
Dining Table	1
Dining chair	5
Writing desk	1
Round Table	1
Rocking Chair	1
Divan with mattresses	1
Carpet large Green	1
Vase with peacock feather	1
Cushion	4
Wooden box	1
Fancy Lamp shades	3
Table mat [very dirty]	1

BEDROOM

Bed with mattresses & rubber sheets	2
Bed covers	2
Side Table	1
Picture	1
Curtains	5
Dressing table with mirror	1
Chair	1
Carpet	1

BATHROOM

Ironing Board	1
Dining Table pieces [boards]	2

Iron [not electric]   1
Table mat [?]   1
Round mirror [rectangular]   1
soap dish   1

FRONT BEDROOM
Bed with 2 mattresses [mat. & springs]   1
Curtains   2
Side table   1
waste papper box [sic]   1
Folding Chair with Cushion   2
Writing Table   1
Chest of Drawer   1
Table lamp [one broken]   2
Rug [ancient]   1
Yellow small Bowl [not there]   1
Jug [not there]   1

KITCHEN
Hot plate [not working]   1
Broom [Indian style—two feet high]   1
Kerosene stove   1
Tin oven [rusted out]   1
Picture [lions]   1
Deksha [?]   5
Saucepan [dirty]   3
Lids   12
Double boiler   2
Saucepan WITH HANDLE   3
Fry pan   2
Basin [rusted]   2
Bread tin "   2
Pie tin   "   2
Squire [sic] tin [dirty]   2
Cake Cup tin   "   2
Tea Kettle [blackened & crusted]   1
Garden tool   3
Biscuit tin [dirty]   2
Coffee pot [suspect]   1
Plastic bowl [old]   1
Measuring cup   2

Bread board	1
salt & pepper	7
glass pie dish	1
juice glass	2
water glass jug	1
Bowls china [1 lid]	3
Wick burner	2
Small yellow jug	1
Glass bowl	1
Salt Dish Glass	4
Tin Tray	2
Flower vase, brass	2
Flower vase, China	2
Grater	1
Platter, large	1
Biscuit molder	5
Tin Cutter	3
Measuring Spoon	3
Kitchen spoon	1
Egg beater	1
Pottato [sic] masher	1
Spriying tuner [?]	1
Meat grainder [sic]	1
Soup Spoon	1
Spoon Stand [toast rack]	1
Plastic butter knife	2
Wooden Spoon	1
Small Sauce pan	1
Strainer [horrible]	3
Sweeper tray [dustpan]	1
Plastic tumpler [sic]	1
C. I Bucket [?]	1
Plastic bucket [new]	1
Lantern	2
Empty tin	2
Jug	1
Funnel [unbelievable]	1
Brush	1
Spring balance	1

Lacto meter [milk tester]	1
Plate Stand	1
Cup, China	2
Sive [sic], old [prehistoric]	1
Table Spoon	7
Large Spoon	3
Fork	5
Knife	5
Tea Spoon	11
Plastic Tray	1
Brass Finger Bowl [!]	6
Fruit Dish	2
Small saucer [plastic]	9
Small cups	9
Sugar Bowl, steel	2
Quarter Plates	8
Full Plates	13
Saucer, Porceline [sic]	8
Glass Dish, square	8
Wine cups, glass	11
Small glass	2
Sugar Creamer [1 set]	1
Tea Pot	1
Sauce Dish	5
Green Bowl [1 broken lid]	2
Water Glass	3
Steel Sweet dish	2
Candle stick [1 broken]	2
Glass with tray	1
Salt & Pepper [more]	3
Porceline cups [sic]	8
Bell, small	2
Glass plate	1
Butter dish	3
Porceline Plate [sic] big	8
" " " large	1
" " " quarter	6
" " " soup	7
Sauce dish white	4

water [glass] jug   1
Milk Jug [!]   8
Ironing Golden words [trivets: "We grow too soon oldt und too
                                 late schmart" and "The hurrier I
                                 go the behinder I get"]
Vegetable dish   1
Sugar & creamer set [another]   1
Plastic Tray [small]   1
Vegetable dish, handle   1

I estimated the total value of the kitchen equipment, based on my
yearly garage-sale enterprise, at roughly six dollars in a good year.

Fortunately, I had brought a number of kitchen items along, sensing the total absence of any sharp knife (I was correct) and the need
for a good tea strainer, some large plastic spoons, a wine-bottle
opener (complete waste of time—no wine here) and my own
kitchen silverware. I also had packed, thanks to Divine Providence, a
good jackknife with all the blade sizes, and a multipurpose tool that
combined a hammer, pliers, can opener and screwdriver. This last,
alone, was worth its weight in gold in India.

The inventory finally completed, and after Job, patient as his
namesake, slowly described each wonder of the "de luxe house," I was
able to dismiss him at last, he promising that Major Lal would materialize the next morning. Regina and I went to Spencer's, the local
store, and purchased scrubbing brushes, plenty of soap and insecti-
cide, and some towels, rags for cleaning, a new kettle and large basin,
and some brown paper for the shelves. I had no intention of using
anything in that kitchen without a thorough cleansing. I think
Muthusamy was rather surprised when I required all of the contents
of the kitchen to be placed outside and the entire cupboard space
cleaned with hot water and soap. After this was done, every item in
the vast and imposing inventory was scraped and scrubbed clean of
former meals, foraging mice and soot. The shelves were lined with
brown paper, after which the items were rearranged within. I did not
intend to use many of them anyway but could not bear the thought
of the colonies of microbes gaily increasing amid my foodstuffs.

Firewood was an immediate problem. Aelred came to our aid
again with a load of wood from the abundant supply at Shembag.
Regina had just scrubbed the kitchen floor when the wood arrived

and was stored in a corner of the kitchen. Outside, she said, it would walk away in the night. Regina proved talented at managing the wood stove and soon had it blazing away. The kettle, new and shiny, was given its ritual baptism of black soot immediately as she boiled water for drinking purposes and for tea. The bread from Shembag was our first meal. This recalled the important role bread had played in every move I had made since I was married.

Al and I had a third-floor apartment when we were newlyweds. After the parade of furnishings and clothing had ascended the three flights and we were gasping for breath on the little rear porch in the June evening, we dined on the finest bread I ever tasted, a crisp whole wheat bread from the local baker. In afteryears, we often looked back on that meal, on the delight of that delicately flavored bread that was the first sacrament of our new life together. Now, once more, in a strange house, in a strange land, I began the life there with delicious bread: the bread of Shembaganur.

I was weary after the events of the day, and the fresh mountain air filled my lungs and closed my eyes. I headed for the double bed and night's rest under the fresh sheets and blankets, courtesy of Shembaganur. Regina retired to the other bedroom. During the night, which was very cold, around 45 degrees according to the thermometer, I heard her coughing. I reflected that she had no cold before, and reminded myself to inquire about it in the morning. It was then I discovered she had no blanket and had tried to sleep under a thin bedspread (the one without the holes) and had been disturbed by bugs during the night. I scolded her for not letting me know immediately, and sent to Shembag for another blanket when Aelred appeared in the morning. He promised to bring it, but added, "It's her own fault. I asked her if she had everything she needed, and she said she did." But he was unable to return that day, due to the work at Shembag, so I gave Regina one of my blankets. She indicated she preferred to sleep on the floor of the living room in front of the fireplace, which she kept warm all night with fresh logs. Knowing that this was probably more natural for her than the bed, I did not protest but told her to go ahead.

But, the next day, I had her turn out the bedroom mattresses (rubber pads and spreads 2) on the lawn behind the house, scrub the beds down with hot water, spray with disinfectant and then put everything back. Now I realized that the large hole in the spread had not been the work of a dog but of the tiny silverfish which infest India. And I also realized I was getting a reputation as a fanatic in Kodai, as the story of all this scrubbing went forth in the town.

Kodai, in season, has a number of foreign visitors. However, this was February; the season begins at the end of March. As the first in the troupe of entertainers, I was the object of deep and careful scrutiny everywhere I went. Children followed me down the road. Little groups of men pondered my clothing, my age, my nationality, and my reason for coming in the cold weather. Before long it was obvious that everyone in town knew the American lady, where she lived, and how long she would stay. Any gap in the dossier was noted, and someone was delegated to inquire. In Spencer's I met a man who asked what I was paying for rent. I told him. By afternoon this valuable piece had been fitted into my file.

A stream of peddlers found their way to Snyder "B" from opening day onward, and continued with unflagging endurance. At first I answered the door myself. Later I asked Regina to do so and to say that madam did not need further chattels. But merchants in these parts are not easily put off. They tend to hang around outside awaiting the first glimpse of madam to hear from her own lips that she will resist jars of jellies, biscuits, watercolor paintings or carved statues. I had been forewarned by Father Nevett that my presence in Kodai would be taken as a sign of great wealth, and that I would be expected to share my riches with the poor. It was little use, I found, to explain that I was a poor widow, on a limited income, and that I had to be frugal with my money. The jelly-and-jam man, finding I was not going to purchase his wares, followed me down the road in the bazaar, with a pathetic whine, relating the story of his family life and the empty larder at home. I had only enough for my shopping and the postage stamps I needed, and told him so. But later that afternoon, in the pouring rain, while I was beginning my simple meal of rice, carrots, peas and bananas, there was a gentle tap at the door. I opened it to find him again, this time under water, pleading for ten rupees to buy food for his family. I didn't have the heart to refuse him. But I realized quickly that he was but one of hundreds. I was only allowing myself fourteen rupees a day for food, and would not be able to continue these dispersals. I told him this. He thanked me, praised God, and departed with the ten rupees.

My landlord, Major Lal, having come to meet me in due course, proved to be a tall man from the North, with a daughter in Des

Plaines, Illinois. He laughed deprecatingly at my novel dismay at the kitchen dirt, and blamed it on Muthusamy, whose education in hygiene was defective due to "his low caste." I was determined to have the blame placed squarely where it belonged. I told him that, as a real estate saleswoman in America, I was aware that no house should be rented in anything but completely clean condition, and that I found the quarters at Snyder "B" sadly lacking in that respect. He found my attitude rather quaint, and launched into a tale about his Des Plaines daughter returning home to India and saying to her mother, "Oh, Mummy, this is so antique!"

"Antique is all right with me, Major Lal," I said with determination. "It's dirt I can't stand. The place was filthy."

Then I brought him out to the kitchen to point out the electric plate, which did not work.

Job, also present, rather anxious about the interview, unplugged it, plugged it in again, and said firmly, "Now it will work, you will see," withdrawing his hand from the surface as if from unbearable heat.

I put my hand on the plate. It was stone cold. "Please take this away and bring me one that works," I asked. "It's a nuisance to have to start a fire just to get a little hot water for tea."

Major Lal told Job to pick up a working model to replace it.

I did not realize while the landlord was on the premises that the geyser in the bathroom was decorative only. After many attempts to obtain more than a cup of hot water for my bath, I gave it up and had Regina warm the water on the wood stove in the kitchen. The rental for the house was, after all, purely nominal; I did not want to be any more critical than necessary. I knew very well that most of the country was without running water, and it seemed a bit much to insist on its being hot.

After the house was cleaned by Regina and Muthusamy, and fresh flowers had been arranged in vases, and I had put a few things from the shops in the bazaar on the mantel, it seemed very nice indeed, and the desk was just the right height for my typewriter. I settled in after a few days with an air of contentment. The birds in the trees, the beautiful hills all around me, and the endless variety of livestock and modes of dress on the road beyond my gate were riches indeed. The fresh air of the hills, the warm sunshine in the garden awakening the roses to a promised bloom under Muthusamy's gentle care and guidance, all more than made up for the earlier tensions. I felt myself putting down a tentative root into the brown clay.

CHAPTER 8

To Find an Ashram

One of my prime objectives in coming to South India was to visit the ashram of Dom Bede Griffith, the famed Benedictine monk who had come to India and embraced the life of a sannyasi, or holy man. I had heard of him for years, and when I found and read *Return to the Center* and discovered the inspired work of synthesis he had done in finding within the Hindu faith certain strains of clear inspiration from the Holy Spirit, which he related to the Christian faith and tradition, I knew this was one man I must meet. I packed this book in my suitcase when I came to India, and, again very fortunately, it was among the few things that arrived with me, rather than sitting in some airport cargo room with my three missing bags. I had only to mention this desire to Aelred when he came up with a solution.

Saccidananda Ashram, Shintivanam, is situated near a village called Kulithalai; Aelred made it sound as though it were just around the corner. He told me Sister Lydia, a doctor with a dispensary in Kulithalai, was at Shembag to confer with her spiritual director, Father de Mello, and that she would be returning there by bus the following Friday.

"You can surely go along with Sister Lydia. She will drop you off at the ashram. I will bring her to see you beforehand, so she can tell you about the ashram, what you will need to take along for your visit, and so on."

On Thursday evening Aelred knocked on the door, and I opened it to find him with a very small little lady with chestnut hair and lovely hazel-gray eyes in a very pretty face. She was wearing a brown nylon sari, and over it a woolen shawl against the night chill. I was delighted to meet her, and very happy to have visitors in my little house. The fire was blazing in the fireplace, and Regina served tea, crackers and cheese. I brought out my only bottle of sherry for the occasion, and we each had one ounce.

Sister was worried that I would not find at the ashram many customary comforts. "It's a very simple place, you know, and no hot water; you may have to share a little room with another lady, since so many come to the ashram."

I told her I was accustomed to simplicity; however, I really would prefer a private room, but neither a second occupant nor the lack of hot water would be difficulties. I thought ruefully of the reluctant geyser in the bathroom.

"Then we must wire to Dom Bede and let him know you're coming, so there will be a place reserved; also, we should let the sisters at Trichy know you will be staying at their convent overnight." This was my first inkling that the trip would be more than a brief one. Together we discussed the journey, involving three buses, because Sister Lydia had to go to their Trichy convent en route to visit her provincial. I said Trichy would be fine with me, since I had children in the school at St. Joseph's there and could visit them before going on to the ashram. Aelred, the minister par excellence, watched the plans being made with satisfaction. He had once again made workable arrangements that would be carried out pronto.

The following morning, I found my way to the Presentation Convent for early Mass, at six forty-five, in company with the schoolgirls. I had discovered their chapel on my own the day before, by the simple expedient of following two sisters up a very steep hill. They left me, panting and faint, at the convent gate and cheerfully hiked on to their sewing classes. They had *walked* from their convent, at Shembag, about four miles uphill and were not even out of breath. I promised myself that, within a few weeks, I, too, would win that kind of stamina. Then I limped up the vast hill path to the convent door, where I was given a hearty Irish welcome and was invited to attend Mass there each morning, and the sister in charge arranged that I should be driven up with the priest from La Providence. More of this later. This Friday morning I told them I was going to the ashram, and they all said I would love the place; Dom Bede is very well known throughout India.

Aelred appeared around 10 A.M. on Friday, drove me to the bank to cash a traveler's check, stopped at the post office for me, and

cheerfully brought me back to Snyder "B," where Regina had
prepared my lunch to take on the trip. I also brought the movie camera and film, some sheets and a coverlet, and a change of clothing.
We piled into the car again, and Aelred dropped Regina and me at
the bus stand and loaded us on, and we went by bus to Shembag to
assure ourselves of seats for the journey down to the plains. We
picked up Sister Annie en route, and at Shembag, Sister Lydia. John
de Mello was at the foot of the hill to shake my hand through the
bus window and wish me Godspeed. Regina remained at Shembag
to weekend with her family while madam was at the ashram.

The bus ride down to the plains was very interesting. Having come
up in the dark, I had had no chance to see the awesome beauty in
sunlight. Monkeys sat on the low wall, below which the drop was
many thousands of feet. Flowers I remembered from my visit in '71
lined the roadway: Lantanas in many colors, but called "lady's pest"
here because they had been planted many years before by an
Australian lady and had gone wild and taken over whole areas in the
eighty years since the original planting. We pulled into Dindigul
hours later and changed buses for Trichy. Sister Lydia told me of her
work as a doctor.

"When I had been in India two years," she told me, "I felt I knew
the Indian people, loved them, and understood them. Now I have
been here ten years; I know the people, love them, but I do not understand them." She described her village, where the life is extremely
primitive (I was to see it firsthand two days later), and a little of her
own life. Born in Belgium, she had studied at Louvain and had come
to India as a member of the Medical Missionaries of the Immaculate
Heart of Mary (I.C.M.) congregation. She is of the same order as
my good friend Sister Stella, of the School for the Deaf and Blind,
Madras. After a time, she felt called to do medical work in a village
setting, working and living as one of the poor. It is a very special
calling, far removed from the sterile, modern operating theatre of
their hospital at Dindigul, where they had also recently lost their beloved surgeon, Mother Franciscus. "Why don't you go to St.
Joseph's and take her place there?" I asked Lydia. "Surely they need
a sister doctor very badly." From the small smile and the hesitation
in her answer, I realized it was not an original idea.

"I have been asked," she said quietly, "but I came to India to serve the poorest people. In my village I am the only one they have, and I think God wants me to do that work."

It was obvious there had been a history behind that decision of hers, and I sympathized with the congregation of medical missionaries who must have counted on this educated nun to continue their work in a teaching hospital, training nurses for India's future. Yet this small lady, with the strength not found in many men, had quietly chosen to follow her beloved Lord in a vocation to the poorest of the poor. The hospital would always find personnel. The villages could hardly find a single Indian doctor willing to undergo that kind of hardship.

She related her attempts to teach hygiene to the villagers and the importance of good nutrition to pregnant women and small children. I thought of the birth-control issue and asked about it.

"When they ask us to teach birth-control methods, I say I am a sister and know nothing of these matters. It should be for the Catholic lay people to discuss, no?"

It seemed a bit of a cop-out, since birth control's pros and cons were hotly discussed all over the country and since Indira's son had chosen a disastrous and politically fatal method of enforcement.

Then Lydia continued, "In the village when I first came there, many women said to me, 'I have had ten children, two living, or nine children, with three alive,' and I saw immediately that something ought to be done for them. What to do? Rhythm method they will not follow. Mucous method is useless for them. They are too simple. They do not count, they only live." Finally, she decided that when such a case came to her with the inevitable illnesses and deaths and tragic inability to cope with life, she would arrange for them to go to the clinic for a birth-control device. "I cannot do it myself, as a Catholic," she said, "but I feel very certain God does not want this tragedy for them. So I tell them where to go for help."

I looked at this tiny woman, and thought of all the arguments and discussion in the post-Vatican II world about the Pill. Of the older school myself, I suddenly realized that the old method was a luxury only a very few in India would be able to manage. There had to be a solution for the very poor, so that somehow they could climb out of the pit and begin to live on a human level. Rhythm had worked for me. It could not work here. Lydia had used situation ethics wisely, and I felt quite strongly that she was correct. This represents quite a change in my opinion. Previously I had not properly understood the poverty of the Third World.

A ride in an Indian bus is an experience worth having . . . once. The engine sounds powerful, strong as a bull, roaring down roads aided by the horn, which is capable of emitting various sounds from a high-pitched whistle to a very long quack. In addition, the journey is enhanced by an auxiliary horn with a rubber bulb attached, to be used in dire emergencies. These features are the only ones calculated to provide any degree of assurance. All else is strictly utilitarian. The seats are provided with a thin cover of leatherette over solid steel, and springs in either the seats or the underpinning of the vehicle would be considered nonsense. The distance between the edge of one's seat and the back (steel) of the seat in front is approximately seven inches. The aisle is about one foot wide. A metal bar is provided on the back of each seat, neatly calculated to remove the teeth of the person behind in case of a sudden stop. Otherwise, it is used as a very necessary handle to hang on to around the curves and over the bumps in the road.

The drivers seem very experienced and capable. Conductors stride up and down the aisle, counting heads and conferring at intervals with the driver, who makes small notations in a little book. These figures are compared with those taken by the conductor, and often it is necessary to halt by the side of the road, count all the heads again, and engage in a little banter with the passengers before the vehicle can chug off again to the next village, where the process is repeated.

No one boards a bus empty-handed. Parcels range from baskets of bananas to sacks of potatoes, and include the entire range of food-stuffs in between. Before long the aisle is completely blocked with parcels, and the conductor executes a kind of leapfrog getting to and fro during his frequent consultations with the driver. When the aisle is completely choked, parcels are lifted to the roof of the bus, and in some instances their owners sit aloft atop sacks of potatoes for the ride up or down the mountains.

Since my legs are very long, even by American standards, I soon found both of them completely cramped, since there was no way to avoid pressing my kneecaps on the steel back of the seat in front and no place to place my feet underneath, that space having been used for more storage. At every village, food hawkers came alongside, selling little twists that resembled doughnuts, and the beggars who live in the terminals did a rather futile round of each window, asking for alms. My white face attracted more than my share of them. I was soon cleaned out of change. At places where the stop was a bit longer, we alighted and stood awhile in the hot sun to permit circulation to return to the lower limbs, and thus give the beggars easier access.

The sudden heat of the plains after the blissfully cool air of Kodai was a shock I had not expected, though I should have been prepared for it. February in Dindigul or Trichy is like Chicago in July or August. In the station, I noted a wooden box marked URGENT—RUSH, which was addressed to some hopeful and which, having gathered about three weeks' worth of dust, was destined to be quite late in arriving at its final station. I thought again of my three bags, and wondered wistfully about their whereabouts. I had begun to think of them as three poor pilgrims, their brown sides stained and dusty, engaged in an arduous journey to Mecca. Yet I had paid in advance for their swift air transportation, and had been assured they would be in Madras before I was. It was now twenty-three days since I had last seen them.

At Dindigul we changed buses and became the unwitting center of a large donnybrook. This being a long stopover, some men had left their seats to go out for a coffee break, and the three of us entered the bus and sat down in those seats. The rule in India is: no lady is required to sit with a man. If a lady enters the bus, she is to find a seat next to a lady. If no such seat is available, the men are expected to move to the long side seat and make room for her. Usually this is done quietly, with little commotion. Occasionally the lady will stand in the aisle next to the desired seat and if the man does not move, she looks mournful until the driver notices and makes the man move. But the three of us, being together, took these seats immediately. The men returned, shrugged and found other places, all but one fellow, who was traveling with his wife and child. He stood in the aisle and shouted, gesticulated and called on all the gods to witness how he had been cheated of his seat while answering the call of nature. The entire busload got into the act.

Sister Lydia whispered that we should pretend not to notice. This became increasingly difficult, as the roar became deafening and passengers from nearby buses began to notice it too. Finally, glancing up with an angelic smile, Lydia told the man in Tamil that his wife was welcome to share the seat with us; we would all compress ourselves, she told him, and he could sit in the empty seat just in front of her. This solution only enraged him, though the other passengers found the solution to their liking. The judgment of the crowd going against him and his throat beginning to give out in the heat and strain of shouting, he finally motioned his wife to take the offered seat, and she did so, with the child on her lap. He plunked himself down in front of her and continued growling about the injustice of life until the next bus stop. Lydia turned and whispered to me, "He was quite right, you know. This was his seat." The journey proceeded while I pondered this in my heart.

Many bumpy, cramped hours later, during which oranges and sandwiches were shared, we reached Trichy, at around five in the evening. We got into a bicycle rickshaw, miraculously, three of us and my bag in that tiny seat, and bumped off again to the I.C.M. convent. I reflected with some satisfaction that the weight-reducing machine I had paid for that day must have melted off many pounds.

At the convent, I was welcomed and given a most comfortable room belonging to a nun. The convent was fresh and clean, as all convents are, and most attractive. There was a wonderful poster on the wall which said, IF YOU WERE ARRESTED FOR BEING A FOLLOWER OF CHRIST, WOULD THERE BE ENOUGH EVIDENCE TO CONVICT YOU?

A shower restored me to normal, and a quiet dinner with the sisters revealed that I had been received at the door by the Mother Provincial of the order herself, Mother Matilda. She is a very good-looking Indian lady with a businesslike air of no nonsense about her who must be a very good administrator. As we ate, I was introduced to the other nuns in residence there: the superior, Sister M. Agnes, in a beautiful azure blue sari, Sister Jeanne Devas, Sister Agnes Logghe, Sister Berthe and Sister Annie. They were in regular dress, not habits, and hence were a mixture of saris and European clothing, since two of the nuns were from Belgium. A spirit of holy poverty and practicality prevailed, and as the meal was finished, Mother Matilda washed the dishes in a little open-air veranda, while we all lined up with towels to dry. I phoned Father Besses, S.J., but since he had not known in advance of my arrival, he was unable to arrange his schedule to visit with me. He said he would come to Kodai after Easter to see me.

Two Muslim women appeared at the convent door in the evening and were admitted quickly. Mother Matilda told me that they lived across the road and this was the only place they were permitted to visit. This was allowed because it was known that there were no men here. A small girl was with one of them, and we sat in the little parlor under the fluorescent light and smiled helplessly at one another. They spoke only Tamil, so the nuns told me their story in English while the ladies smiled and smiled. I was horrified to learn that they were virtually slaves in their own homes. Their husbands were wealthy, and their homes lacked nothing in the way of comfort and decoration. The nuns had visited them and assured me this was so. Neither of the women had gone beyond the second grade, and both had been married at thirteen years of age to older Muslim men. One of them had lost her first husband, and his brother, a man of forty, had then taken her as his wife when she was fifteen. They had a number of children, and the other lady, who seemed around thirty or thirty-five, had grandchildren already. The women were not blessed with features that would drive a man wild, I decided. Both had very large protruding teeth, as though from constant thumb-sucking. Their clothing was of silk and lace, not overly clean, and there were ornaments everywhere that hinted of wealth: nose ornaments, earrings, pendants, ankle bracelets and rings gracing the bare feet.

When I expressed my shock at this slavery, the nuns told me that in the house next to these two poor creatures were a Muslim and his wife, both doctors, who sent their little girl to the best schools and who were living the usual life of a twentieth-century professional couple. "So it is changing gradually in some instances," said Mother Matilda.

"Tell them that I have five children, am a widow, have a very responsible job, seven grandchildren, and that I have traveled to India from America alone, and that this is my third visit." I watched to see what expression this bit of news might engender. There seemed to be no response whatever.

Instead, their next question was translated as, "How is it that you are all living here together, some Indians, some not Indians? How are you doing this?" Mother Matilda translated this one for me.

I found myself eager to reply. "Tell them that we are related through Christ," I suggested.

Mother Matilda's face closed. "That I cannot do," she answered, and then explained to the women that some were nuns and some (myself) were visitors. This seemed to satisfy them, though I wondered why Christ could not be mentioned. Later I found that if any mere suggestion came to the ears of their mates that Christ or religion had entered the discussion, they would have been forbidden to come again, and the sisters knew this small contact with the outside world was important to them both. Apparently, every detail of the visit would be related and re-related at home.

We watched them take their leave, silently flowing through the convent doorway into the dark road to the house opposite. A small boy there answered the door and admitted them; before entering their prison they turned and waved to the little band of nuns in the convent doorway. What a world!

I retired to the quiet of the guestroom, noticed the tasteful arrangement on the floor in the corner of the room for private devotions, and wondered which nun I had displaced from her bed. The bed was a marvel of austerity. After trying unsuccessfully to arrange my outraged bones on the thin felt mattress, I decided to see what was holding it up. It was a shock to find that unlike the Jesuits' woven frames under their straw mattresses, the nuns had opted for solid steel. It looked like a metal cabinet door. I pulled the mosquito netting down and lay in the dark, my muscles quivering still from the seven-hour bus ride. At 2 A.M. I arose and decided to find something to read. On the desk I found Tagore's *Scattered Birds*, a most beautiful collection of haiku-type poems that was new to me. I read it from cover to cover. The quiet beauty of this poetic genius filled my heart and soothed my mind. I fell asleep afterward and did not awaken until the Muslim/rooster ecumenical worship aroused me. I dressed quickly and went off to early Mass with Sister Agnes.

The sisters have a tiny chapel for prayers and devotions together, where we had met before bedtime the night before, but Mass is not said there. Sister Agnes and I hurried down the lane at six-thirty to Campion School and watched the sleepy schoolboys file in for Mass. Two of them, clad in shorts and white shirts, were easily seven feet tall, and I wondered if they had a basketball team. The boys were most devout at Mass, and were led in prayer by a white-cassocked young priest. Returning down the road to the convent, I saw a small boy feeding a little brown dog by holding a cup to its mouth.

"What are you giving him?" I asked the boy.

"Coffee, madam," he replied. The dog seemed to love it, judging from the excited gyrations of his tail.

Breakfast was very pleasant, with all the sisters present, and we chatted awhile over coffee. Mother Matilda shared my sentiments about Mrs. Gandhi. I felt sorry for this woman who had done so much for India and was now being reviled by the press throughout the country. I had seen India during the early days of the Emergency, and had been very impressed by the progress I had seen everywhere: trains and buses on time, public offices well manned and open the entire business day. Of course there were signs everywhere, too, which are still pasted on all the vehicles and post offices: AVOID LOOSE TALK; DO YOUR DUTY and IT'S NICE TO BE IMPORTANT; IT'S MORE IMPORTANT TO BE NICE. These, I felt, were a bit much, but in the general air of efficient functioning, I had not minded the propaganda. Now Mrs. Gandhi is being blamed for many things she had nothing to do with. I thought it sad that her stupid son had brought her to such a state, after her many years of devotion to India. The nuns agreed, and said they thought she would stage a comeback. It will be interesting to follow the situation. She has rejected her former associates and has formed a new party, it seems. The new government had done nothing anyone can mention to solve India's overwhelming problems, with the exception of issuing new statements daily on the corruption of the former government. When this issue is finally beaten into the ground, one hopes to see some much-needed rural aid and employment opportunities for the vast population. Mrs. Gandhi has unwittingly left a legacy the people can compare the new government to, for the signs will remain until they moulder into dust, this being India.

I left the convent with Sister Agnes accompanying me on my next stop en route to the ashram: St. Joseph's School, in Trichy, where we have a number of Harijan boys being educated on the Nevett Fund. As we rode there on the rickshaw, Sister Agnes Logghe, a lovely Belgian nun with many years of service to India behind her, pointed out the flood damage that had left its black high-water mark on the buildings. At the school, we waited for the rector, who came finally and sent us across the road to the semiboarding school, to confer with Father Thomas. I asked him about the flood. It had done terrible damage at Trichy, he told me, saying it had created an irretrievable loss to the Jesuits at St. Joseph's. He gave me a paper containing details of the flood, which follow:

November 13–15, 1977 Floods. The Events and Their Effect on Persons and their Belongings, by Dr. G. A. Savariraj:

INTRODUCTION:

On Saturday, November 12, 1977, for about 7 hours between 11 A.M. and 6 P.M. a severe cyclone ravaged all the coastal and some of the inland districts of Tamilnadu State in South India. Before people could take note of the cyclonic havoc, the next day on November 13, 1977, uncontrollable floods ransacked the same regions of the same state; 10 out of the 14 districts of the state have been more or less seriously affected by this cyclone and floods; besides the loss of about 500 human lives, the material loss is estimated to be Rs. 2,000 millions, the most seriously and grievously damaged districts are Tiruchirappalli Town (Trichy) and Tanjore; in the district of Tiruchirappalli itself, one of the worse hit areas of the town is the St. Joseph's College and its surroundings as it is situated on the bank of the river Cauvery in a low-lying area bordering cultivated lands on its northern and western sides.

In this report we describe in Section II the events that overtook the College and its surroundings quite unaware. . . .

II. THE EVENTS:

Already the Saturday Cyclone has not only blown off the thatched roofs of hundreds of huts in the town but also uprooted trees in large numbers, obstructing normal traffic; in the St. Joseph's College itself about 70 trees, victims of cyclone-havoc were hindering the usual passage through the roads and alleys in the college campus; student volunteers spent the whole of Sunday in clearing the roads and alleys; little did anyone realize the worst had yet to come. At 6:30 P.M. on Sunday there was some water about 1 foot deep in the Harijan Colony and in the New Hostel, which was an annual feature during the monsoon season. But within half-an-hour unmanageable waters from the Cauvery in the north and from its uncontrollably breached feeder canals in the west crashed into the college campus in mad fury; the furious waters engulfed the entire college complex and its surroundings, and the towering college and school buildings looked as if they were floating on 12 to 15 feet deep water for two nights and a day. Some details are given as follows:

A. *Harijan Colony:* From the human point of view the most painfully affected were the inhabitants of the three harijan units, Chintmani, Venice and Preaton Battery; there were 400 mud-walled thatched huts sheltering about 2,000 people. Some of them are working in the St. Joseph's College or school as peons, marteers, sweepers or manual labourers. Since flood waters rose up to more than 15 feet in these areas, all the huts have been washed away. All the people took shelter in the dry areas of St. Joseph's College and School buildings. Another 1,000 villagers from the neighbouring village Kambarasampettai were also given shelter in the School buildings. The latter had gone back to their village after three days, while the former were living in the college campus till December 1, 1977. But since the education of 4900 students could not be postponed indefinitely, the inhabitants of the Harijan Colony were obliged to leave the college and find shelter in a nearby municipal building; indeed at present they have nowhere to lay their heads (Luke 9:58) which they can claim as their houses.

Then follows a description of the damage done to Teresa Colony, Joseph Colony, Britto Colony, and finally this note on the College departments:

Narrating the panic in the New Hostel a student pointed out that within half-an-hour water rose very fast to 15 feet around the New Hostel, 12 feet around the college library and laboratories, 8 feet near the Sacred Heart Hostel and 5 feet near the Father's House on November 13, 1977 night. The Mahe Grounds were a vast expanse of water, a mini-ocean. The torrential fury of the current played havoc every-where and even inside buildings like the library and laboratories, knocking down and scattering pell-mell everything in its way. One PUC boy from distant Changanacherry, Kerala, was swept off his feet by the murderous current near the community Centre and his body could be found only 36 hours later. It was only on November 14 evening that Fr. Principal could reach the 230 inmates marooned in the New Hostel, bringing some biscuits and water. Volunteers from BHEL, NCC and the Army rescued 60 of them on November 14 evening and the remaining 170 had to stay in the hostel itself in pitch darkness with water all around them below.

III. THEIR EFFECTS

The people of the Harijan Colony had very little material possessions; but what little they had, they lost it all; let us earnestly hope that they have not also lost hope of a better future. Any rehabilitation or reconstruction work must instill in them an unshakable hope of a brighter future through self-help, supported by the help of others.

In the *Teresa Colony, Joseph Colony and Britto Colony*, every family has lost its food provisions (rice/paddy, grocery items), utensils, clothes and jewels, and the books and note-books of the school/college going children.

From the material point of view the damage and loss sustained by the *College Departments* are colossal. The worst-hit part of the campus is the *Library*, one of the best-equipped collections of books in the whole country, containing not only the best books on almost every subject of study but also rare and precious books gathered in the course of the last 132 years. In every rack consisting of 7 shelves, books kept in 5 shelves have been completely damaged. We have lost over 40,000 precious volumes including very valuable international research journals; both in Physics and in Botany, the Research Libraries used by M. Phil. and Ph.D. scholars have been completely damaged. In chemistry the B.Sc. Lab has suffered a heavy loss. In Physics, the Photo-Laboratory and Science-workshop being underground installations were under 15 feet of water for more than 24 hours, and therefore have been wiped out. The college playgrounds, the Mahe grounds are covered with more than 6 inches of silt and mud.

Then follows an itemized list of losses, the grand total being 6,258,000 rupees, or roughly $782,250. When one realizes that this is the report of the loss in only one town, and that a very great number of towns were thus affected, the loss of life and property is indeed staggering.

At the semiboarding school across the road, Father Thomas greeted me cordially and sent for the Nevett scholars; I spent about an hour photographing them and visiting a little while in the shadow of Rock Fort Temple before boarding the bus that would carry me finally to the ashram one hour later.

CHAPTER 9

Saccidananda Ashram

Saccidananda Ashram, Shantivanam, the ashram of the Holy Trinity, was founded in 1950 by two French Fathers, Jules Monchanin, who took the name of Parama Arubi Ananda (the Bliss of the Supreme Spirit) and Henri le Saux, who took the name of Abhishiktananda (the Bliss of Christ). By taking these names and calling the ashram by the name of Saccidananda, the Hindu name for the Godhead, as a symbol of Christian Trinity, they intended, anticipating the Vatican Council and the All-India Seminar, to show that they sought to identify themselves with the Hindu "search for God," the quest of the Absolute, which has inspired monastic life in India from the earliest times, and to relate this quest to their own experience of God in Christ in the mystery of the Holy Trinity. Unfortunately, Father Monchanin died in 1957 before the ashram could be properly established, and Swami Abhishiktananda after remaining for some time alone, eventually settled as a hermit in the Himalayas, where he died in 1973. On his departure in 1968 the ashram was taken over by a group of monks from Kurisumala Ashram in Kerala.

Thus the little leaflet of the ashram describes the early history of the place, to which Dom Bede Griffith has come as the reigning spirit and holy man, and where six young disciples have now joined him in a kind of novitiate. I was met at the gateway of the ashram, after I lugged my little wheeled cart with my bag on it down an embankment, amid a flock of bored water buffalo being driven by a small boy with a stick. The sun was very hot, and I was delighted to enter the shaded garden of the ashram.

A very beautiful young man with long, shining curled hair and a wonderful, Christlike beard, wearing a white dhoti and shawl, introduced himself as Brother Vincent, one of the disciples, and it was he who led me to the little guesthouse, where a room was waiting for me. He brought me bedding immediately (though I had been advised by Sister Lydia to bring my own, and this was the bulk of my luggage) and fixed up the string bed with a folded afghan as a mat, over which was placed a cotton sheet, topped by a woven cotton throw. A plain wooden table and chair, and a rough-hewn shelf for books and other items completed the simple furnishing. There was a shuttered window, innocent of screens, and the roof was woven of coconut palm leaves. Simple, indeed, as Sister Lydia and Father d'Silva had said. A schedule tacked to the door announced the hours for ritual, meditation, meals, and so on, and it began at 5:30 A.M. Two hours are set aside for meditation, the hours of sunrise and sunset, which are traditional times for prayer and meditation in India. There was prayer in common three times a day: morning, noon and night.

Brother Vincent appeared and said if I wished to see Dom Bede, I might come with him. I followed him across a beautifully shady area planted with coconut palms, across a little raised path, narrow and private, and there, on the cement veranda of a little hut, I sat and spoke to the holy man I had heard so much about. He is very remarkable in appearance, being well over six feet tall, with a wonderful face. Classic English features are now somewhat hidden behind a snowy white beard, and his white shoulder-length hair has a hint of blond, which may have been the original color or may be caused by the sun. His eyes are beautiful, deep-set and with very dark lines carved down from them along the aquiline nose. His face gives the immediate and unmistakable impression of the asceticism that has been his life for many years. He was dressed in the saffron shawl and robe, wore no shoes, and greeted me with all the courtesy one has come to associate with the English.

Sister Lydia had told him I was coming, and he was expecting me. I told him where I was from, a little about the Center for Pastoral Ministry where I had worked, and my present mission in India: to examine the possibility of retiring there for at least a part of the year. He suggested that in case a resident visa could not be readily obtained I might use the ordinary tourist visa and then have it extended for another three months, thus making possible a six-month visit. He also told me that some people make a practice of remaining for their full visa and then go to Ceylon for a time, and return to

India on another visa, thus avoiding the expense of traveling back to Europe or America. That, too, seemed a possibility to me, though as the mother of a large family, I would certainly want to be with them for half of each year.

We spoke about prayer, and he suggested the Jesus Prayer as a very effective one to promote a closer union with Christ, Who is within us. I was familiar with the practice, of ancient origin. It consists of sitting very straight, with the spine completely upright. One breathes from the upper abdomen very slowly, inhaling on the words "Lord Jesus Christ" and exhaling on the words "have mercy on me, a sinner." Repeated over and over again, for increasing periods of time each day, great spiritual and physical benefits are claimed; in addition the blood pressure is reduced, and the whole body calmed and relaxed. I longed to ask him about his own prayer, but since I had just met him, decided simply to observe for a time before venturing any more questions.

Having mentioned that I was eager to photograph him with my sound movie camera, I found him very gracious in agreeing, though it must be a pain in the neck to him. I imagine every eager pilgrim to the ashram wants photos. However, there was not the slightest hint that this was the case; indeed, his natural courtesy and charity gave the impression that he would find it a great pleasure. He told me I was to remain at the ashram as long as I wished and that many came to stay for months, and some for years. Knowing my own constitution, however, which does not do very well in the heat, I was fearful of becoming ill in a place far from home and was therefore planning to remain only a few days. He seemed surprised, since I had come so far, but I told him this visit was in the nature of an exploration and that I hoped at some future time to remain longer, now that I had learned how to get there. Such a longer stay, I thought, would be possible when I knew firsthand the climate of the place and could form an accurate idea of what would be needed for my stay there.

Dom Bede told me of the people presently in residence: one American, a man from New York; and a French Canadian, of whom I will add more later. Some sisters from an Indian congregation were there on retreat, a Frenchman dressed in a yellow shawl and dhoti and sporting a long beard, two young shaven Buddhists from France, a young girl from Australia, another from Scotland, and a slightly older girl from Leicester, in England. This last was an Anglican. There were others as well, about twenty in all it seemed, but I did not have time to talk to all of them. The days were quite busy between meditation and walks down to the Cauvery River, which flowed along the side of the ashram in silver beauty and majesty. Later, when Dom Bede and I walked down to see the sunset there, the calm flowing of the river and the blue hills in the distance made a scene of unforgettable beauty. He told me how much he loved the place and that he planned to remain there always, by this lovely river.

The chapel of the ashram is modeled on the South Indian Hindu temple. The tabernacle is almost hidden behind an enclosure at the far end, suggesting the Hindu "cave of the heart," and is always kept dark to signify that God dwells in the darkness. Directly above the tabernacle is the vimana (dome), and on the outside, high above the chapel roof, it rises very like those on the Hindu temples. At the base of the vimana are the figures of the four living creatures of the Apocalypse, the lion, the ox, the man and the eagle "which represent the whole creation redeemed by Christ." Above them are four figures of saints, Mary, Peter, Paul and Benedict, representing redeemed humanity, and above these, four figures of Christ in various postures seated on a royal throne and surrounded by angels. Each of the figures faces a different direction, to encompass the entire world. I asked Dom Bede about angels, so many recently having expressed doubts about their existence. "Oh, yes, there are certainly angels," he said. "I believe that some of the 'gods' of Hinduism are actually angels—and in some cases, demons."

I was greatly interested in this affirmation, which I have always felt myself. So many times in my life I have been helped on the brink of disaster by aid I had always felt was actually the guidance and help of my guardian angel.

To continue the description of the dome, as given in the ashram literature:

"Above these figures of Christ and the saints is the throne of God, represented by the dome covered with peacock feathers and above this again the lotus, symbol of purity supporting the 'kalasam,' an ancient symbol of the four elements, earth, water, air and fire, pointing upwards to the 'akasa,' the infinite space, in which God dwells in 'inaccessible light.'

"Thus," the leaflet continues, "at the entrance of the temple the mind is directed to the mystery of the Godhead as three Persons adored by angels. Then, through the mystery of the Cross and Resurrection, it is drawn to contemplate 'the new heaven and the new earth' which is the destiny of man, and beyond this the mind is finally turned to the ineffable mystery of the Godhead beyond name and form to which all earthly images are intended to lead us."

The inner sanctuary, down a few steps from the "cave of the heart," has an inscription in Sanskrit taken from the Upanishads: *"Param arthastvam evaiko nananyosti jagatha pate,"* which means: "You are alone the supreme Being; there is no other Lord of the world," and under this the words *Kyrios Christos,* the Lord Christ, in Greek letters. It is in this inner sanctuary, on the red tile floor, where mats are placed in parallel lines, that Dom Bede and his disciples sit, yoga fashion, facing one another, for the liturgy. Between them is a tall brass oil lamp that is lit for prayers, containers for incense sticks, bowls of flowers and a brass bell. Just beyond this area is the outer court, where the congregation assembles. All of this is surrounded by a low curving wall; it is all open to the sky and the breezes off the Cauvery. Flowering vines and birdsong complete the decoration. I also noticed two chipmunks, apparently greatly attracted by the liturgy, which had choice seats above the inner sanctuary, on the high beams, and which scampered about all through the services, hanging down sometimes by their hind legs to get a better view.

The gate leading to the chapel compound is adorned with a gopuram, on which is sculptured an image of the Holy Trinity in the form of a Trimurti, a three-headed figure, which according to Hindu tradition represents the three aspects of the Godhead, as Creator, Preserver and Destroyer of the universe. This is taken as a symbol of the three persons in one God of the Christian Trinity. The figure is shown emerging from a cross to show that the mystery of the Trinity is revealed to us through the Cross of Christ. In pointing out the figures on the gopuram to me, Dom Bede called my attention to the fact that the Holy Spirit, third person of the Trinity was shown as a woman; the spirit of love and inspiration having, for him, a feminine form. This last innovation would provide much satisfaction among the feminist theologians, I am certain.

Meals at the ashram were all taken on the floor, using the fingers rather than utensils. A concession was made in my case, and I had a little table and chair. Thus I sat in the front of the room, like the schoolma'am, while Dom Bede, his disciples and all the other guests of the ashram sat on mats below me. I was also given a spoon. The food was very simple, but tasty. It consisted of a big meal of rice and vegetables at noon, sometimes with chapatti—a thin, flaky wafer—and the drink served was boiled water. The evening and morning meals were lighter: at night, wheat rolled into a large pancake and served with a spicy sauce, and in the morning something similar with a milky kind of rice water over it. I ate everything in sight, and enjoyed it very much. I glanced down at Dom Bede and noticed that in the evening he had a cup of curds as well; probably a very good thing for his health.

After this evening meal, during which silence was observed and an excerpt from either a Hindu or a Christian work read aloud, we all trooped out with our stainless-steel plates to a circular sink outside fitted with many faucets, where we washed our own plates and cups. Afterward we took them over to a large pan of nearly boiling water, where they were rinsed and then dried. It was, I thought, a neat arrangement, and one I would like to inaugurate at home, though I doubt whether anyone else would be very enthusiastic about it.

During each afternoon, there was tea served in the garden, in the center of a great circle of benches, where Dom Bede came to join in conversation with everyone. These conversations with Dom Bede during periods of relaxation were most enjoyable. Each evening after supper, we gathered on a little veranda in wicker chairs and simply talked together. Mayor Daley, Mother Teresa, good books and events of international interest were lightly tossed between the guests and Dom Bede. It was here I encountered the many guests, and learned a bit about their lives. One guest in particular, the French Canadian, will remain in my memory a long time, for he proved to be a curious fellow indeed. I had been talking about my experience involving the Muslim ladies and how the Mother Provincial had told me she could not tell them about Christ. I was expressing my regret over this when he burst out, "That's the trouble with you Catholics! Always shoving Christ down the throats of everyone!" I was surprised, and said it was rather a question of sharing something I knew to be the highest good. Dom Bede agreed. But this fellow went on in a very loud tone about religion, and how much he hated it. Dom Bede changed the subject, and we spoke of snow, and other cool things. We retired when the stars came out, at about 9 P.M., and I noticed a beautiful full moon sailing over the velvet sky through the coconut palms. I had a quick cold shower in the women's shower room, courtesy of a barrel and a small dipper, and then went to my room. With the light on, of course, I was soon joined by a great number of mosquitoes, and I turned if off quickly and tried sleeping under the net. It was much too warm, so I threw it back over the rod and let the mosquitoes do their worst. Actually, it turned out that they, too, were feeling the heat and were not much interested in American fare. They droned awhile, and like me, soon fell asleep.

It was no trouble at all to arise for meditation at five. I dressed quickly and went down to the riverbank to watch the sunrise. It was magnificent. All of nature seemed to be conspiring to add to the glory of what was happening here. Along the bank, amid the sheltering trees, I could see the ashram guests absorbed in prayer, and one of the disciples, the one who walked with his pelvic bones a full six inches ahead of the rest of his body, doing his yoga exercises on a little mat. It seemed quite proper and fitting.

Coming back for morning devotions in the chapel, I again saw the French Canadian, this time with a dirty undershirt on and with a blue rag wrapped around his loins, hairy and barefoot, arguing with one of the young Buddhists. It was obvious that meditation held no charm for him.

That day, I armed the movie/sound camera and Dom Bede kindly gave me some of his time, speaking for the benefit of the film. But as luck would have it, very shortly afterward I saw that the batteries had failed, so the portion I was able to shoot was quite limited. Luckily, before this session I had taken some shots of the place, capturing the birdsong and various scenes of the ashram, including one of Dom Bede striding toward the tea garden. The camera was new to me, and I had not realized how short-lived the batteries were. The young man from New York told me it was the sound feature that took the power.

During devotions in the chapel, I was amazed to see a very small little boy enter briskly and take his place among the disciples on the matting. He seemed to be about six or seven years old, and very devout. He responded to all the prayers, sang all the hymns in Tamil or

Sanskrit, and reverently took the sacred ash to place on his forehead. I was intrigued, and when Sister Lydia appeared on Sunday morning to take me to visit her village across the road, I asked about him.

"It's a very sad case," she said. "He came with his mother and sister to my village, having walked about thirty miles from another place because they knew I was a doctor. The mother was dying of TB. The case was so far advanced I could only make her easy until she died. The daughter, who is eighteen, I sent to Madras to learn needlework, and the boy I placed with Dom Bede to keep until we can find a home for him."

Since the mother's death, Sister Lydia had been trying to figure out what to do with Renganathan. Later, Dom Bede spoke to me about the boy.

"This is no place for him to grow up. He needs a woman's care and an education." I thought of the Fund.

"Is there any place where you know he would be well cared for?" I asked him.

"In Madras, where his sister is, it would be possible to find a place, I think," he told me. Lydia also confirmed this, adding that if the sister, at eighteen, eventually managed to obtain a dowry, she would then marry, and the boy would have a home with her.

I thought quickly. Ted Huebsch, a great friend of the Nevett Fund, had given me money, before I came, with one express purpose: find someone you know needs help, and provide it! Here was certainly one such case, and I did not hesitate a moment. "Make whatever arrangements you can for him in Madras," I told Dom Bede. "Send word to me of what it will cost, and I will see that you have the money." He said that he would do so, and the matter was settled. Thanks to a pair of truly holy Charismatic Christians, Ted and Mary Huebsch, the ashram child would find a home in a good place, near his sister, and eventually be able to live in his own family again. It had clearly been the Holy Spirit, so alive in their hearts, that had prompted the gift, and led me, all unknowing, to the child who needed this help.

Dom Bede took me on a little tour of the ashram, and pointing out the temple dome, told me that the Hindus believe that temple domes have a very special attraction for spirits, both good and evil, and that a blessing of the vimana is necessary before a Hindu temple can be used. Honoring this custom, Dom Bede had conducted a blessing of this vimana when it was constructed. He had to climb aloft and say certain prayers and bless it, while five thousand Hindus and Muslims and Christians gathered at the ashram to witness the deed.

I asked him about the rumor of De Nobili's recovered grave, but he had not heard it. He took me to the fine library he has gathered at the ashram, set in a lovely octagonal building with a glory of bougainvillea curtaining one side of it. A little veranda surrounds the entire structure, and, inside, bookshelves are fitted into the walls around an open center where tables and chairs permit study and reading. I noted the great number of books there from every faith and wished I could spend many months there, just reading and learning.

All around the ashram were fields under cultivation, since the ashram owns five acres of land, on which are grown the rice and vegetables they feed their guests. They also have a small herd of cows. They helped establish two nursery schools and a dispensary in the village nearby, thus sharing in the concerns of their neighbors, but, as the little booklet says, "We have to keep constantly in mind that what people need more than food or clothing or medicine or education is knowledge of God. An ashram must above all be always a place of prayer where people can find God, where they can experience the reality of the presence of God in their lives and know that they were created not merely for this world, but for eternal life."

When I mentioned leaving, Dom Bede told me that it would be well if I remained over Sunday, since their monthly dialogue would be held that day, during which Hindus, Muslims, and Christians of many denominations would gather to spend some time exploring the areas in which agreement could be found. I thought this would be most interesting to hear, and agreed to remain another day.

On Sunday, at around 9 A.M. (I had already been up for four hours) many cars began arriving, and from them poured a variety of gentlemen dressed in everything from sport shirts and slacks to cassocks and sandals. A special place had been arranged the day before for this meeting, a huge circle about sixty feet in diameter, around which had been planted very fresh green plants, and around the inside perimeter of which the chapel mats had been placed. One of the brothers of the ashram brought a little bench for me to sit on, and I perched at six o'clock, with Dom Bede at high noon, and about thirty-five people all around the clock circle sitting quite comfortably yoga style. It made me wish I had continued with yoga. I had done it regularly for about two years and then given it up. Now I knew that though I could assume the lotus position, my legs would go to sleep and I would never thereafter be able to regain my feet. I was grateful for the little bench.

The meeting began with a very solemn prayer asking God to bless the dialogue and to bring forth from it renewed understanding and appreciation for one another's faith and convictions.

As Father Francis, who had been invited to speak first, was beginning his statement, which was to be confined to the topic of where and how he saw his Christianity in relationship to Hinduism, the French Canadian, in his dirty undershirt and tattered rag stepped into the circle, aimed for the two o'clock position, and caused several women to rise and move their mats over to make room for him. Father Francis continued his statement.

This was followed by a statement from a Hindu, who said that his faith in Hinduism was no longer as great as it had once been, and that he was impressed by the social works and charity he had observed among Christians. Then a Jesuit from St. Joseph's, Trichy, began to speak. With great earnestness he related his childhood experience in a family half Christian and half Brahmin. He told of the respect the Brahmin portion had for the sincere love of God they had seen in his own Christian relatives, and how, when cousins and uncles, aunts and grandparents came to visit, each religion held appropriate devotions within the house with mutual respect for the God they both served. He mentioned the word "Christ" again, and immediately the French Canadian was shouting, "Christ! How can you call Him the Son of God? How do you know He even lived?" I suppressed a sudden desire to go over and brain him with my bench. No one else was even surprised. Evidently they had heard all of his act before.

The visiting Indian Jesuit turned toward him and said he had never met Churchill but believed that he had lived because of the historical evidence that existed. The historical evidence for the existence of Christ was irreproachable.

"I don't believe in Christ," the undershirted wonder shouted. "You insult people by even mentioning Him, when many in the world do not believe in Him."

The Jesuit quietly said that scholarship proved that Christ had lived, and had died in a certain place at a certain time. Of this there was no doubt whatever. "My faith," he continued, "tells me that He was not a mere man, however, but the Son of God."

The discussion then centered around "faith," and I found the Jesuit's arguments very clear: "A son must accept the word of his mother even about who his own father is," he stated pointedly. "The butter is present in the milk, though it cannot be seen. We accept these things on faith."

The French Canadian was trying to muster all of his elementary school education to deal with this one when Dom Bede Griffith interrupted gently, "You will have plenty of time to discuss all points this afternoon. This morning's session is given to statements on the part of all our guests as to their own religious belief."

The Muslim then spoke, relating in detail the fasting all Muslims undergo one month out of the year, which was, he said, in order to be able to feel the hunger that the poor man experiences always. He spoke of the system of giving a portion of income for the poor and said that he was very friendly toward Christians, a fact that had often gotten him into trouble with his own religious brothers.

The young Anglican woman from England made some very good points, particularly when she stated that the Hindu seemed to stress the vertical relationship from the individual to God, while the Christian stressed the horizontal one to his fellowman. She said she thought what was needed was for these two directions to be more widely stressed by both Hindus and Christians, unaware perhaps that as she illustrated these directions her hands were outlining the Sign of the Cross.

There were unintentionally humorous statements made too: for example, the Hindu gentleman, in trying to express that there are many valid paths to God, said, "All roads lead to Rome." Another remarked that Gandhi had said, "If God were to ever visit the earth again, He would have to come in the form of a loaf of bread." I wanted to remind him that that is exactly the form He took—bread—when He visited the earth, but in view of the Canadian's time-consuming interruptions of the dialogue, I refrained.

Father Lawrence Sundaram, the Jesuit from St. Joseph's Trichy, made a statement I found wonderful: "The devotee seeks sanctity; the saint seeks God."

We broke for lunch and resumed the discussion afterward, continuing until 3 P.M. The general air of understanding, charity and hospitality of Dom Bede and the ashram made a profound impression on all the visitors, and they all expressed this with gratitude and rather elegant phrases of thanks.

At evening prayers in the chapel that night, when all the invited guests had departed, Dom Bede spoke for a short time on the subject of not judging one's neighbor but simply giving him love. I was moved, remembering my anger at the French Canadian, so after dinner I sought him out to try to speak to him, hoping that if I could understand him better, my dislike would vanish.

He was very willing to talk—even eager to see if he could shock me. "I am a criminal, and have been for twenty-six years," he grinned.

"Have you been in prison, then?" I asked.

"No, but I am a thief, a pimp and a murderer."

I asked if he had tried prayer.

"I don't believe in all that hogwash," he said flatly.

We walked over to the veranda, where the chairs were waiting for the evening conversation. Dom Bede and Father Francis were there, and gradually we gathered around them and sat down. Dom Bede expressed his belief that the day had gone well. The French Canadian crossed his hairy legs, slouched down in his chair, and began again the by now familiar refrain.

Dom Bede looked at me with a smile. "He has his own religion, you see," he explained.

"You're damn' right—and what's more, it's a damn' good one. I don't take kids and make them learn catechism or any of that rot. Kids don't need it. They only have to be natural and happy. Education has ruined more guys than anything else!"

"Did you ever have a child?" I asked, remembering how we had struggled to educate our own children.

"I had a daughter. Brought her up myself. She was goin' real great, too, until . . . ," and here he stopped suddenly. No one wanted to inquire what had happened. It was obvious that the Great Experiment had failed somehow.

I told him I thought children, like small pets, had to be trained properly from the beginning of their lives if they were to grow up in society and be able to hold their own. "That's what civilization is all about," I said, "the transferring of what one knows as good and true to the next generation, so that they can build on it."

This began another diatribe against what the older generation does to kids: making them "go to school, teachin' them prayers, and all that garbage.

"I think a guy who works eight hours a day is a nut. He gets nothin' out of life. I remember guys in my class in school. They knew all the answers. I see them now, smug in their jobs and fancy houses. Hell, they don't know what life is all about!"

"What work do you do?" I asked him. "How do you support yourself?"

"I told you already. I'm a thief," he said with a snort.

"So you let others support you," I said.

"I live to be happy, that's all. I seen my mother prayin' and going to St. Joseph's in Montreal, every day of her life. Then she was paralyzed for the next thirty-five years!"

Suddenly I saw it, the cause of this hatred and bitterness. God had not answered his mother's prayers. She had died an invalid. "And yet," I said, "here you are at this ashram."

He laughed harshly. "That's another story altogether."

I realized then that he was here simply for the free food and shelter, a traveling hippie, an all too common phenomenon in India. The other guests examined their hands and did not look up. I wondered how often Dom Bede and his hospitality has been abused in this way.

That evening, as I left the group, heading for my little room under the thatch, I stopped long enough to wish him well. I told him I thought his mother was praying for him. His face lost for a moment the hard sneer that was its usual expression. "But if I were to base my life on that . . . ," he began. That was all he said. We parted.

Next morning, arrangements were made for Father Francis and me to get the bus for Dindigul. We were taken by horse cart to the bus stop. I dangled my legs off the back and enjoyed the experience I had not had since childhood, when I once had a ride on a horse-drawn ice wagon.

The bus station was filled with people, and we had missed the ten-o'clock bus, which had come at nine-thirty by some strange chance explainable only in India. I recalled Father Nevett's story of his first days in India, fresh from Britain, where great care was taken with schedules of public vehicles. He stood waiting for a bus in India, where it was always late, and was greatly surprised when the bus appeared promptly at the appointed hour.

"Congratulations," he said to the driver, "the bus is on time for a change."

"No, sahib," said the driver sadly, "this is yesterday's bus."

While waiting, and chatting with the brother from the ashram and Father Francis, I noticed a palmist squatting in a corner of the station. He had piles of very dirty cards in front of him, and a cage containing two parrots. Father Francis said that for one rupee the parrot would pull out one of the cards and tell my fortune. This was of no interest, but I had seen the sign with the palm all mapped out on it, and I have always been interested in palmistry. It seems to me plausible that the spirit or psyche of a person leaves certain clues on the body itself, and that it is possible that the palm might contain hints of this inner spirit, which could be discerned by one who had made a study of it.

We went over to the man and I offered him my palm to read, first crossing his with the required rupee. He spoke only Tamil, so it is fortunate that I had others with me who could translate. The man flattened out my hand in his, and began to read.

Brother spoke. "He says that you will have a long life, until eighty-three, and that you enjoy very good health." I knew this to be true, at least the health part, and waited for him to go on. More Tamil, and then, "He says you have lost all interest in material pleasures, and that you will devote your life to seeking higher knowledge." This impressed me no end. Then, "He says you are thinking of leaving your family in one place, and seeking a life of solitude in another place. A decision must be made, and will be made soon." And, "A problem is troubling you [my missing luggage?] and soon will be solved very satisfactorily." I asked him if I would live in India. "No, madam," he answered.

There was a bit more, quite flattering, and I was filled with awe until I realized that this station at Kulithalai was the only connection with the ashram, where no foreign lady would come unless she were seeking "higher knowledge" and was disinterested in material pleasures. This took the edge off the thing; however, the other bit, about my family and the life of solitude, stumped me. I found myself examining my hand with new interest. Father Francis and the brother also returned to their seats to wait, and studied their own palms. The brother knew something about palmistry too, and "did" Father Francis' palm while we waited for the bus to come.

The ride back bypassed Trichy and led straight to Dindigul. I was squashed into a seat shared by three small women and a little girl with silver bangles on her ankles who was intrigued by my yellow cotton hat. She wore it part of the journey, and could be induced to relinquish it only by being lured by one of the greasy fry cakes being sold at the bus stop. I enjoyed the country scenes once again: green paddy and bent workers, who have no difficulty whatever bending straight from the waist to work in those fields. Sudden and surprising outcroppings of huge rock erupted along the horizon, some with temples set atop them, and one with an imposing fort and wall that probably went back to the time of the English and French wars. I wished that Bert Nevett were with me to fill me in on the history. No one else on the bus spoke English.

I alighted at St. Joseph's Hospital, Dindigul, where the Fund has educated a great many nurses. I had visited there twice before and was looking forward to seeing again the Belgian sister-nurses I had met in the past. Sister Lena greeted me with a small cry: "How? Now you come?" I knew I had not given warning, due to the speed with which the trip had been planned. She had expected to see me only in April. I was led through the high-ceilinged, cool rooms of this beautiful hospital and brought into the dining room, where I was stuffed with the best food I found since landing in India. Meanwhile, Sister Lena told me of Arulee, one of our most prized nurses, who had married a fellow no one thought much of, and of her worry that the marriage would not succeed. I recalled that Bert, too, had mentioned this, how dowry money had been sent to her, how she had given it instead to this fellow to pay off his gambling debts, and how he had then written to Father for more money, evidently under the impression that he had found the horn of plenty. Arulee was working as a nurse again, Lena said, and lived far from Dindigul.

Lena also related, a bit ruefully, how the hospital was changing. Indian personnel were rapidly replacing the older Belgian staff, and the resultant differences in value systems were rapidly becoming evident. What the future held, she did not know, but simply went from day to day, doing her accustomed efficient job and trusting God for the rest. She told me too of the tremendous work being done in Dindigul and other cities of the South to help the Harijan villages recover from the effects of the terrible cyclone. Workers, all of them Indian scholars from Madras, had poured into the area and were being fed at the hospital while they struggled to rebuild and aid the suffering masses of people. The hospital compound had had much water, but fortunately not a great deal of damage had been done.

A bicycle rickshaw pedaled me uphill to the bus stop, where I found the Kodaikanal behemoth and climbed aboard. Unwisely, remembering the swaying, neck-jerking movement one finds in the rear of the bus, I headed for the front seat, and sat down. It was only seconds later that I found that there was no space for my long legs in that spot. But by this time the bus was completely filled with passengers, bundles, chickens, sacks of potatoes and many very dirty coolies, and so I was condemned to that seat for the ride up to Kodai. It seemed a very, very long ride. The driver had been told at Dindigul (by one of the sisters at the hospital who spoke Tamil) that I must be dropped off at Shembaganur. And as night fell, and the numbness of my legs increased, my only consolation lay in the fact that eventually I would arrive at Shembag and the warmth and friendship of Aelred and John de Mello.

The hours passed. Amid the stench of the coolies, and the sound of spit being delivered to the roads from each open window, and the knowledge that now, with the hot sun gone from the sky, every pestilence known to mankind was infesting the air around me, I thought of home, and the bus system there, which, though it was a million times better than India's, I had always scorned to use. How I longed for the Greyhound and their motto I had always ignored: "Leave the driving to us." I thought of my beautiful little shiny Datsun, asleep in the garage at home, under a roof that held one foot of snow. And it was during this ride that I also faced squarely the inconsistencies of my nature. In America it was easy for me to believe that I loved the poor, that I could see the face of Christ in their needs, and that I would be able to share their poverty and always help them. Now I saw how greatly I had overestimated my ability to share even the hard realities of an Indian bus ride.

At length, some thousands of years later it seemed, the driver stopped the bus and indicated by a curt nod to me that the hour of my deliverance had come.

"Shembaganur?" I asked hopefully.

"Shembaganur," he said.

I began climbing over the sacks in the aisle, heading for the rear door, holding my bag and purse awkwardly as I negotiated the difficult route on numbed limbs. As I got to the rear, and was almost out, I said to the conductor, "Sacred Heart College?"

"Sacred Heart is one furlong from here," said a passenger. I sat down on my bag in the aisle and waved the driver on. Finally the bus stopped again, and I was extruded into the pitch-black road, with the stars and moon high above but no other light whatever.

"Sacred Heart Seminary?" I shouted to the conductor, who watched from the rear of the departing bus with some interest. He pointed straight up as the bus disappeared around a corner.

I knew I could not remain in the road, because a truck or another bus would surely be whizzing around the corner, so I maneuvered myself over to the side away from the dropoff and tried to figure out what to do next. My eyes are not good in the dark; they never were, but at fifty-seven their early brightness had somewhat dimmed. The moon came sailing out from behind a cloud, and in that light I made out a very steep incline about fifty feet ahead. I decided that this must be the "up." I lugged my baggage along, ascending slowly because of the cold mountain air and because of my congealed legs, and suddenly I was laughing out loud. It was really quite an adventure.

Perhaps my laughter did it; at any rate, after what seemed a long climb, I glanced up, and far, far above me I made out the outline of a man against the sky. Cupping my mouth, I yelled, "Can you help me?"

He yelled down, "What's wrong?" I pondered how to answer this. There didn't seem to be an adequate vocabulary. Evidently the fact that a lady was mountain climbing, dragging her baggage along the road in the middle of the night was not in itself a matter for concern. I went right to the heart of the matter. "Where is Sacred Heart Seminary?"

"Up here, madam." And within seconds he and a small boy had bounded down that hill, in the darkness, and were carrying my bags up. I almost embraced him, so happy was I to see another human being, and one who could speak English. He was the father of one of the scholastics, I discovered, and had come to visit his son. He led me into the bright dining hall, where Aelred was having his dinner. I was all right again.

Aelred and I drove in the seminary car to pluck Regina from the midst of her family, and she brought some of them out to gaze at me. We drove to my little house in Kodai, and I unlocked the door and stumbled into my "home." It was very, very good to get back to it. I went to bed with no dinner, and fell asleep immediately.

CHAPTER 10

Kodai Woman's Day

The routine of life at Kodaikanal was taking on a form and character of its own within a very short time. Each morning, I awoke without being called, having retired at nine the night before. I quickly washed, dressed, wrapped my woolen shawl around my shoulders, and ventured down the early-morning road to the point where by kind arrangement the Presentation Convent driver would pass, with his other passenger, Father Montaud, from La Providence. A few sleepy greetings exchanged, we would drive uphill to the Presentation Convent and the magnificent chapel set like a jewel in the hills. There I attended six forty-five Mass, embellished by the sweet singing of the schoolgirls and the rich French accent of the liturgy as performed by Father Montaud. Afterward, drawn into a circle of warmth and friendship that seems the exclusive property of the Irish, I was given breakfast and the chance to talk to the nuns, who, like myself, were far from home and who cherished cleanliness as just one step removed from godliness.

Downhill is my best style of walking, and after Mass each morning I would descend along that interesting road, my spirit refreshed and my tummy nourished, and smile at everyone I met all the way down. Past the house of the local dentist, also a daily Mass-goer, past many good-looking homes with well-kept compounds behind their gates, past a little bridge on which was the sign DO VOTE FOR A.M.G.E—DON'T FORGET, past the kids from the town en route to school at the convent, and the youth on motorcycles or herding cattle to pasture, past the "auto repair shop," with the two yoked bullocks and a load of huge gray stones for the road repairs as the only transport in sight, past the "micro-wave station," which turned out to be the source of all telephone activity in Kodai, none of it in working order; and finally past the fine home of Gemini Ganish, a film star from Madras, and in my own gate again.

Regina, during my early-morning absences, learned to get all the sweeping and dusting finished, and was always in the kitchen creating my lunch when I arrived. Lunch, I gave her to understand, was to be fixed eternally at rice boiled with vegetables, a piece of fruit (banana, orange or apple) and tea. We did not deviate from this pattern. It seemed wiser, and safer.

I worked at my desk until lunch, and often for several hours after it. Regina was plainly disturbed by the constant clacking of the typewriter. "Madam all day long typing, typing, typing. What's wrong, madam?"

"I'm writing a book," I told her.

"A book, madam?"

"A book," I repeated, driving it home.

"Why, madam?" I found this too difficult. I changed the subject.

Generally I had a brief nap, and with the aid of the bounteous quantity of hot water Regina kept on the wood stove, a kind of bath. The geyser, so envied in the hills as a luxury feature, was completely useless. We had many summit conferences on this topic—Job, Major Lal and I. Inspections were made, always with the same result.

Job would painstakingly go over the manual of instruction again. "Two hours before using, put on switch. After finished, turn off switch."

I tried telling him that even with the required two hours switched on, only a cup of warm water dribbled out of the shower head.

He removed the shower head. Now a thin trickle appeared. Triumphantly he turned to show me this marvel. "See, madam, working perfectly."

The trickle, at home, would have indicated that there was a defect in the closing valve or that a washer needed replacement. Here it was the extent of the hot-water pressure. Two cups of water trickled out, and then stopped completely. "See?" I asked him, "That's all the water I get. It's no good at all!"

He looked accusingly at me. "Small tank, madam. Doesn't hold much water."

I looked up at the five-gallon tank above the toilet. It surely could hold more than two cups. But I knew when I was licked. The geyser was completely clogged, with five gallons of rust inside; in the long history of its existence it had been left innocent of maintenance. I would not disturb this system, I decided, knowing the strength of two thousand years against the fragile thread of my American plumbing experience. Thenceforth, Regina carried buckets of hot water to the deluxe bathroom, and I took what the other Americans in Kodai called "teacup baths." It certainly saved soap.

Each afternoon, after my small nap and a cup of hot tea, I took a walk around Kodai in the bracing, clean air. The hills were visible wherever one wandered, and I never tired of seeing their terraced sides, dotted with villas and enhanced with dark forests, rising up to the beautiful, blue sky. I had not seen so clear a sky since a brief sojourn on Sanibel Island the previous year. Chicago was choked with fumes, smoke from a thousand industries, and blanketed in a dirty gray mist one could see over the city while approaching from a long way off. Countless times, coming down from our cabin in Wisconsin and seeing this pall in the distance, we had felt our lungs cry out and our hearts fail before that dirty haze surrounding Chicago. Kodai air, like that of Wisconsin, was clear and bright; I loved to walk and just breathe. No wonder the Jesuits lived so long here, I thought.

The bazaar was, however, anything but lovely. Like every place where man comes in large numbers to trade, it had an ugliness and squalor I had seen in the streets of every large city. Dirty little shops, attended by dark men who spat frequently and argued incessantly, lined a hillside leading down from the American School. I visited the place many times, and then relegated this chore to Regina, who knew how to bargain and purchase the rice, vegetables and fruit we required. Not far from the house, Spencer's had a good store, with much higher prices of course, where one could find all manner of household supplies, canned goods, umbrellas, thermos bottles or candles, and it was there I did much of my shopping for Snyder "B." There were a number of Kashmiri shops too, where one could find unset gems, beautiful papier-mâché plates and boxes, numdah carpets and carved trays and bowls. More of this material would be available from Kashmir when the season opened, in March, I had been told, so I limited my purchases to a lovely rosewood statue of Christ as preacher seated yoga style on a little carved wall, a magnificent oil painting of Mahabalipuram, some brass candlesticks, and a set of carved elephant bookends to hold my small collection of paperbacks. With these arranged in the Snyder "B" living room, the place began to look more homelike. I removed the horrible "picture" on the living-room wall, stored it away in a cupboard, dusted the wall, which retained the outline of the frame, and awaited an opportunity to find something I could enjoy looking at to place on the single nail. One did not remove a nail from these walls. All had been counted in the inventory.

Word from Winnie in Madras brought the startling news that my bags had not even left America until February 16—a circumstance that certainly explained why they had not preceded me to Madras. She was still hot on their trail and would inform me when they came down from Delhi. I began to ponder the logistics of that situation: They would have to clear customs in Madras. I had given Winnie my power of attorney to act on my behalf; would this suffice? I swiftly sent a note to her informing her of the combination-lock numbers on the luggage and my hope that she would be able to send them the fastest way when they arrived at Madras. But I was still uncertain whether or not this would work, and shuddered at the thought that I might have to return four hundred miles to Madras myself, in the terrible heat there, to do the necessary clearance through customs. Pan Am would certainly hear from me.

Strangely enough, though, by some fluke I had managed to bring with me to Kodai just enough to get by on. My two pair of hose, it is true, were in shreds, from all the walking, climbing in and out of buses and rickshaws, etc. But I had with me a pair of slacks that nicely covered the runs. I also had a warm woolen cape, several changes of clothing, a warm robe (mighty necessary there at night), the typewriter, a good lamp, a ream of paper, a flashlight, and the bare minimum to outfit the kitchen: some silverware, a vegetable steamer, a sharp knife, my all-purpose tool, a wooden spoon and a larger, plastic one. With these and the strange collection of odds and ends that the house was equipped with, I managed to maintain myself quite adequately.

Regina served me her simple meals three times a day, using more plates and saucers for each than I would have used at home in a whole day. For example, breakfast: one hard-boiled egg, in a bowl, with a plate under it. Two pieces of toast, on a plate. A jar of honey on a plate, with spoon. Salt and pepper, in little crystal containers, on a plate. Horlick's malted milk jar, on a plate with spoon. Teapot with boiled water, on a plate. Peanut butter, on a plate with knife. Bowl of fruit with my trusty little potato peeler, on a plate. I did not use anything but the egg, toast, a little honey, an orange and the Horlick's, but all of this array of "porceline" made the simple meal seem quite a feast. Burning always on the dining-room table were three sticks of incense stuck in a little brass container I found in the bazaar. The flowers might be massive arum lilies, with fern and some other broad-leaved background. The coffee table often contained chrysanthemums, daisies, begonias, roses, or poppies. In my bedroom might be two lovely camellias. I was becoming quite fond of my little house. Chipmunks raced over the tile roof, leaving a little thrill of noise with each passage; outside, the wonderful birds in the great pines sang strange songs.

Sometimes I sat in the sunny garden and read, dried my hair or just watched the life on the next terrace below. There were several Indian homes there, and many chickens and the rooster that summoned me at 4 A.M. each day, the wandering cows and dogs and a few children. The women were often outside in the space behind their house "doing up" the pots and pans with a mixture of mud and clay. This seemed to give them a beautiful bright finish, if not entirely germ-free. I noticed Regina did our pans outside the house too, but she used the "Vim" I bought at Spencer's and a pot cleaner. There was sometimes a terrible howling from the dogs, and I found myself lying in wait for the culprit that was responsible. The dogs of Kodai all have a highly individual air, marching up and down the hills with great purpose, as though on a mission of importance. When one calls to them, however, they turn tail and run. I think they are afraid of humans, perhaps with good reason.

One day in the bazaar, as I was returning up the hill, side stepping the manure and puddles of red spit, I saw some dogs running across the road ahead. A jeep came out of a side road with great speed, ran over one of the poor dogs, and kept right on going. I yelled with all my strength and ran in the direction of the jeep. It came to a stop slowly, to see what would happen. Catching up to it, I said to the driver, "You hit that dog. Didn't you see it?"

He knew very well what I was saying, by the look of shame on his face, but indicated that the dog had been at fault and there was nothing to be done about it. "The dog is dead," he said.

I looked back at the suffering animal, which was struggling to its feet weakly. Suddenly I was furious at this callous disregard for life. I drew myself up in an effort to calm my rage, but it was no good. "You are a barbarian," I shouted at him.

He smiled and drove on.

This encounter, witnessed by many of the Indians along the road, was also added to my dossier. That afternoon, there were many more beggars at my door.

I discovered another insight into the nature of the Indian worker when I came to realize that, coming up the road from town or from a hike, I could always see Regina and Muthusamy sitting on the stone near the gate, chatting and gossiping together. Sometimes they were joined by some of Muthusamy's family and grandchildren. Yet, when I rounded the corner, in plain view of the house, all melted away like mist. I would go through the gate, find Muthusamy digging furiously around the flowers, Regina in the kitchen scouring something, and both very surprised to see me. I said nothing about it, but forever dispelled was the belief that any work at all would be done in my absence. They were like very small children in this regard. Regina, in her evening conversations with me, always revealed she knew exactly where I had been, what I had done, and to whom I had spoken in town. I filled in the gaps obligingly for her, in case there was a point or two she had missed. Muthusamy's son worked at the boat club, so whenever I walked near the lake, my whereabouts could be duly reported to his father.

I still recall my great surprise when I got into a boat on the lake, asked to be rowed to the other side, and heard the young rower ask politely how I had enjoyed my trip to the plains last weekend. I asked how he knew of it.

"I am the son of Muthusamy, madam," he said. No other explanation was necessary. I realized he knew what I had for lunch, which clothing had been laundered today, and numerous other details of my daily life.

Regina's brother worked in the convent kitchen, so my attendance at Mass and breakfast conversation with the nuns were subjects of note. Thus the network of information was quite good, sometimes accurate, and always an excuse for conversation. No wonder no one complained about the poor telephone service. There was no need of a phone in Kodai. The mysterious "microwave station" might have been tracking satellites for all the effect it had on the life of the town. You want a taxi? Send a runner to the taxi station. A new baby is born in the family? Tell one person; by evening the gifts will begin arriving. But what is happening in the world outside Kodai? Who knows? Who cares? The bus coming up from the plains will bring all information of vital importance, such as another flood or a serious accident on the road. It will also bring supplies, potatoes, maybe Indian tourists, and sometimes an American who suffers from strange leg cramps. Musing one evening, before the fire, about the bazaar and what ought to be done there to improve conditions, I created for myself the vision of a Kodaikanal Bazaar Chamber of Commerce.

Possibly I was merely homesick for Oak Park, where such matters are taken seriously. At any rate I had fun with it:

PLAN FOR THE KODAIKANAL BAZAAR
CHAMBER OF COMMERCE

I. Form a committee of at least 6 of the most influential merchants of Kodai, 2 Hindus, 2 Muslims and 2 Christians.

II. Hold a meeting with these men at which:

1. a movie is shown describing the action of microbes, and their effect on public health.

   a. a talk by the local doctor on the conditions of the bazaar which make disease among the people a certainty.

2. A talk on the real allure of Kodai as a tourist attraction, and the effect that filthy conditions have on the European or American tourist who might come here.

   a. The banker discusses the effect of greater income on the community.

   b. The bus and trucking concessions speak on the effects of increased employment opportunities.

3. Presentation of a plan to form THE KODAIKANAL BAZAAR CHAMBER OF COMMERCE:

   a. To remake the environment for the following reasons:

      1. To improve the health of the community.

      2. To increase the income of the merchants.

      3. To attempt to match the beauty of Kodai's hills and trees.

      4. To foster pride in a bazaar that will indicate a people of discrimination and taste.

4. Discussion of these aims and objectives.

5. Vote on the desirability of implementing this plan.

III. Formation of the Kodaikanal Bazaar Chamber of Commerce, consisting of:

    1. All the merchants who have permanent stands in the bazaar.

    2. All those who bring goods to sell there from other towns.

IV. Funding to depend on contributions (dues) from each member, based on a percentage of his annual income. This sum to be determined by the joint committee.

V. The plan to be announced throughout Kodai, together with a time schedule for the improvement plan.

    1. This is crucial, so that all concerned with the bazaar as a source of supply would know of the plan. Customer aid might also be solicited to build up the fund.

VI. The Chamber of Commerce Fund (see IV) to be placed in the Kodai State Bank to form a credit-union fund.

    1. Each merchant—member would have the right to draw a loan from this credit union at a low rate of interest, provided:

        a. The loan is used exclusively for the beautification of his shop and its immediate surroundings.

        b. Inspection of the work done would be the province of the Loan Committee.

        c. The time schedule of the work to be done must be clearly stated, and exactly followed.

VII. An additional Maintenance Fund should be set aside (raised by popular subscription) for the following purpose:

    1. Hiring a MAINTENANCE CREW for daily clean-up of the bazaar street. This crew should also plant flowers along the sides of the road, where there is now trash and dirt, and provide maintenance on a daily basis.

    2. An annual prize—to be awarded each March for the best-kept shop in the bazaar. A Prize Committee chosen from the shoppers. They alone can be the judges.

VIII. A continuing-education program on hygiene, personal cleanliness, decoration skills, and better business methods should be carried on weekly, in some central place where all the merchants could gather. Could be combined with lunch.

IX. Very heavy fines to be imposed on anyone in the bazaar area who:

    1. spits on the road

    2. permits his animals to wander on the bazaar street

    3. sells unclean food

    4. is himself not clean

    5. cheats a customer.
  X. Each shopkeeper should be an example of cleanliness, having bathed and donned clean clothing each business day.
 XI. Beggars should be cleared from the bazaar area.

A large billboard in the bazaar would be erected, where shoppers could note various impressions of the shops, where violations occur, as well as where great improvements have been noticed. I believe the implementation of such a plan would greatly add to the beauty of Kodai. News of it would certainly increase trade and retrieve the lost customers who now refuse to shop there.

The year 2500 seems a likely target date.

CHAPTER 11
Presentation School

The visitor learns very quickly that, once the little lake has been explored and viewed from various spots that highlight its lovely contours, the real treasures of Kodai are much higher up; one must climb the hills to see them. A case in point is the Presentation School, up a steep hill from the town and set like a jewel with a wonderful vista between the giant trees of its terraced campus. The buildings are quite old, having been there for about sixty years, but are in excellent repair and evince constant and intelligent maintenance, without which nothing lasts for very long. A beautiful little chapel, decorated with great charm and simplicity, dominates the school grounds, and here a priest from La Providence, the Jesuit house, comes daily to celebrate Mass for the sisters and the students.

There are about two hundred and twenty-five boarding students and forty-five day scholars. Most of these girls are from seven to fifteen years of age. The atmosphere of the school is charming and very homelike and reminds me strongly of my own convent school, Our Lady of Angels Academy, in Clinton, Iowa. A principle of self-discipline is in effect here, with the school divided into three houses, each with its own captain and prefect. In this way the girls are encouraged to self-government and given the opportunity to learn self-reliance.

The curriculum consists of English language, English literature, Hindi, Tamil, French, biology, Scripture, physics, chemistry, math, commerce, history, geography and art. There is an excellent sports program, which gives every girl an opportunity for physical activity daily, as well as courses in music and dance, household arts and flower arrangement; in short, nothing that would enhance the formation of a woman's mind and heart has been neglected.

The girls wear a uniform, which immediately removes the competition natural among a group of girls, many of whom are wealthy, while some have only modest means. The dark green pleated skirt, white blouse, green sox and black shoes are becoming on all the girls, and they also have special uniforms for Sunday and for weekends, and cardigans in their own color. Most of the girls are not Catholic, but Hindu, with some Muslims and Protestants mixed in. But all are given the opportunity to praise God in chapel, and all sing the hymns with clear and joyful voices. Daily Mass in that chapel is a wonderful experience, especially when the "smallies" sing.

Presentation School was founded by Presentation nuns out of Ireland; Sister Ethna, Sister Eugene, Sister Aloysius and Sister Carmel are the only representatives of that happy race on the premises today. The order is now enriched with many lovely young Indian nuns. They adopted me from the first day I appeared on their doorstep, immediately arranging with their driver to pick me up. And after Mass I had breakfast with them each morning. Thus was begun a friendship and companionship with these wonderful women that was doubly precious since I was far from my family. They made me part of theirs.

They lent me books: Father Powell's *He Touched Me* and T. J. Walsh's *Nano Nagle and the Presentation Sisters,* the inspiring story of their foundress, a young Irish woman of wealth who spent it on building first an Ursuline convent, and when it was functioning with nuns from France, another convent, which she herself founded as its superior, the Presentation Sisters, in eighteenth-century Cork, when the faith was being effectively stamped out by the British, and the Irish were bereft of any educational opportunity except the hedge schools operating in defiance of the law. This Catholic laywoman's lifelong struggle to improve the lot of the poor in her country, so successful that her work has spread all over the world through her seven thousand nun followers, was several hundred years in advance of the Women's Liberation movement, and stunning testimony to the power of one solitary woman. For Nano Nagle was a woman fired by a love of Christ in His poor, and she succeeded in changing the face of her country and making possible the benefits of a Christian education to most of the known world. She concentrated her efforts on the education of girls, and her sisters describe the importance of this emphasis in this way:

To enable all women to realize the exalted supernatural dignity of their role, it is necessary that the education of girls be geared to a practical fulfillment of the ideal of womanhood. It must make the girl aware of all that she is supernaturally and all that she owes in loving allegiance and dependence to Mary, her Mother. It must emphasize the fact that woman is essentially a mother, that biologically and psychologically she is fitted for motherhood, and in motherhood she will normally find the fulfillment of her being. Her natural tendency is to give herself to love and service. Thus, whether she marries and bears and rears children or whether in virginity she serves others through works of mercy or of education, she can best fulfill herself through the expression of her maternal instinct. Only an educational program which imbues pupils with such concepts as these is worthy of woman. (T. J. Walsh, *Nano Nagle and the Presentation Sisters*, M. H. Gill and Son Ltd., 1959)

I realize that the above is in direct contrast to the strident preachments of many "libbers" today; it is nevertheless a true statement of the nature and role of women as created by God and recognized by the wise of every age since the beginning of the Christian era. I am in complete accord with it, having lived for fifty-seven years and observed not only myself but my sisters and friends. Woman was made for nurturing and caring, man for creation and invention. The care of her own young is not the only service she is called upon by nature to perform; the care and nurturing of every child on earth is ultimately her sphere. Not only children but all in need: the sick, the old, the discouraged, the burdened, the weary—all are the proper sphere for woman's care and concern. This is not a second-class citizenship. Rather, it places woman in the forefront of all creation, since without her ministrations in the home, the business, the office, the industrial plant, the factory, the bank, government departments and presidential halls, every forward motion would come to a grinding halt. Try to imagine the effect of a worldwide women's strike. Countries would collapse.

Most women do their jobs naturally, for love or money. Sisters do this nurturing for the love of God. And sisters like these at Presentation School are a joy to be with, so rich are the humor and the laughter, and so deep is the concern for their students. Being drawn into that little circle of love was for me a tremendous gift, and one I cherished more each day of my stay in Kodai.

One day, walking briskly in the bazaar, I turned my ankle on a stone and went down in the dust with a bang. My glasses and hat flew off, the small boys on the street laughed with glee, and a small crowd gathered to watch the entertainment. I suppose there *is* something funny about a woman falling down, though I must confess it escaped me at the time. However, kindly hands reached under my elbows and helped me up. An elderly man inquired if I was all right, and found me a place to sit for a while while he picked up my hat and glasses and restored them to me. I watched my ankle swelling up with some concern, and found that I could only walk on it with great difficulty, though it was obviously not broken. So I hobbled back to Snyder "B" and, it being Regina's day off, heated some water on the electric plate, put it in a basin and, with another basin of cold water, began the treatment I remembered Al using when the kids turned an ankle: hot water, as hot as one can stand it, then cold, then hot again, and so on. Meanwhile the skin was turning a lovely shade of purple, and the pain was quite intense. I knew I would not be walking for a day or two, so I wrote a small note to the sisters and then went to bed until Regina came home, at 9 P.M. She wanted to rub it, but the thought of even the slightest pressure was unpleasant, and I told her I would keep it elevated and see how it was in the morning. I asked her to go down to the meeting place at six-thirty the next morning to give the driver my note, so the nuns would not worry.

Next day at teatime, the four Irish nuns appeared at my doorway, filled with concern for the ankle and filling my little house with their lovely, soft voices. Father d'Silva had also come, so I had plenty of company during my enforced confinement. The following day, the ankle was better, and two days later I was once again climbing up and down the hills of Kodai, enjoying the sunshine and the fresh, cool air.

One evening, the sisters were having a movie for the students and invited me to come. The movie was to be shown at seven-thirty and be over at nine. Realizing it would then be too late for me to walk down to the house again, there being no streetlamps in Kodai, they invited me to come prepared to spend the night as their guest. At six-thirty Regina accompanied me up the road to the convent, carrying my little overnight bag. She left me with the nuns and went down again, after saying she would return for me in the morning. Sister Ethna and I sat together in the school hall to watch the movie. The hall was filled with the girls, their captains keeping order among the various schools and seating themselves last, as is proper for Those in Charge.

The film was of great interest to me in spite of many broken segments, during which the light had to be lit while the sister projectionist mended the break with Scotch tape. An Egyptian film called *Seven Daughters*, it provided an interesting glimpse into modern Egyptian life. The father of seven daughters was shown as a timorous clerk in the office of a ruthless boss. The poor man was desperately afraid of losing his job, harried at home with the family's need for school clothes, books, new shoes, and in the case of the older girls, husbands. I found the interiors of the Egyptian home very much like ours. The characterizations were very good, from the "arty" uncle who insisted on playing his "symphonies" for the girls (who always disappeared when he sat down to play) to the youngest child, who was a kind of Shirley Temple, Egyptian style. Reel after broken reel went on, with the audience deeply appreciative and attentive. I found myself engrossed in the plot, which thickened quickly as romantic young men appeared for several of the older girls, and the course of true love ran far from smoothly. Matters reached a climax finally when the father was forced to refuse his permission for the hoped-for engagement because of the ruthless employer, who wanted the young man for his own daughter. The final reel was placed on the machine, the lights were dimmed, and we found ourselves being treated to an Egyptian travelogue! Sister explained that the last reel was defective, and the company who had rented it had sent the travelogue instead. Surprisingly, none of the students moaned or complained. They seemed quite satisfied to make up their own ending to the story. I was the only frustrated spectator.

Sister Ethna led me down a steep stairway to the terrace just below the convent, where a little stone bungalow served as their guesthouse. Opening the door, I found the pleasant combination of cleanliness, taste and order that was evident in the rest of the school: a beautiful little Queen Anne desk and chair, an antique dresser and mirror, a narrow bed with an embroidered coverlet (now made up with three pink woolen blankets) and, glory of glories, a hot-water bottle tucked under the sheets. The house also contained a spacious and immaculate bathroom, with a large porcelain tub and geyser. Some books in a case on the little porch absorbed me for a time before I went to sleep.

CHAPTER 12

Neighbors

One afternoon, when the day was crisp and cool, I climbed one of the hills behind my house to find the home of a Danish couple the Presentation nuns told me I should know: the Tubros. The hill was very steep, and as one ascended, the view of the lake district of Kodai was truly beautiful and serene. All along the road I met small kids playing; coolies ran down the hill with large bundles of saplings on their heads, all smiling, "Salaam, madam," as they passed. I found a very impressive gate with the Danish name on it, and entered to climb still farther along a lovely lane lined with shrubs and evidences of the gardener's hand. At length, through a second iron gate, I found Abernyte (the name of their estate) and went to the door. A gray-haired lady appeared, greeted me kindly when she learned the nuns had sent me, and brought me inside. This was Mrs. Tubro, and after cordial introductions were exchanged, I glanced around her entrance hall with admiration. It was impressive. Dark woodwork, a staircase leading to balconies above, high, cool and dim, with the kind of furniture that has been gently used and that rewards its owner with an ageless air of dignity and simplicity.

In the drawing room a fire blazed in the large, friendly hearth, and Mr. Tubro sat reading the paper. They made me very welcome. We sat down for a half-hour chat, during which I discovered they had lived in India a part of every year for the past forty years and that their daughter had attended Presentation School and was soon to return to Kodai on a visit with her husband and children. The gardens were all blooming, and everything was being made ready for their visit. Tea was served by three servants, two of whom carried the tea cart into the room. They put it down and flowed out again, whereupon Mr. Tubro said with a laugh, "They have only recently come down from the trees. The cart has wheels, but they must carry it in."

I told them of my interest in the possibility of one's living in Kodai in retirement, and they said it was certainly not only possible but a very good place for retirement. They had bought this house in 1945 and had done extensive improvements; Mr. Tubro was founder of a large construction business. He had, as a matter of fact, built a number of beautiful bungalows on the estate, and these were used by executives of the company when they came to Kodai on holidays. I knew these bungalows must be excellent, judging from the refinements of their own house, in which nothing was lacking that would have made it a desirable home anywhere in America. It was clearly old, perhaps one hundred years or so, and thus had the high ceilings, the huge sliding doors between the rooms and all the features now so rare and in such great demand at home. It was heated well, by electricity along the baseboards, and contained four bedrooms and four bathrooms, in addition to the usual rooms of the first floor. All around were acres of garden under careful cultivation, and the scene from their drawing-room windows of the mountains beyond was magnificent. I asked if they knew of such a place for sale. Mrs. Tubro knew of one, built by another Danish couple, the Mortensens, and told me where it was.

Not long afterward, with the aid of Mickey, the bearer at Presentation, whom the nuns sent with me to find the way, I entered the high world of Constansia Estate. It is difficult to describe the effect this elegant home made on me, for it was set on eight acres of fruit trees, all terraced down a very steep slope, the highest hill in the district. Set in about the middle terrace was a beautiful little bungalow with outbuildings and a portico and surrounded by the finest lawn and garden I had yet seen. It would have done justice to Barrington Hills. I glanced around me at the view of Perumal Peak, blue and violet in the distance, and the incredibly wonderful puzzle of farms and trees grown on terraces in the wide basin below. I stopped to catch my breath, and took photos of it, so I would always remember its loveliness. We went to the back door and met Cooper, the caretaker.

Cooper seemed to be part Indian and part Chinese. There is the look of Nepal on his features, not India. He is respected widely throughout Kodai as the finest manager in town. Two minutes in his company told me why. He was completely knowledgeable and eager to show me the wonders of Constansia Estate. Mickey left me there, and I began to survey the place, beginning with Cooper's own quarters, which were American-style clean, with a very good kitchen, a large bedroom and bath. These were attached to the bungalow but had separate entrances, so that Cooper, or any manager, could enjoy privacy. Every inch of wall, window ledge and flooring spoke of high quality and excellent care. We entered the main bungalow through the kitchen, and my heart lifted at the sight of the immaculate and very well equipped room, with a gas stove, cabinets along the walls, a good double sink with windows over it looking out at the flower garden, a necessary porcelain water filter, and tile walls. The living room was a dream. About thirty-five feet in length, angling the corner in L shape, and about twenty feet wide, it boasted a fireplace, carpeting, wood paneling on some walls, built-in cabinets, very comfortable and well-chosen furniture, marvelous antique chests here and there, and brass hardware on the solid doors. There were two bedrooms, and two bathrooms lacking nothing that comfort, intelligent decorating or imagination could conceive. All the cabinets were equipped with fine linen, fluffy towels, soap, and everything else associated with gracious living. It reminded me very much of the model houses Marshall Field's loves to decorate for the despair of young brides.

We inspected the outbuildings, which included servants' quarters and bathing rooms, an empty cow barn, a very large and shelved storeroom (equipped with a bank-vault-type lock) and a little stone house that had been used for poultry. A pigeon roost with perky occupants lent life to the place, and two black dogs roamed about this paradise like squires.

By this time, I had realized that whatever price the absent owners had placed on it, it was clearly a millionaire's playground and far beyond my modest means. I intended to inquire about the price, however, when the owners returned to Kodai, later in the season. The most intriguing discovery I had made was this: it is, after all, possible to build a really fine-quality house in Kodai, in spite of the negative impression I had of the local concept of "de luxe." With such a home, and given the very modest cost of living, wouldn't life here be a dream come true? It began to haunt me. From what I knew of real-estate values in the States, such a place as Constansia would cost about half a million dollars. Perhaps by finding out the local cost, I would be able to make an accurate estimate of the disparity of prices between the States and India.

The dream of living in India for a portion of every year while retaining a solid base in America for the sake of my beloved children was still very strong. I began making inquiries about what obstacles I might find in purchasing a house in Kodai. Everyone was quite pessimistic. You can buy, with difficulty, they told me, but you can't then sell. Or, if you do, the money received back from the property must remain in India. This was, of course, entirely against my plans. Whatever I had left when my "eighty-three years" were over, I would leave to my children. Not that there would be much left, but anyway.

One day, I asked to see the bank manager, to ask him about this. Once again, I encountered the strange sense of "Indian time." I was placed in an office and told to wait. I did, for about half an hour, and then inquired where he was. "He's out making inspections, madam. You just sit here and wait." I got up and left. Several times after that, I saw him in his office, but there were always about ten people waiting to see him, so I gave up on that source of information.

Major Mohan Lal was often referred to as the person to see regarding property, but I found him more elusive than the Scarlet Pimpernel. Our supply of firewood was running low, we needed new light bulbs, but no messages, visits to the Kodai Club or requests for interviews resulted in action. We began on Monday to negotiate for what we needed on Thursday, but with very little success.

With dreams of Constansia still in mind, however, I began to think of the possibility of renting such a house, perhaps from the Tubros, and resolved to inquire if a long-term lease would be a possibility. I found, however, their rentals to be completely tied into the corporation and unavailable to others.

Meanwhile, from Winnie came the news that my errant luggage had finally arrived in Madras, and now I must send her: my passport, via registered mail; my landing permit (I didn't have such a permit), and authorization for her to act on my behalf and claim the luggage. She said she would send it via air to Madurai, where I could then go and pick it up. Thus it became necessary to plan another trip to the plains, in the heat and discomfort I knew I would again find there, magnified by the summer sun. A young cab driver in town, Raja ("My sister is in the Holy Cross Convent, madam"), had a good car and seemed intelligent. I asked him what he would charge for the round trip to Madurai. "Two hundred forty rupees, madam," he told me. This is roughly thirty dollars. I knew it was too high and told him so. Immediately, the price was adjusted to two hundred rupees, and I told him to plan on the trip. I would wait until Winnie had time to clear the luggage with my passport, and then we would drive to Madurai for a day trip, get the luggage, and return to Kodai. Pan Am was going to hear from me. The stuff had been shipped from Chicago on the sixteenth of February, instead of on the first, when I brought it to the airport. I was for one month without the things I needed here, including the fund records, and much that I had to replace with Indian goods.

Winnie had also cautioned me, in her luggage letter, about the inadvisability of coming to Madras in April for the ordination. She had been in India for twenty-six years and still found the summer heat all but unbearable; she thought it possible that I would become ill if I came down from the cool hills. I took this caution to heart. I knew that illness here would place burdens on everyone concerned, and that I must guard my health if I wished to complete my three-month plan. I wrote to Bert in Darjeeling for his advice, but even before it came, I had almost decided that the plan to go to the ordination would have to be canceled.

But I needed my passport to get American Express checks cashed, which could only be done between the hours of ten and twelve daily; therefore I would go down to the bazaar next morning, get many rupees, then mail the passport to Winnie, and get Raja lined up for the following Wednesday's trip to Madurai. Life was not dull.

Yet even as I prepared to get more rupees and send the passport and authorization to Winnie, I found myself pondering the fact that there were now three more bags of chattels to worry about, to buy back from the airlines, to lug up the hill, unpack and use, and eventually repack, and ship home again within two months! I began to see very clearly the wisdom of having only a few possessions. Certainly, in spite of the delay, I had gotten along with the few things I had (except for hosiery, the tape recorder and the fund records). I really didn't need all the clothing I had packed, in my desire to "cover" all situations from a hike in the woods to a government ball. The strange instinct that had worked to select the few things I had succeeded in carrying to Kodai had been exactly right, and the fact that now my closet would be bulging did not please me. I recalled Bert's favorite travel hint: "Bring one half the clothing you think you'll need, and twice the amount of money." I realized it really made good sense. He's a wise man, Bert. He can pack into a small bag the stuff he needs for three months anywhere on earth (staying in Jesuit houses, he can always borrow what he forgot to bring), though it's sadly true he tends to leave a trail of possessions behind, which have to be then shipped to his next stop. Twice now, following visits, I have had to send him his jacket. The last time, it reached him only when he had returned to Darjeeling.

I began to sense, too, that I had too much stuff, particularly when I looked around Kodai and saw the tribals here and their tiny pittance. Still unweaned from my habit of shopping all the interesting stores in my search for useful or beautiful things for gifts or for my house, I began to suffer from pangs of conscience when, coming from a shop where I had paid forty-five or fifty rupees for a wood carving, to meet the wood carriers coming down the hill at a half trot, their bare feet blue with cold, and remember that what I had purchased was the equivalent of three weeks' work for them.

At night, when the lights were out except for the candle before the borrowed crucifix, when I fixed my mind on Christ and sought to bring Him the day's events and listened to His voice in my heart, I began to hear with greater and greater clarity the call to poverty and renunciation of the world's goods. These people were my brothers and sisters; I began to realize that all the stupid "standards" I had carried around in my head had no real value whatever. What mattered was the fact that Christ had died for all of us, that His love extended from the finest house on the hill to the meanest hovel, even to the repulsive black beggar man I stepped over daily in the road. This man is spectacular. I do not believe he is Indian at all; his skin is coal black, his clothing solid black, his hair, which stands on end in spirals of grime and grease like a fright wig is jet black; only his eyes and teeth are not ebony, but red. I knew that the charitable organization in town, Corsock, had a home for the destitute, where they were cared for, fed and given a clean place to sleep. But so ingrained is the begging habit in many of the Indians that they are no sooner placed in the home when they are back again, pestiferous and grimy, whining in the town after every foreigner. Whether or not this black beggar has been through that route, I do not know. I only know he can be seen daily sleeping on the side of the road, an inelegant and terrible contrast to most of the tribals, who are small and neat. Yet Christ had died for this beggar, who, for all I know, may be much closer to God than I am, who have had many advantages. It was a sobering and serious thought. India was changing me slowly, as the constantly running stream begins to round off rough stone.

I had not yet realized the inestimable favor Aelred had done when he sent me from the seminary supply a carload of wood, neatly cut for the stove and fireplace. The magnitude of this gift only hit me when we ran out of wood and began negotiations to renew the supply. This time, rather than impose on the Jesuits, I asked Muthusamy if I could buy some wood.

"Certainly, madam. I am telling Job." I was foolish enough to think this meant that he was telling Job the same day. Not so. Monday passed, no wood. Tuesday dawned, and I noted with some concern that the supply was down to three pieces. I found Muthusamy in the garden, digging disconsolately amid the begonias. "Muthusamy," I said sweetly, "how about the wood?"

"Coming, madam, coming. I will tell Job," he said, and went on digging. Tuesday disappeared forever into history.

Wednesday I was busy all day away from the house, and told Regina to lie in wait for Job, should he show up. When I returned, she told me Job had indeed come, said he must "measure for the wood" and that he needed sixty rupees for this transaction. I gave her the money, in case the wood would arrive from God knew where while I was away and we might pass another week without action. But when I retired on Wednesday night, Job's measurements had not produced anything concrete, or wooden, either.

On Thursday, with no wood left and thus no possible hot water in the house, I left for early Mass and instructed Regina that if Job showed up again, she was to hold him there, by force if necessary.

"Job coming this morning," she said with confidence.

"Well, while he's here, tell him we need three light bulbs, too," I said, and left for Mass, reassured. But alas, when I returned home again, the kitchen was innocent of wood.

"Didn't Job come?" I asked Regina.

"Job say he coming. Job no come," she said. "No wood, madam." I sat down to my lunch of fruit and curds, and thought it over. Perhaps Job was angered by the fact that the first load of wood had been delivered without his ministrations, and now he was pouting.

"I guess I'll have to ask the Jesuits for more wood," I told her. It would serve him right, I thought indignantly, for making me wait four days for a single load of wood. But as I was thus ruminating, and peeling bananas, a knock on the door announced Job. He came in and announced he had come about the wood. "It's been four days, Job. What took you so long?"

"Only yesterday I heard about the wood, madam."

I looked at Muthusamy, and knew which one was lying. Muthusamy had made three trips (of three furlongs each) to this miscreant's house. I decided to let it pass, but filed the knowledge that in addition to everything else, truth was relative in India. "Do you have it on the truck?" I asked him, fully prepared to hear that he would bring it tomorrow.

"The wood is behind the house, madam." I gasped in astonishment and went out to look. There, at our back door, was a supply of six-foot logs that had been there all the time and could have supplied the whole hillside. I inquired through clenched teeth why Muthusamy had not brought it on the first day I asked for it.

"Muthusamy doesn't know how to measure it, madam," said Job with an air of sweet reasonableness. Obviously this measurement was an extremely technical procedure that necessitated the attention of an expert.

"I want two loads," I told him and retired to a window to watch the measurement process. It consisted of Job standing amid the woodpile and tossing out huge logs onto a haphazard pile, until he decided he had tossed enough for one day. Muthusamy and Regina respectfully watched this highly scientific measuring.

"That's two loads," announced Job, wiping his face and hands with a dirty rag, obviously worn out by the unaccustomed exercise. I looked at the pile of quartered trees he had selected for my little wood stove, fully expecting him to begin cutting them to size so they would fit. But Job was preparing to leave. He had moved the wood about three feet from the main pile and was now through with the transaction.

"Just a minute," I called to him. "Who is going to cut this wood to fit the stove?"

This was, in Job's view, an entirely different department. Madam would have to hire a woodcutter. "Don't give him more than seven rupees for this work, madam," said Job in a burst of confidence.

"Don't give *who* seven rupees?" I asked. "Do you cut wood, Muthusamy?"

Muthusamy looked injured. "I do gardening, madam," he replied shyly.

"He has no ax, madam," supplied Job.

I had visions of another four days wasted trying to get my new treasure cut to size.

But Job generously offered. "When I go out on the road, madam," he said brightly, "if I see somebody with an ax I will send him to you."

I had been in Kodai for a long time and had never once encountered anyone carrying an ax. I began to realize that this was going to be a long siege, and that if the nights continued chilly, a very cold one as well. I could visualize using the tiny electric heater for water, but I would also be paying for the current used, and the rate on electricity was high. Meanwhile, Regina gathered sticks on the hill behind the house and tried to make do.

My social life began to pick up, following an interesting meeting Aelred took me to at the American School. This was the monthly gathering of Corsock, the organization that concerned itself with charitable work around Kodai. Aelred was the newly elected treasurer. The president, a pleasant-looking American lady, Mrs. De Jonge, told me she was from Iowa, which sounded reassuring. She conducted the long business meeting with dispatch, and I reflected that some woman's club at home was probably missing her a great deal.

She called on me the next day, when I was busy standing in line at the bank trying to cash my American Express checks and so missed her. But she left a nice note inviting me to drive over to the Holy Cross Convent the following day with her, to attend the World Day of Prayer. Sister Innocentia had already invited me for this, and I had hired a cab in the bazaar to get me there, but I looked forward to seeing her again. In my absence that same day, Jon Kessler and his wife came to call, to invite me to tea. Later I met him in the bazaar, and he delivered the invitation in person from the seat of his shiny motorbike. Things were definitely looking up. Later that afternoon, I heard the sound of an ax out back. I ran to the window. Someone was actually cutting the logs into small pieces.

"Who is that?" I asked Regina.

"Muthusamy's son, madam," said Regina.

Subsequent inquiries revealed that the usual price for a load of wood was twenty-five rupees, and that it was only sold cut to size. Ah, India!

The tea at Kessler's was very cozy and friendly. The Kesslers are the house parents of a hostel connected with the American School, High Clerc, and share their large and comfortable quarters with a number of boarding students—about fifteen, it seemed to me. Very friendly and genuine. I liked them on sight, and knew I had again fallen into the good fortune that had accompanied me all along the way. Their living room was charming, filled with the Indian things they had collected during their stay: a pierced folding screen that divided the "office" from the rest of the room, and an impressively hand-carved coffee table covered with marvels of animals and trees, which had taken its creator six months to complete. Mrs. Kessler served very good cake and turnovers from her own kitchen, and we chatted of Illinois and India for a pleasant hour or two. They had been presiding over a Lutheran congregation around the Aurora area, and knew Oak Park and the western suburbs well.

Two more guests came in, Dr. and Mrs. Lichtenecker; he from Vienna, and she from River Forest, the suburb adjoining Oak Park. A delightful couple; we found in conversation that we knew the same people, and Dr. Lichtenecker proved a wonderful resource in helping me seek out people in Kodai who understood the town and its people. In particular, he recommended I find M. S. Kalyanasundaram, whom he considered a true Renaissance man and who had written a book, entitled *Indian Hill Stations*, that had much material about Kodai. I made a mental note to find this gentleman and introduce myself. He sounded like the very person to teach me more of this beautiful town.

I left this refreshing afternoon determined to explore my little wood stove thoroughly, to see if in its black depths I could find an oven where I might bake a cake and have a tea party at Snyder "B." I knew I would have to rely on Spencer's for flour, and on my own very poor memory for the ingredients of some simple cake; I had no cookbook with me, and had always been the kind of amateur who

slavishly followed *The Joy of Cooking* or the strict dogma of *The
Art of French Cooking*, two of the scriptures enshrined in the
kitchen at home. As far as I could now recall, it seemed one had to
separate eggs, beat the yolks until they were lemon-colored, gradually
adding butter and sugar to them. The flour, I thought, must be
sifted, baking powder and a pinch of salt having been added, and
then mixed carefully with the egg yolks. Finally, it seemed to me,
the egg whites must be beaten until stiff, and then folded into the
mixture, adding a few drops of vanilla. This mixture was then
divided into two pans, which had been prepared with butter and
sprinkled with flour, and baked in a 350-degree oven for about forty
minutes. Once finished, one removed them from the pans, let them
cool, spread one with some kind of filling—custard, frosting or fruit
—placed the other one on top, and then spread the entire thing with
frosting, made by mixing melted chocolate, sugar, butter and flavor-
ing. Whether or not I could duplicate this process on a wood stove,
and whether I could find at Spencer's anything approximating these
ingredients were still to be seen. I thought that I would set aside a
day of experimentation, and if I succeeded, have a tea party, serving
cake and coffee or tea.

News from home, which took fourteen days to reach me, revealed
that Barb was fine (or had been fourteen days before), had enjoyed
the tickets I gave her for the Joffrey Ballet—in the fifth row, orches-
tra, "so close I could hear their shoes creak," had also heard the
Chicago Symphony, seen *Close Encounters of the Third Kind*
and thought it mind-boggling, and was taking the two dogs to Clinton to visit her sister Laurie. She had also spent an entire day paying
the household bills, wondered how I had done it all these years, and
had received roses from Ted Kawa on Valentine's Day. She was
loving it.

Dom Bede had told me to look up his friend Richard Keithahn,
who has an ashram in Kodai. I had Raja take me there, near the golf
club, very high up in the hills, where a dense fog had ascended above
the trees, swirling through Green Valley View, formerly called Suicide Point. The government, sensing the subtle influence of place
names, had changed it to the more picturesque one, to attempt to
change its image. Raja told me that one of the drivers had driven a
young couple from Madras to that point, let them out to see the
view, and having waited for them for more than an hour, went up to
investigate. He found only a kerchief and their sandals. Walking

along this very narrow strip of grass, and feeling my stomach rise in protest at the miles of distance below, I wondered how anyone could actually step off the edge voluntarily. I asked Raja about this.

"Some have many troubles, madam. Life not good. They just go."

Not far from this point, we found a series of low buildings with a little flower garden in front. There I found Richard Keithahn. He is an elderly man, American, born in Minnesota, who has spent over fifty years of his life in India as a Christian missionary. He was bundled into a heavy jacket, having just come from Van Allen Hospital, and he spoke to me in his office/bedroom/library, which was crammed with books on every available surface: tables, chairs, mantel and bookshelves. He seemed happily surrounded by a great deal of knowledge, so I asked him what he considered the most important thing on earth.

"The Kingdom of God," he said. He told me he was a Benedictine Oblate, though apparently not a Roman Catholic. He said if he could be said to have a guru, it was Dom Bede Griffith. His ashram is devoted to a fellowship among all who worship and strive to serve God; together they seek to understand the importance of "bread labor," the growth of creative personality, the ways of working for a balanced diet for hungry India, the need of hard study and group thinking for a working democracy. There didn't seem to be much activity there the day I visited, however, and I left with the vision of a rather sick old man, in a disorganized room, looking distinctly lonely.

Brother Paranjothi drove up from Manalur one bright Saturday morning, to take me on a day's excursion to the Jesuit's coffee plantation, called St. Mary's Estate. We were accompanied by Father Augustine, who was celebrating his thirty-fifth year as a Jesuit and who had been invited to Manalur for a special dinner. The ride down was very pleasant, the driver being an expert at hairpin turns, and I was able once again to marvel at the many spectacular views of hills and plains as we descended in the bright morning sunshine.

St. Mary's Estate was acquired by the Jesuits in 1831 and has been under cultivation continuously, with coffee, oranges, bananas and some spices. Pineapples are now being introduced, but coffee is the main source of income. After about three hours, we arrived there to meet Father Peter Ryappan, the manager, who has been in charge for about twelve years and under whose careful hands the estate has flourished. Brother Xavier, his able right hand, is foreman of some four hundred workers—men, women and boys—who pick the coffee fruits and deliver them to the pulp mill, where they are reduced to the coffee bean and then sent to another plant, in the plains, for drying. The Indian Government has a strict control board that sets the prices and buys the entire crop. The Soviet Union is the largest customer.

Brother Xavier took me around the plantation in a car to see the new sprinkler system they set up with hydraulic pumps to send water enormous distances through aluminum pipe from America; this irrigation is making possible better yields not only of coffee but of pineapple. I inquired about how large the crop would be and was told that one hundred sixty tons is about the average yield yearly, though much depends on the rainfall. I was led through the nursery, where new varieties are being nurtured under leaf roofs until the proper age and hardiness can be achieved. These will then be planted where old coffee plants have been uprooted. A plant yields for about fifty years.

Back on the veranda, Father Ryappan told me of the pruning operation, which must be completed every three years, and the constant, intensive spraying to protect against insect predators.

Along the shady lanes of coffee bushes, we met several men carrying rifles; they had been hunting wild boar. Father Xavier told me a panther was roaming the neighboring forest and that two cows had been killed during the past two weeks. The hunt was also on for the panther.

Father Augustine's jubilee feast was served: soup, carrots, chicken, cauliflower, rice, curry and potatoes, followed by rice pudding and cakes with fancy icing. It was a huge success, we laughed and told funny stories, and lingered over our tea. One of the priests had been to America, and he described the John Hancock building to an amused, but disbelieving, audience.

Later, on the shaded veranda, after the tour of the plantation had been completed, a handsome young Indian came in, bowed his knee before Father Ryappan, and waited for the hand in blessing on his head. I thought he was a seminarian but found he was a neighbor, Pajus, member of a large extended family. His people were also coffee planters, and deeply devoted to the Jesuits because of the help that had been given to them in the early days of both plantations. His name had been given to him in honor of Father Pajus, one of the early Jesuit managers. He spoke English very well, and I detected about him the air of wealth, education and refinement that proclaimed the higher-caste Hindu. I was wrong. He was of the Nadar Caste. But so successful had been the coffee business that, at his brother's recent wedding, the guests had numbered ten thousand persons, who had been fed and entertained for two days. Father Ryappan saw my astonishment, and told me the cost had exceeded three lakhs. This is roughly forty thousand dollars. Pajus, when we were parting, asked me to come to his village. I was very eager to do so, not having previously met an Indian who was not extremely poor. Brother Paranjothi said he would arrange it and let me know. I put it on my agenda as a "must."

Returning home one day, after a small dinner with the De Jonges, I was rounding a bend in the road when I saw a very large crowd of men and boys around a grotesque tangle of rubber, metal and logs. I saw it was one of the private carrier trucks, which had smashed, demolished a wall, and come to rest in the ditch upside down. The cab was badly smashed in, but it appeared that the occupants and driver were not killed but had been taken to the hospital. Considering the very bad curves in these roads, the crowded conditions where animals and coolies choke all but the narrow space in the middle, it is surprising that there is not a greater number of accidents. Everyone says this is nothing compared to the "season," when many more tourists will be here and the roads become very hazardous indeed. Indian truck drivers are skilled with the same kind of careless abandon I have seen among parking-lot attendants at home. They never slow in the presence of traffic but come ahead full speed, with one hand on the horn, daring anyone to dispute their superior bulk. The problem is that there are no places for pedestrians to walk except on the road. All along either side, tangles of grasses, cow dung, rock and sewers make it impossible for the pedestrian to find any footing. The road at least is a smooth path.

Early morning, when I went out and down the road to await the ride with the driver from Presentation, was really the only safe time. Standing in the clear, cool morning light, I could hear the wonderful birds in the trees and the strange song of the Hindu who had a dirty little coffee shop on the opposite corner, set in a grove of trees; watch an emaciated pony wandering around near the lake, feeding on the grasses there; and salaam to all the cleanly dressed men and women who hurried along to their jobs in the American School. Jogging seems to have caught on here, too. Many young men would come puffing along, their sandals slapping on the road as they jogged past me, their eyes fixed on some eternal prize.

I found that walking up and down the hills was gradually becoming easier for me. I did not have to stop continually and "admire the view," but could pace my breathing in harmony with my feet, and was soon walking quite easily for long distances. Time has a way of spinning out into a silken web in India. At home I would have considered it disgraceful to spend an hour walking to and from the store: time was money, the essential stuff of my life, and must not be dribbled away in useless activity. It was to be measured, carefully doled out to the many tasks of the day, and driving was more efficient. One even had to budget one's time to "do some exercise" in that busy, mad pattern of life at home. Here, I found that the hour I spent walking to and from the bazaar was anything but a waste. Not only did it reward me with interesting sights and encounters with my neighbors on the hill, but it also paid a bounty in birdsong, weight reduction, increased stamina and a buoyant spirit. I began to feel younger, more alive, more intensely aware of life, the faces of beautiful children, the inquisitive, shy little tribal ladies, and the sometimes insolent but always curious young men. We were having a fine education, getting to know one another. I could hear them discussing my clothing, my age, my origin and my religion. Some words were continually repeated as I passed a group: "amah" and "American." The elders in town always raised their folded hands to their forehead when they saluted me in the road. I was told this was a sign of respect given to teachers. Apparently they believed I was a teacher at the American School, since I had friends there and was often in the library.

Sister Cecilia, the appropriately named music sister at the convent, asked me one morning if I would have time to look in on her class and say a few words to the girls. It sounded very casual and informal. I thought it might be fun. It was a distinct surprise, later, to find that the "few girls" had increased to about a hundred, and that several of the other sisters and teachers had also gathered to hear my words of wisdom. I feared I was going to be a huge disappointment to them, but I plunged in anyway, giving them a bird's-eye view of the life of an American housewife, a brief description of my various jobs, and a little credo, and then asked for questions. They seemed interested in America as a troubled civilization: the drug problem, the racial question, crime in the streets, unemployment, etc. As I warmed to the task, I found that the thirty-five minutes allotted to me slipped by unnoticed by anyone, and we spent a full hour in discussion. Whether anything of value slipped from me to them I have no way of knowing, but at least they had met one American who believed in God, still prayed, thought America wonderful, believed that the blacks were being given an increasingly fair opportunity for education, jobs and housing, and was unwilling to consign her country to criminals and dope addicts. They seemed genuinely surprised to learn that I never locked a door at home, had never been robbed or mugged, and that only in India did I feel constrained to guard my meager store of possessions. Someone had certainly been giving them a very black picture of America, I decided, and when I remembered the obscene comic-book garbage I had seen being sold as "literature from America," while the classics and great poems and drama of the Russians occupied all the rest of the bookstore shelves, I wondered at the distribution of reading materials, and pondered who might be behind this kind of subtle propaganda. One child asked me about the hoards of "tramps" in America, an obvious reference to the great depression years of the hobos and other boxcar riders. I told her that problem did not really exist anymore. It turned out to be a learning experience for us both. As I was leaving, one of the sisters asked if I would address their "leadership" meeting the following Sunday.

Later, one of the American residents at Kodai told me frankly there had always been drugs in India, taken in small doses daily even by the poor. They made it themselves, she said, from poppy. Bombay parties for young people, she said, were often quite gay, due to the drugs slipped into the sweets "to make the party go better," and that sometimes the unsuspecting guest was unaware that the food had been thus poisoned. This sneak attack seemed to me even more insidious than the deliberate act of getting stoned, since it was perpetrated on the innocent, who were given no choice in the matter. The greatest deterrent in India at the present time seems to be the extreme poverty of the populace, who simply cannot afford the drug habit on the same scale as Europe or America—one of the unexpected benefits of poverty. I have no doubt that when and if the country becomes prosperous, they will be left defenseless against the vices of affluence. For what is termed morality in India is often merely a conforming to the local culture of the village or tribe. The effect of such a fragile moral sense when the individual is transplanted to a new culture is a question for the future, when Indians migrate to other nations rich enough to breed criminal drug use.

CHAPTER 13

Down to Madurai

Faithful Winnie at length wired that my luggage had been passed through customs and was now in Madurai. I contacted Raja, who polished up his taxi, visited the petrol tank and arrived at Snyder "B" at 6:30 A.M. for the descent to the plains. I wore a light cotton shirt and skirt, anticipating the heat there, and brought along the sound movie camera. I knew the journey down the ghats would be scenic, and with Raja at the wheel I could ask him to stop where I wanted a shot of the valley below. I bought fresh batteries, since the camera had been running rather strangely.

The road was clear at first, and then patches of fog began to obscure the distant hills. Lorries and taxis began honking around the hairpin curves, and since Kodai road is very narrow, we were careful to sound a blast on the horn at each curve. Several times, lorries sped past us with what seemed like a two-inch clearance. Raja had a healthy respect for the tortuous route, though his relating of the more spectacular accidents did little to reassure me. Two years before, a busload of passengers had fallen over the side and down one mile. There were no survivors.

At one of the villages, Raja pulled into a gas station to get water for the radiator. The sound of early Mass in Tamil drifted up from the village church by means of a loudspeaker, which thus shared the liturgy with the whole village. A large blue bus from Madras took the road immediately ahead of us, and for about fifteen miles Raja gamely tried to honk his way around it. The driver, obviously terrified by the steep, corkscrew turns, held the exact center of the road grimly, and slowed down to about five miles per hour. The thick black diesel smoke issuing from the rear of the bus all but choked us, but Raja patiently kept within one foot of the blue hind end and tooted his horn in the accepted manner of the hill driver. He explained to me that this driver from Madras did not know what he was doing. Then he related an incident when he was in a car driving a police inspector down and a truck refused to give way to permit them to pass. At the first opportunity, the policeman had instructed Raja to not only pass the truck but block the path in front of it. The truck driver had then been arrested for his bad driving manners. Finally the blue bus got the message and moved over so Raja could pass, and we shot forward down the hill again, leaving the blue bus far behind.

As we went, Raja told me a little of his family history. He was one of five brothers and four sisters. His father was a doctor of Tamil medicine, an expert in herbs and tribal remedies. He has one brother a priest, and two sisters who are nuns. The clean taxi had already made a very good impression: there were blue plaid slipcovers over the seats and three sticks of incense burning before a little shrine on the dashboard: Chambers's rather sickly portrait of the Sacred Heart wistfully gazed from a little chrome frame surrounded by a garland of fresh coral flowers, underneath which a sign read: JESUS LOVES YOU. I felt I was in good hands.

Raja himself is a very handsome young man, taller than most Tamilians and with very even features, excellent white teeth (which are often in evidence), carefully combed curly hair, and a courteous manner. He is of the Adidravada caste. He is twenty-two years old, "a bachelor, madam," but hoped to marry in three years.

After government high school in Kodai, he had tried three or four times to gain entrance into an industrial school but with no success. Finally his elder brother obtained a loan at the bank, bought a secondhand taxi for him, and after driver-training he was now in business.

As the fog thickened and the windows steamed up, I began to worry a bit and mentioned this to Raja.

He laughed, "This is nothing, madam. During rainy season cannot see edge at all."

I was relieved when we arrived at the roadside shrine of St. Paul and Raja got out to light a candle and murmur a brief prayer for a safe journey. He also cleaned the windshield.

Farther on, the fog lifted, monkeys scampered along the low wall at the edge, and I tried, unsuccessfully, to take a few feet of film.

They were too quick for me and headed for the trees. Raja knew of the most scenic spot where there was room for the car to park safely and where I would have an unobstructed view of the plains below: coral and blue and violet in the distance, with a nice pool of water shimmering in the sunlight, and with a waterfall drifting down from the hills.

"This Dum Dum View, madam," said Raja as he helped me from the car.

I assembled the mike on the camera, preparing to record Raja's description of the scene, when out of the ground came a small crowd of men and boys. It was incredible. Even at this altitude, people appear out of nowhere. One has only to halt, whether walking or driving, and one is surrounded with a highly appreciative audience. I felt like the main attraction at the zoo. It is understandable in a place where so little else happens. I quickly took a few feet of film and climbed back into the taxi again, amid much waving and cheering.

"Why is the place called 'Dum Dum'?" I asked Raja.

"When rock falls down, it say, 'Dum dum,' " answered Raja with beautiful logic.

This time I took the front seat, and when we left the hills behind, Raja cleaned the windshield again so I could shoot from the car in case of interesting scenes along the way. But any drive along a country road in southern India is so filled with beauty and pastoral charm that one would have to focus and shoot continually. I was conscious of the limitations of my camera, and of its anemic batteries, and found myself mentally moaning as we passed wonderful Hindu shrines and villages of picturesque dilapidation, where a sudden bright flash of blue or red sari in the door of a hut drew the eye to domestic scenes that included what seemed to be the delousing of a child's hair, and where many small boys could be seen peacefully urinating on the roadside. Down one avenue of overhanging trees, I saw a group of people walking toward the car, the women with pots balanced on their heads.

"Field workers," said Raja. "Work in paddy near here." I made him stop while I photographed this stately procession as it came toward us, and again when four young girls came up the road with haystacks on their heads. A group of men and women winnowing along the road made another scene worth recording, and then the camera stopped for good. Raja said I might be able to get more bat-

teries in Madurai, and so we proceeded past vignettes that shouted
for recording while I mentally cursed the maker of my camera, and
all shoddy workmanship. Large flocks of goats rambled by, driven by
small boys, and men with marvelous faces, and I ground my teeth in
disappointment. Tiny donkeys, the size of collie dogs, accompanied
the dhobies, with their bright loads of washing, down to the streams.
Roosters with proudly brilliant feathers strutted between the red clay
huts; flashes of copper jugs in the bright sunlight gleamed like gold
against the soft dark skins of the young girls, who balanced the precious water on their heads as they slowly moved under the coconut
palms. The bullocks of the area still wore brightly colored horns,
remnants of a feast during which these had been painted. At one
small pond, I saw four water buffalo and seven or eight small boys
happily bathing together in the bright morning sunshine. The plains
were very warm, but it was not until the car stopped that I realized
how drastic had been the sudden rise in temperature. It was 100 degrees F.

At length we came to Madurai. This ancient temple city seems to
have sprung up as a series of little shops around the towering
gopuram of the Temple of Meenakshi. The streets are narrow,
crowded with bikes, cattle, pedestrians and pedicabs. There is a fair
selection of goods obtainable in Madurai, center for the entire
South, and we threaded our way up a street to the Indian Airlines
office, where I went to get my bags. There they were! I paid the cost
of their ride from Madras, plus their demurrage charges (at Madras)
and checked the contents, which seemed all there. I had Raja place
them in the trunk of the taxi. I was interested in buying cotton
cloth, and we found the shop of Hadji Moosa, across from the red-
and-white-striped temple wall, in the shadow of the gopuram.

Hadji Moosa's emporium looks rather unprepossessing from the
outside, and except for the recommendations of Kodai residents, I
would not have known the treasures that lie within. One enters a
small room where courteous, English-speaking male clerks stand
behind the counters, in front of walls lined with shelves of fabric. It
looked like a very limited inventory to me, but I then found that this
room gave way to another, where clerks were seated on the floor. I
investigated, and discovered magnificent silks being sold there. Beyond it was another, still larger room, where customers on the floor
were being shown saris; behind this a third showroom, for silks. Up-

stairs was a revelation of hand-woven toweling, blankets, bedspreads, drapery fabrics and upholstery materials. I could have bankrupted myself for ten years had I bought all I craved. I contented myself with two marvelous double-woven bedspreads, with reverse designs on the two sides, some beautiful woven cotton saris to be used as summer dresses and as gifts for my daughters, a little wraparound skirt with elephants on it for my granddaughter Miss Laura, and cotton gauze for dresses. There was a black chiffon sari embroidered heavily in gold, costing many thousands of rupees, which would have been an evening gown of great splendor; I bit my lip, glanced at my fifty-seven-year-old face in the mirror, and reminded myself that evening gowns and expensive fabric were no longer my style. Barb wouldn't have worn it either. I realized suddenly that I knew of no American who was engaged in the kind of social life that required this harem splendor. The West, when I had seen it four weeks before, was featuring simple, peasant-style clothing. The cottons I had purchased would be in style. Glancing around at the young women seated before these wonders of needlework and color, I guessed they must be brides-to-be planning dowries. Older women with them would be their mothers, and I regretted the fact that only in the mysterious East were such magnificent ornaments being made and purchased for the beauty of women. Western women were wearing slacks for evening dress; Paris had made poverty chic for the season. The Third World alone still values gold embroidery, fine lace and pure silk. The affluent West wears blue jeans.

I had a quiet lunch at the Taj Restaurant, nearby, Raja having gone to his family's home for lunch. We met again in an hour, and Raja was accompanied by his younger sister, Rosemary, a shy, pretty girl with jasmine woven into her braid and wearing a violet sari. He explained that she must go to Kodai to visit the rest of the family, and hoped I wouldn't mind taking her along. I had no objection; she sat in the front seat, beside Raja, and for the next four hours said not more than two words. I decided she must either be in love or ill; but Raja said she had always been a quiet girl.

I wanted to visit Boys' Village, which I had heard much about at Kodai and from Dom Bede, so I told Raja to stop there en route to the hills. Batalagunda is the village nearest the ghats; Boys' Village is on the outskirts of Batalagunda. We left Madurai and pointed the car toward the ghats. The sun shone down unmercifully on the fields and road, and I was longing for a shower. Rosemary, however, in the front seat, with her fresh flowers and lovely dress, seemed totally undisturbed by the heat. Her heavily oiled hair remained in place though the car windows were open and a hot blast circulated around and caught my hair in a whirlwind. I put a scarf on my head, and wondered if fresh flowers might have helped me, too.

A bullock cart heaved into view, and I noted with envy that its driver was not at the controls but sound asleep on a sack under the basket-woven awning. The bullocks apparently knew all the rules of the road and were properly licensed.

In midafternoon we arrived at Boys' Village, immediately noteworthy because of the startlingly fresh white little houses, with the new red tile roofs and the general air of southern California landscaping; it reminded me of Carmel-by-the-Sea, an incongruity this far from salt water. A tall, youngish man in shorts, a white shirt and sandals came down from the shade of a veranda when our car pulled in, and identified himself as Brother James. He invited us in, but Raja and Rosemary elected to stay with the car; he out of a sense of duty to guard, and she, I thought, from sheer apathy.

Guiding me over to his own little hut, white and fresh, like all the others, and facing the newly planted red fields, Brother James told me a little about his work and this wonder village he had created in three years' time.

He is well qualified for the job, having been in India since 1952, a member of the De La Salle Brothers. Many years' experience with a similar Boys' Village in a different location gave him the sure touch he exhibits here. One has the feeling there is nothing he cannot accomplish. As we walked about the place, he told me he has fifty-four small boys, whom he provides with a family orientation, rather than that of an institution. The boys themselves make the rules and live by them. A Boys' Panchayat, or village form of government, meets in a large hall, where the seats rise in a semicircle. His aim is to foster initiative, competence and self-reliance, and judging from the boys I met, busily planting, watering their small beds of marigolds, or bathing a smaller boy in a tub, and generally looking like very efficient Lilliputians, he has succeeded admirably. All of these boys are orphans, and destitute. They range from eight to fourteen years of age. He sends them to the local schools, and as they become older, arranges for them to be placed in industrial schools for craft training, so they will become independent. The work they do at Boys' Village is not free. They are paid for it. Their money is carefully saved, along with the weekly allowance he gives them, and when a boy has saved thirty rupees, it is placed in the bank in his name. This bank account, added to continually, is his. In this way, when a boy finally grows old enough to leave Boys' Village, he has enough saved to get a modest start in life. Several families also live there, and the women of these families care for the very small boys as their own.

A beautiful open-air chapel, much like the one I saw at Dom Bede's ashram, with marvelous pillars holding up the roof and, above the altar, a beautiful portrayal of Christ with children, caught my attention. Brother James told me he bought the pillars for a few rupees each and had used them widely in his building projects; they were ancient, with lovely carvings on them, obviously centuries old, and now very suitably holding up the roofs of a chapel and a meetinghouse for small boys. The painting was his own work. Brother James is not only a gentle, enthusiastic and youthful fifty-two-year-old man of God; he is also an artist and architect and village planner of tremendous talent.

The Christ-centered work to which he has given his life has not stopped at Boys' Village. He has considered the plight of the poor neighbors in his area and reached out to touch them in as many helping ways as possible. His conviction that the food shortage is crucial has resulted in his creation of a demonstration model farm, where he has, by example, shown the neighboring small farmers the techniques of multicropping, intercropping and the use of hybrid seeds, the use of waste land for fruit trees, the simple irrigation methods possible for every available source of water, and the intensive use of animal and green manures, tank silt, and coconut-fiber dust. He operates an excellent dairy, goat herd, and poultry farm, and breeds sheep of high pedigree.

His most recent project involves the rebuilding of an entire village nearby, where the Harijan population was living in untold filth and squalor. He interested a group of college girls at Fatima College, Madurai, in this scheme, and now has two crews of young women who are actually themselves building a new village. If I had not seen this with my own eyes, I would have found it hard to believe; yet there they were, these young college women in their colorful saris, working amid the ruddy bricks and under the blazing sun, while one worker mixed mortar and slapped it on the bricks as the girls passed them along. The hut they were working on would be finished within a week, Brother told me, and the older woman in their midst, also working on the building, was to be the occupant, along with her husband and children.

The funds for this project had come from England, where a group of wives in a large corporation decided that the excess profits had better be put to a good use, and asked if he would take them and rebuild a village with them. Brother James never says no. He has been answering yes to life for many years now, and empowering hundreds of children and young people to do the same. He will make an enormous difference in this part of India, where his joyful leadership and example will become part of the legend of this place and take root in lives still unborn. He will never be content with what has been accomplished, however; his mother-and-child clinic and his dispensary for what he calls the common diseases have now been expanded to care for TB, leprosy and eye diseases. The boys from his village go voluntarily to visit and help the forgotten aged in the nearby villages, and he told me with surprised delight that they had recently discovered that in their school many kids had no lunch, so they themselves organized a lunch program and are now feeding these hungry classmates.

We parted friends, with the promise of a visit during Holy Week, when he comes to Kodai. I left with the feeling that I had been conversing with a modern saint. There was nothing in his manner to suggest that he considered the village *his* project; he was simply making it possible for the boys and the villagers to reach a higher potential. I left the place inspired and more than ever convinced that this work among the poorest castes is the real core of the Christian message. The Indian upper classes are wealthy; there is a growing middle class who are able to care for themselves with increased education and opportunity, but the vast majority of this land, the poor, need the help of the Christian West, not to give them handouts but to share in their lives, to live as they do, and to gently teach what the West has learned over the centuries since the great industrial and economic expansion while India was still struggling against foreign invasions and exploitation. It is a special calling, requiring the kind of love and commitment only a few manage to muster; Brother James is one of these special people. I found myself wondering if I might find this kind of call in the depths of my soul, and if, having heard it, I would ever have the courage to simply settle down in a village, like James, Sister Lydia, the Presentation nuns, Dom Bede, and the Jesuits from Europe and America, and share the trials and hardships of the poorest of the poor.

CHAPTER 14

A Day with Father Minister

Aelred d'Silva is Father Minister, in charge of the everyday affairs of the community at Sacred Heart College. He has reached out to the community around the college, and spends his free time doing works of charity, acting as treasurer for Corsock; everyone in town waves as he passes. He drives the car and the jeep himself, taking the driver along with him only to mind the car while he conducts his business at the bank, or at the government offices, or at the home of some poor family who look to him to solve their immediate and terrible problems. I was touched and grateful when he offered to come for me on a Saturday, when his work did not demand too much attention, to show me some of the sights of Kodai and of Shembaganur. He arrived at 8:30 A.M. I had returned home from early Mass, and was ready, wearing walking shoes, comfortable clothing and a wide-brimmed hat. I brought the camera for whatever scenes the day might unfold.

The most spectacular view of the plains from Kodaikanal is to be seen at Coaker's Walk, a very narrow pathway near Van Allen Hospital, where great clouds of fog often obscure all but the tips of the hills. We were lucky. That Saturday morning, the view was marvelous: Sacred Heart College far below, surrounded by its eucalyptus forest, seemed from that height an accessory for a child's train set. All around, the terraced hills sensuously curved around each plateau and held little fruit trees or vegetables on their steps. Distant mountains turn purple in the haze and are so far that not even the forest colors can be seen; little wisps of smoke often proclaim a hut there, where a poor man may have settled down to clear the land in hope that the government would eventually recognize his squatter's rights and deed it to him.

We stood for a while to gaze at this lovely scene, while Aelred pointed out the Carmelite Convent in the distance, the parish church, and the stark drama of Perumal Peak, lofty and lonely, dominating the scene. A little group of tourists, Indians in their finest clothes, the ladies glittering with gold necklaces and lovely saris, the men in sport shirts and white dhotis, stood close enough to hear Aelred's remarks, thus gaining some information free of charge. Looking down is definitely dizzying. The only other time I experienced the queasiness of height was when at St. Peter's in Rome I ascended to the inside top of the great dome and looked down at the altar, far below. I was grateful for the handrail there, and backed away from the edge.

We viewed this valley from several points; farther on, at Green Valley View, and then from Pillar Rocks, where the granite rock of those hills can be seen in its naked strength and massive durability. I stood there, after taking some photos, and remembered Bert telling me of the tragedy that happened there when he was a young novice, in the thirties. The seminarians had walked from Shembag to Kodai with their picnic lunch, as they often had done. With them was a young Belgian novice who had arrived only three days before from Europe. Somehow, during the picnic, he had failed to jump across a crevice and had fallen to the rocks below. He was killed instantly. No one was around when the accident occurred, and it was only when all had joined to return to Shembag that he was missed, searched for and found. Nearly fifty years have passed, but the tragedy of that young life lost is still remembered and spoken of at the seminary. Pillar Rocks has claimed many lives, but most of them are offered voluntarily. The most recent was a Hindu businessman who suffered financial losses and went there to end it all. Today only the murmur of a waterfall echoed in this place of awesome and fierce beauty.

Passing the golf course, we saw Mohan Lal practicing his swing with gusto, and stopped to chat with him a bit. He invited us to the club for coffee, but Father explained that we had a lengthy program planned for the day, so we took a rain check.

We stopped at La Providence, the Jesuit residence, where we found Father Augustine watering the roses. I walked through the garden, marveling at the flowers, every variety from exotic flowering cactus in huge pots to the most delicate of tea roses grafted on trees.

Delphiniums, poppies, strawflowers, daisies, cineraria in every hue, swayed in the high breeze from the cliff, and bloomed in this sanctuary of quiet and peace. Later in the season, many of the Jesuits from the plains would come up for their holidays; the garden would then have its proper audience. I asked for some seeds, and Father Augustine gave me many varieties in envelopes to carry home to try in Oak Park.

We drove to the post office at Shembag, and found Brother Peter, postmaster par excellence. I had some cloth and other items to ship to America, which would require his attention. Knowing that they had a special method of wrapping, I brought them all in bags and dumped them out for inspection and discussion about the proper method of shipping. One of the brothers, a friendly gentleman in a long coat, scarf and cap, came along to assist, and we were soon weighing material on the scales and printing labels for the young man who would do the wrapping in the bindery room. There is something definitely regal about being the only customer in a post office and having the entire attention of the postmaster and three or four assistants. As we worked, Brother spoke of other parcels I had sent from this post office, in 1971, 1973 and 1975. He remembered them all. It was flattering, to say the least. Among the parcels to be shipped would be the special vestments for Kanikairaj, to be sent to Madras; the nice wool shawl and long skirt lent by Winnie for the ashram; the parcels to America, and the cloth for Sister Stella's workroom in Madras. It was quite a long time before all were properly wrapped and labeled and the cost totaled. Brother Peter presided over the event like a benevolent monarch, his long beard lending great dignity to the affair. I found myself tending to whisper in his presence, as before the Dalai Lama. But he was gracious, kindly and supremely in control of his minions, who share his love for order, exactitude and the sacred character of mail. Someone should make a movie of this post office and show it in America to our Postal Service as a training film.

Lunch at the refectory followed: rice, curry, a special plate of prepared vegetables for me, and the excellent bread of the seminary. There was another visitor besides myself: Brother Aloysius, from Poonamallee. He was a classmate of Kanikairaj's and would be ordained in May. I conveyed to him my regret at being unable to stand the heat of Madras during April, having experienced it in Madurai in March and finding it unbearable. I asked him to explain this to Kanikairaj. Then I remembered the vestments that had just been packed, and arranged with him to take them back to Madras and personally give them to my friend. This he promised to do.

While we were talking, Father Ugarte came in. This priest is in charge of the museum at the seminary, and I began telling the visitor of the marvels to be seen there. Father Ugarte promised to give him a tour the next day. Suddenly I remembered that one of my goals was a visit to the dolmen sites, and I asked Father Ugarte how this might be arranged. Within seconds he had fixed it for Monday, which was before the exams at the seminary, and by the time Aelred found us, we had a party made up that included Brother Aloysius from Madras, myself, Father Ugarte and Brother Robert. They would send the car to pick me up at seven thirty Monday morning.

As we left Sacred Heart, Aelred drove up the lane where the college servants lived, to show me Regina's house.

"She'll be furious with me," he laughed. "She will say, 'I wasn't there to clean it' and make all kinds of bother about it."

I recognized young Philomena, who had Regina's eyes and face, leaning on the wall as we approached. We entered the dim little two-room hut, where Susai Mary, the elder daughter, was keeping house in her mother's absence. My heart sank as I looked at the poor string bed, the only bed in the house, and saw the clothesline slung across the room with the few pieces of ragged clothing on it, the pile of books, papers and notes on a table, and on the floor, beautiful white drawings made by Susai Mary to lend some kind of décor to the dark hut. The small door at the back gave way into a still darker little chamber, where a hearth was set into the wall for cooking. Outside, surrounded by a wooden fence, were the pump and pots for water, washing, bathing, and, I presumed, toilet facilities. A few shelves held some stainless-steel plates, cups and tumblers. That was all. I thought of Regina's puzzlement at my disapproval of the kitchen at Snyder "B." No wonder! It must have seemed like a dream kitchen to her. Father spoke a few words to Susai and Philomena, and we stepped into the sunlight again. Neighbors had lined up along the walk to see the strange American lady. We got into the car quickly and drove away. I felt vaguely uneasy at having visited Regina's home without an invitation.

Aelred wanted me to see an orphanage nearby which he had taken

under his wing. It had been begun some years before by a group of
sisters from Pondicherry; they were terribly poor and one evening
had been forced to walk to Shembag, ring the Jesuits' bell and tell
them they had no food at all for the one hundred children they were
trying to care for. The hills are very chilly at night, particularly in
the winter months, and the orphans had nothing but the rags on
their backs. Many were severely undernourished, filled with sores
and scabies. The result was that Aelred had taken up their cause,
provided them with blankets, sweaters, medicine, slates, school
books, notebooks, food and money.

As we approached up a narrow dirt road in very bad condition, the
jeep rocking and bumping along in teeth-jarring rhythm, Aelred told
me the history of the place and the present state of the water there.
For months the sisters had had to collect water from a nearby stream
when their miserable hand pump failed. Next to food and shelter,
water is the most essential need of mankind, and when children are
involved, great quantities are necessary to keep them clean, wash
their clothing, and create the kind of healthy environment they
require. An electric pump seemed the most sensible solution, and I
inquired why none was there. Aelred said they were looking into that
matter, and trying to raise money to purchase the motor and provide
the cement needed for a reservoir when the electric pump would be
installed.

There was a great cry of welcome as the jeep approached the low
gray buildings behind the rock wall, and as we drove in, the children
came running up to Aelred to grasp his hands and to welcome us.
They were pathetic little creatures, large heads, tiny, emaciated bodies, barefoot and ragged. Some had very dirty woolen sweaters on, all
had running noses, and the freshly swept mud compound bore marks
of their little feet. The buildings were in bad condition; charac-
teristically, no electricity was working that afternoon, so they were
dim and dark inside when we went from one building to another.
The classroom, with low wooden benches, blackboards and lessons
on the walls, was also their sleeping and eating room. It was in a
frightful state of disorder, with a few larger girls in very dirty saris
trying to create some kind of hospitality for us. No sister was in evidence.

Aelred walked through the place with the easy familiarity of one
who is at home, and at length we found three or four of the nuns.

They had been directing some work in their quarters, where the roof had been leaking. Piles of wood shavings covered the floor of their poor little chamber, with its six or seven small hard beds and a few holy pictures on the walls. I was dismayed to see that their condition was not much better than the children's: barefoot, with very dirty white saris on, old shawls wound around their thin shoulders, and in their eyes a kind of desperate plea that I would understand. I could not understand how they managed to live in these conditions.

Aelred introduced me, and we went down to the children again, to the classroom, where one of the sisters told the children to sit down. Aelred and I were given the only chairs in the room. After much excited conversation, they began to sing for us in clear, piercing voices which displayed an amazing energy and joy. I fought tears as I looked at them, eyes shining, offering from the depths of those undernourished bodies the age-old appeal of children's song. There were some very good voices among them. A small boy, with the agility and theatrical know-how of Jolson himself, began a song-and-dance drama he had clearly picked up from the Indian films. He sang in a high, clear voice, used his arms, hands, limbs and body in an amazingly sophisticated manner to tell some story, the words of which escaped me, though I could follow the general idea. The kids loved it, and he played to them and to us in full confidence that his was a rare and sweet treasure in that forsaken place. The applause was deafening. A word from Sister, and another "act" came on, several small girls singing with three little boys, who portrayed the monkeys who see, hear and speak no evil. Act followed act on those wooden boards, to a highly appreciative audience, all of whom were capable of supplying a verse momentarily forgotten or a cue the comic might have stumbled over. When it was over, and the kids became aware that the bag I carried contained a camera, they shoved themselves forward in the manner I have come to associate with Indians everywhere: they love to be photographed. Luckily, I had an electronic flash on the camera and was able to do without the phantom electricity.

We tossed a ball around in the compound for a while, and then the sisters asked me to come in for tea. Their plain little parlor was clean and neat, and the tea excellent. But the sisters were very shy, and did not sit with us. After pouring and serving, they left us to eat alone. I left them some rupees, and told Aelred I would give him a hundred dollars of Ted's bounty toward the purchase of the electric pump. We left in a flurry of good-byes, ta-tas, and namastes.

The road back led us near the home of Bob Stool, and since Dom Bede had told me to make sure to visit him, I asked Aelred if we might stop there. He was quite willing, and we drove through the gate, near which a statue of Our Lady leaned out of a little shrine, and found a very pleasant, low house that seemed to sprawl about a large area, surrounded by a beautiful and well-kept garden. We entered a pleasant room and were greeted by a servant, who went to tell Mr. Stool we were there. He sent for us to join him in the library, and we went through a series of corridors opening out into interesting rooms I had no time to examine. In the library a large and friendly Alsatian dog was lying on the floor, and beyond him, seated at the desk, a bearded Scotsman who greeted Aelred joyfully and held out his hand in a warm welcome to me. He was genuinely happy to have company, and complained that Aelred had not been there for some time. Aelred explained he had been busy, and since he knew the other Jesuits visited, had not availed himself of the pleasure. They talked for a while of mutual friends, while I glanced around the masculine room and longed to read the titles of the old books in the cases around the room. Bob Stool noticed my interest and handed me the book he was presently reading, by Cardinal Hume, *Searching for God*, which he pronounced excellent. "Mae is reading it too," he said. "She's a Presbyterian, but she thinks it is deeply spiritual." Mae, I found, was the sister of his deceased wife, who was in Shembag for a visit. He sent the servant out to the garden to fetch her. "She'd never forgive me if she knew we had visitors and she missed seeing them," he said with a grin.

Mae came in, introductions were made, and we settled down with gin and lime to get acquainted. Bob Stool was interested to know what I might be doing in Kodai, and when I told him I had hired Regina, I was interested in his reaction. Regina had worked for him for many years, and had been let go when it became apparent that the male servant's new bride was being bossed around by Regina in a manner that made it very unpleasant for all of them. "Mind you," he said, "Regina is very good—I've been at a complete loss since she left here. Can't get anyone to take care of things as she did; but the situation was impossible, and I had no other choice." I could understand it, having found myself more than once wondering who was boss at our house and knuckling under to her in the matter of when to dine and when to wash my hair. I told him, however, that on the whole I was pleased with her, since her care of the house left me free to write and to see Kodai, which was why I had come.

I gave Bob greetings from Dom Bede, and he said, smiling, "Is that broken-down old Benedictine still at that ashram?" I was rather shocked until I realized that this was love talking, that they were old friends. Bob was also a Benedictine Oblate, and when I said I had met Dick Keithahn, he laughed and said that they three had all worked together at Batalagunda years ago. What a team that must have been! We had another gin and lime while Bob related some of his family history, gave the Scotsman's view of India, detailed some of the more scenic and impressive places worth visiting in Scotland, and patted his dog, Timothea. He and Aelred compared notes on mutual friends, some of them Jesuits, and on local quarrels and donnybrooks that had taken place. Just as I was about to say we should be going, this canny Scot looked at me and said, "And now, darlings, I'm going to throw you both out," and we said our good-byes and left with the promise that he would find his way to my doorway soon.

Aelred brought me home in time for my fruit-and-curd dinner, which Regina had ready for me. She was most eager to know where I had been. I told her I had visited her house, and she beamed. I told her I had met Bob Stool, and she said, "What he say, you tell him I work you," I busied myself with my apple peeling and told her he said she had been a very good servant, and that he missed her.

"He nice man," said Regina gratefully.

CHAPTER 15

The Day of the Dolmens

"They'll be wondering at Presentation why I didn't come this morning," I thought as I sped by the Telephone Exchange in the seminary car. The driver had been sent for me at 7 A.M., and I had packed a bag with the cameras, some coffee and my floppy hat. I was to see the dolmens, finally, in the company of an expert, Father Ugarte, who was in charge of the museum and the collection of burial urns, ancient bones, and tools and jewelry from the Stone Age.

We picked up Aelred d'Silva, who drove the car, with the driver squeezed into the front seat beside him and Brother Robert on the other side. In the back, Father Ugarte and I enjoyed a bumpy conversation as we descended the Kodai road in search of the site where the most accessible dolmens were to be seen.

Father Ugarte had come to India from Spain at the age of eighteen, and except for a brief period of study and an assignment as rector in Trichy and another five years at Poona, he had spent all of his fifty-six India years at Sacred Heart in Shembaganur. He had worked under the famous Father Anglade, the genius who had collected, classified and memorialized the contents of the Jesuit museum. A native of the Basque country, he found the climate there very agreeable, and had never been adversely affected, as were many Indian Jesuits, by the fog or cold. His special fields were biology and psychology.

"About these dolmens, Father, can you give me a definition of what a dolmen is?" I asked him.

"That means a stone building. But here in this country, they have their own names for them; they call them forts."

"You think they were used as forts?"

"When you see them, you will realize that is not possible. You have to see them first. Otherwise, it is easy to build up theories. It was impossible to live in them, so they cannot be forts, you see?"

We honked our way around a few hairpin curves, and some over-laden buses sped past us. The air was crisp and cool, and the fog began to lift, giving a beautiful vista of the plains below.

"Who first discovered these dolmens?" I asked him.

He told me they had been commented upon ever since the first Europeans came to the Palni Hills. At Kodai the American missionaries had come here first for holidays; even before the Jesuits. The first Jesuit, he told me, was a man named Pierre St. Cyr, who had one parish at Dindigul and another at Palni. He had crossed these hills to get to his people, and at Shembag he found a little bungalow and settled down there, in 1870. I recalled seeing his grave in the chapel near Coaker's Walk, La Salette, which he had built.

"Surely when the news of these dolmens reached Europe and America there must have been scholars who wanted to come and investigate?" I asked him next.

"On the whole," he said, "this is a type of structure that exists in many places: Ireland, England. I've been here for fifty-six years and we've never had foreigners coming here to study dolmens."

I was surprised, and realized again how very elementary was my knowledge of archeology. America does not contain many such antiquities, as far as I knew, while in Europe and Asia, apparently, they were old hat. "How old would you say these dolmens are?"

"The general theory is that they date from 5,000 to 2,000 B.C., which is a very large margin, at the beginning of the Stone Age, the Mesolithic Age, that is, taking in the range of the dolmens from Europe to Japan. Those in these hills are impossible to date. We found nothing inside, such as bones."

"What about the burial urns in the museum? Aren't these connected with the dolmens?"

"They are a different matter entirely. They're a much later development. The urns are never found near dolmens."

"They are an independent find?"

"Yes. Usually you get the kind of stone circle, pieces of rock jutting out, and these formed into a circle. Digging on these sites, we found bones."

I asked whether or not he thought the dolmens might have been astronomical calculators, and told him of the theory about Stonehenge.

He did not think so, but added: "I will show you one thing, however, that is a bit puzzling. There is always at the dolmen center some kind of little box structure, square or rectangular; practically, we have not been yet able to see the use of it."

"Has there been any digging on the site of the dolmens, or would this be permitted?"

"Digging is almost impossible there. The dolmens are on sheer rock, granite. The dolmens just sit there. The stone circles, on the other hand, the moment you dig in these you are sure of getting urns. These were certainly burial places. We have many of these urns and pots at the museum. You must have seen them; we have a shelf where they are all represented, every kind. After a while, you get tired of these pots. But at the dolmens themselves, nothing. We never find anything there."

I became interested in the subject of accurate dating of their findings. Father Ugarte told me that, several times, people had carried pieces of bone and pot back to America to get them carbondated, but nothing further had been heard.

I told him I would like to try to get this done for them. Would they give me bits of material to see if I could succeed in having them dated? He readily agreed, and later on gave me a piece of bone, a bit of a pot, and best of all, a copper bangle, heavily oxidized in green crust, which I hoped to have dated in America.

Later, at home, I contacted a scientist in Arizona who told me that large quantities of bone must be reduced to ash to get carbon dating; that the shards and copper were useless. He gave me the address of a lab in Bombay where the work might be done, and I have passed all of this along to Father Ugarte.

Then I began to wonder about the tribal people of these hills, who might be the descendants of the dolmen builders. I asked Father if anyone had studied the folklore of these people; whether there were myths or legends that might point to explanations of the dolmens. But he said that acculturation was pretty complete in the hills. The Palayans, who were the original settlers of the hills as far as anyone knew, had been integrated with the Tamils from the plains, and nothing remained that could be considered the pure tribal race. They

1. Author at Pushpanagar with Harijan (outcaste) children being educated through the Nevett Fund.

2. La Salette, Jesuit chapel at Kodai built by Father Saint Cyr in 1866.

3. Feast-day procession at Kodaikanal.

4. Typical street in a Harijan village—Pushpanagar, near Madras.

5. Harijan child caring for her young brother.

6. Author with Father Albert Nevett, S.J., organizer of education project for Harijan children.

7. Ancient temple at Madurai, surrounded by modern commerce.

8. Temple chariot pulled through the streets on Hindu feast days in South India; similar to the one that almost ran the author down in Madurai. Note the children along for the ride.

9. Heroic figures inspiring appropriate awe and reverence in front of a wayside shrine in South India.

speak a kind of degraded Tamil. "But we have been mostly curious amateurs in this study," he said.

I asked if he thought it might make a good doctoral study.

He did not really think so.

Meanwhile we came to the spot where Father Ugarte told Aelred to park the car. A low wall at the side of the road contained a number of tribals in ragged clothing, chatting in the sunshine. "Cowboys," said Father Ugarte. They were . . . minding cows.

We brought the cameras and coffee, and climbed up the granite rock some little distance, higher and higher above the roadway. Brother Robert was cautioned to go very slowly; he was a heart patient, and his brothers were very solicitous about the effect of the exercise. But as the assistant in the museum, he was eager to join us on this excursion; he had never seen this particular dolmen site.

Father Ugarte, at seventy-five, his white cassock flopping about his legs and his black beret tight on his white head, loped ahead of us with the agility of a mountain goat. I was next in line, panting and "stopping to enjoy the view" every fifty yards, while Aelred thoughtfully slowed his pace to accompany Brother Robert, who took the climb slowly and with frequent rests, as he had been cautioned.

About four hundred feet up, in a clearing of solid granite where nothing grew at all, we came upon the first dolmens. They were smaller than I had pictured but structured of very heavy granite stones placed in a circle, and some of them were uprights supporting huge slabs of granite as roofs. Father Ugarte told me to ignore this dolmen.

"It's crumbling. You cannot see a real dolmen here," he said, adding that the local cowboys brought their herds here and had knocked down much of the walls, searching for God knows what. Perhaps there would be gold there?

We got our breath, Brother Robert gave assurances that he was fine, and we continued our climb.

We were rewarded at length by coming upon a second large clearing, much more spacious than the first, about the size of a large football field, granite underfoot, and there were three dolmens to be seen there, one of them in very good, pristine condition. Father Ugarte pointed out the walls all around the structure. On one side, at least, they were still standing as they had down through the centuries. I gazed with awe at the huge stones placed one on top of another with such precision, without mortar of any kind, and rising to a height of about four and one half feet from the solid granite ground. They enclosed a circle of "rooms" covered with very large slabs of granite that must have weighed many tons. Some six or eight rooms could be seen clearly by climbing to the top of the wall and peering inside. In the exact center of the configuration of these rooms was the curious "box," outlined in granite, the use of which had puzzled so many dolmen researchers. It was not more than two feet square in this one; in others on the same hilltop I noted one that was rectangular in shape. The boxes were at the hub of the curious little "rooms" with their solid-granite tops.

It was very clear that it would not have been possible to live in these dolmens, once the rocks were in place, for the occupant would have been buried alive. There was no way out. And no bones or any sign of human habitation had ever been found within these dolmen "rooms." The only way they could have been used as forts would have been if there had been underground tunnels up and into them, providing a way of escape. There was no water on the hills; today the cowboys graze their cattle there but bring up water for themselves. And the likelihood of tunnels in solid granite is unthinkable.

But what were they, then? Not forts, not burial places. Could they have been places of worship? One curious fact about them is this: they are found on the best hilltops, where the view of the surrounding countryside is unparalleled and beautiful, and often within plain view of the next dolmen, on another hill, opposite. Could they have been stations for communication? But why the rooms? And why so much trouble with the tons of granite? Messages might have been sent by easier means; the fire, smoke and blanket of the American Indians spring to mind.

I photographed them and the Jesuits from many angles before we headed back down to the car, my mind buzzing like an excited bee over the mystery I had just contemplated. As we were coming to the car, Father Ugarte saw some tribals and called out to them. One of them, a man small in stature but with a barrel chest and long, powerful arms and matted hair, came over to see what he wanted. In English, Father Ugarte said to me, "See this fellow's face. This is the only remnant we have left of the original people here. He is clearly not Dravidian, you see?" I looked at the uncomprehending tribal. It was true. There was an entirely different set to his features. The forehead sloped back, while the jaw jutted forward. I remembered the Neanderthal types I had seen at the Natural History Museum in Chicago. It was not very difficult to imagine the ancestors of this man living their simple, tiger-hunting lives in these hills before recorded history. Father Ugarte said a few words to the man, and we got back into the car. While we drove, Father Ugarte told me tales of the early days in the hills, where tiger and panther were hunted of necessity and where the coolies from the plains carried all the food up to Kodai along the twelve-mile, steep coolie ghat road, rested at Kodai, descended, and returned again with another load in the afternoon. One such coolie, with an enterprising turn of mind, eventually made himself rich through the sale of fish from the rivers of the plains and became the founder of the very wealthy family that owns the bus company.

Back at Shembaganur, Father Ugarte took me back to the museum and once again pointed out the wonderful hand-carved models of the dolmens created by Father Anglade. Now they made more sense to me. I had seen the originals and could now understand that in some of the models there were destroyed walls, while others had their walls still intact. He brought me to the cases, where I was given the precious artifacts I carried home to have dated. "If you succeed at this," he said, "it will be of tremendous service to us."

I began to understand then the enormous difficulty of ever dating the dolmens. Even if it were possible to carbon-test the rocks themselves, which would certainly predate their use in the dolmens by perhaps millions of years, nothing could be learned about when the dolmens had been created from them. But the pots found in the stone circles? The bits of bone and copper jewelry? Certainly the age of these could give a clue.

I was determined to find out all I could. I sensed that a whole new world of wonder and learning had been opened before my eyes, a world that could fill years of searching and studying without ever becoming dull. I determined to read all I could on the dolmens, and would begin with the library at Kodai school. From the evidence of my eyes, as the most innocent amateur, I saw no way the granite rocks could have crumbled, as in the first dolmen, after only a few hundred years. Stonehenge is, after all, still standing after thousands of years and bears a striking resemblance to these dolmens.

I finally returned to Snyder "B," tired and happy, and with a

treasure of films I prayed would be good. I had a simple supper of
curds and fruit and retired early, my mind still busy with the problem that had fascinated the Jesuit scholars.

It was probably the coffee I drank before retiring. I could not
sleep. I played some music for a while, reread a portion of a book,
and again switched off the light and tried to assume the proper pos-
ture for slumber. It was no good. In my mind's eye I was again back
on that wonderful hilltop, with a glory of valleys and distant hills all
around, and reexamining the curious stone structures. Suddenly I
thought of the book *Chariots of the Gods,* which had presented the
theory that men from outer space had visited earth in the ancient
past and left there many remainders of their visit. What if these dolmens had been created by such visitors? As landing pads, perhaps?
While we had been seeing "rooms" below the slabs of granite, what
if these were accidental rooms only, created by the need to get a firm
support for the huge slabs themselves? I thought about it for a while.
Certainly the hilltop of solid granite could have been ideal landing
places for round space vehicles. Could there have been small space
ships? Cone-shaped, and thus fitting nicely into the center "box" all
outlined in granite, with the circle of slabs providing a support when
they landed?

I played with this theory for a long while. Finally, I decided I had
been influenced by *Close Encounters of the Third Kind* too deeply,
and went off to sleep. I dreamed of glowing red tops in the sky,
hovering over the Palni Hills.

CHAPTER 16

A Day in Thani

Sundays were Regina's free days, when she took the bus down to Shembag to be with her family. One Sunday, weary of the monotony of fresh fruit for lunch, I decided to walk over to the Carlton Hotel for lunch. However, I needed batteries for the camera, and spent several hours wandering in and out of the dim bazaar stores, asking for penlight batteries and being sent up the road to other places. I finally found them, purchased a quantity, and sauntered over to the Carlton, about a half-hour walk. It was a brisk day, and I was really starving by the time I arrived, around three-thirty.

There was only one table occupied when I entered. The lobby was much as I remembered it from 1971: old-fashioned and comfortable, the dining area raised up about five steps to form a balcony. The waiter came over as if surprised to see anyone at a table. I asked for a menu, and about ten minutes later it appeared, soiled and mimeographed in a rather mysterious arrangement of pages. I read through the breakfast page, in expectation that I would eventually find the lunch and dinner menu, but a brief scanning of these pages proved disappointing. With a sinking heart, I realized I was going to be stuck with rice and vegetables again, since I could recognize no other dish. I summoned the waiter once more.

"I'd like the rice-and-vegetable plate," I said, and added, "Bring me some chapatties, too." I thought they would at least give me a welcome change. The waiter looked puzzled. "You want it now, madam?" he asked, as if I had asked for a shower.

"Isn't it ready yet? In that case, just bring the chapatties and some coffee, and I'll wait for the lunch."

He disappeared into the inner chamber, and I could hear the sound of great discussion. Then he reappeared at my side.

"Chapatties not ready, madam."

I glanced at the clock. It was now 4 P.M., and my stomach was sending up unmistakable distress signals. "How about coffee?" I asked in despair. His face cleared immediately. "Coffee right away, madam," and he toddled off again, contented.

The party at the other table had noticed the negotiations, and were amused. One of them called to me, "We've been here one hour, and no food yet." I indicated that I was now settling for coffee, and they invited me to join them, on the principle that by joining forces we might get more service. I picked up my bag and went over to their table.

The party consisted of a married couple from Bangalore, and a newly married couple, he from India and she from Germany. They were touring the area briefly and were staying at the Carlton. We exchanged information on our origins and business in India, and at length their order arrived, pancakes. I began to wish I had ordered from the breakfast menu, since it was apparently within the scope of the kitchen staff, though the hour for breakfast had long since passed. The waiter brought me coffee and his terms on the proposed order of rice and vegetables: "Madam, why not take a nice walk around the lake. Come back at seven-thirty, and we will have your order ready." Even in my prime, a three-and-one-half-hour walk on an empty stomach would not have been attractive, and I said I would cancel my order. Though this news did little to brighten his day, he took it like a man. I finished my coffee, said good-bye to the tourists, and went back to Snyder "B" and my bananas.

The following morning, at breakfast at Presentation, Sister Ethna said she was going to be driven down to Thani on the following day to pick up Sister Evangelist. She would remain there overnight and return on the following day. Would I like to join her? I was delighted. I could stay overnight at their convent in Thani and thus see more of village life.

The drive down, on the following morning, was lovely. Sister Ethna and the driver in the front, and Sister Xavier and myself in the back. We began the journey with a short prayer, and having commended us to God, the soft Irish voices began relating tales of the hills as we sped along. They showed me the coolie ghat, where the bearers ran up with loads on their heads in the early days, and told me the first sisters up to Kodai had been carried up in sedan cars on the shoulders of the coolies.

"The fat ones were always left till last," laughed Sister Ethna. "The coolies were always fighting over who must take them up."

Meanwhile, the deep, lush valleys and the vista of hills filled the eye with wonder and we saw a crowd along the roadside and ropes being lowered down over the side of the cliff. An accident! A lorry had gone over the side, and a party of men were struggling to haul it up again. It looked like a pretty hopeless task to me. The road was too narrow to stop to inquire; we only had a glance down the cliff, where the yellow truck could be seen tangled in the treetops.

"I hope the driver is all right," I said.

"Oh, they always jump out when the lorry is in trouble," said Sister. "Very seldom is a driver hurt."

Soon we were down in the plains, driving through the arch of trees and dodging farm workers en route to their fields, bullocks, goat herds, and all the busy life of the plains. The heat was intense, but with the breeze of the drive, we did not notice it at first.

We passed cotton fields, and I was surprised to learn that much cotton is also processed in that valley. A number of large ginning plants were pointed out to me. Castor-oil plants on their spindly stalks, sugar cane, paddy, and jaggery provided an ever-changing scene along the roadsides; while on the road itself the usual haying and rice husking were being accomplished by the simple means of spreading the grain on the road and allowing the cars and trucks to drive over it. Women in deep blue saris and an occasional flash of bright crimson bent over the work in the fields, making beautiful pictures, though I realized that, charming as it all looked, there was much hardship in the life under those banyan trees.

The word "Thani," I discovered, means "honey bee." When the sisters had come to Thani twenty-five years ago, to found a hospital and school, theirs was the only building anywhere in sight. They had been surrounded by rice paddy. Now the shops and roadside enterprises had crept up to their gates, their owners canny in the knowledge that many people came there for treatment. Thus, the convent and Holy Redeemer Hospital had served as a catalyst to attract commerce. We drove under the tamarind trees through a gateway and found, behind the high gray walls, the little paradise the sisters always manage to create on any real estate they possess. There were coconut palms and a glory of bougainvillea threading up into the neem trees, confusing the eye with their bright blossoms. Wonderfully variegated leaves of strange plants stood in pots along the garden walk, and a crowd of people in the verandas of the hospital proclaimed the need and the success of the twenty-five-year-long struggle against heat, poverty and disease.

At the convent doorway, where the car stopped under the portico, many Indian sisters began pouring out to clasp the Irish nuns and give them the cheek rubs of welcome. I was greeted with great kindness, and immediately felt like one of the family. Sister Xavier told them I was part Jesuit and part P.C.S. I was given a cool, refreshing room in the hospital, which was lovingly garnished with all the little feminine touches: flowers, beautiful bedspread, and even a little WELCOME FROM THE HONEY BEE card on my table. A flask of drinking water, covered with a tiny piece of net held at the edges with little seashells; a private bath with shower, and pink mosquito netting on the bed. It was beautiful, clean and inviting after the very long, hot drive.

Sister Ethna, who had been superior of this convent before coming to Kodai, took me on a tour of the place. We inspected the fine, modern hospital building, gift of Misereor, that wonderful German institution whose work in India is monumental. I met the staff of doctors, made up of two Indian sister doctors who were members of the community, and a male doctor who was working with them. And it was here, while coming up the corridor toward the maternity section, that I had the experience of a lifetime. A baby was being born, and Sister Ethna held the door ajar so I could see this miracle take place. My whole body ached for the mother; they told me it was her first baby, but I soon forgot my own feelings as I stood in wonderment in the doorway of that room. For the woman made not one cry. Grimacing in pain, and gripping the sides of the table, she was fully conscious. Suddenly there was a triumphant sound from the attending doctor; the baby was there, small, pale by comparison with the mother's mahogany skin, and the woman gave a great sigh. It was a boy! The grandmother, who came rushing from the waiting room at the news, was clearly overjoyed at this bounty of the gods; the birth of a boy is the greatest blessing a woman can receive in India. She said she must go immediately and buy some sweets for the doctor. The tiny newborn was carried to an adjoining room, where a tube was inserted into its nostrils to remove mucus; then also into its mouth. It was some seconds before the wondrous new life was squalling and crying and filling its lungs with great draughts of air. I was exhausted by the time we left this scene, and all the memories of my own five confinements flooded over me. I wished the mother well, and left a small gift for the child.

In a ward where a number of women were being treated, one woman caught my eye. She had earlobes extended, so long they rested on her shoulders. Into these, which caused the distortion, were about three pounds of brass bolts. I asked Sister Ethna about this afterward, and was told that this custom, once very common, is slowly dying out in India. She herself had operated on a great number of these ear distortions, clipping off the elongations, sewing them up again so that the ears were restored to normal size.

"It's quite a simple operation," she said. "We used to charge five rupees for it." Five rupees is less than one dollar.

We walked across a section of the compound where the rain had left the red clay soft and clinging. Reaching a veranda, I entered and found a group of men and women patiently awaiting treatment. A nurse and the doctor were standing near the medicines; I discovered I was in the leper-treatment center. The doctor told me they gave the standard treatment for leprosy, and in addition, an injection of vitamins; the patients refused to believe they had been helped without an injection of some kind. "Even if we only injected water," said the doctor, "they go away satisfied. We inject vitamins. Pills, the lepers believe, don't count. They insist on injections."

Then, as my horror and heartbeat mounted, one by one the patients began holding up their hands for me to see what the disease had done to them. Stumps of fingers, huge sores on the arms, the poor twisted feet, in some cases unrecognizable as human, were there before me. I remembered the scene in Ben Hur—the early version— when the lepers had to call out, "Unclean, unclean," when they met any of the townspeople. I rather nervously asked the doctor if isolation would be in order, or whether they still lived with their families.

"You can't isolate them. They refuse to go," he said. "They live at home. By the time we get them, they have already infected the whole family anyway." They had fifty-one cases for treatment that day. So the charm of the Indian countryside had a sinister aspect too. These people were stalked by the most frightening disease known to mankind.

At lunch I met Sister Evangelist, the ninety-year-old veteran of Presentation Convent, who was at Thani, her "winter quarters," because the air at Kodai was too cold for her. At Thani, she had fallen and cut her head badly enough to require many stitches, and they had despaired of her life. She had rallied, much to their surprise, and was at her place at table, wearing a bib to protect her white starched habit, and looking me up and down.

"An American, eh? What are you doing? Tooling around India, I suppose." I said I was not moving around much but would be at Kodai for some time yet. She returned to her main topic of interest, the packing of her small bag of clothes for the trip back to Kodai. The Sisters had a great time kidding her, and enjoying her replies. She had a soft Irish brogue, and had been one of the founding sisters at Kodai, having been carried up in a chair by coolies on that initial journey long before. I knew she could give me much of the history of the place, and looked forward to a quiet chat with her.

"Shall we go and pack my bag now?" she asked Sister Ethna.

"No, darling. We can do that tomorrow. After your lunch you can have a nice nap. There's plenty of time to pack." The thought of a nap sounded good to me, though Sister Evangelist plainly didn't think much of the idea. I went off to my lovely room to turn on the ceiling fan and have a shower and rest. It had been a pretty full morning, and it was very hot in Thani.

Around 5 P.M., when the heat began to subside, I wandered back to the convent, after visiting the new mothers and babies on the first floor and dispensing praise and good wishes all along the way. I noticed that Indian hospitals permit family members to remain with the sick, to keep them company and to wait on their simplest needs. It seemed a pretty good system, relieving the overworked nurses and preventing too much homesickness, though it must have been difficult at times to keep the noise down. Visiting times were free-for-alls. The crowds at the gates were enormous, all waiting to bring cheer and a touch of home to their loved ones. They had to be held back by gates until the proper times; otherwise the hospital would have been overrun with people all day long, and any routine would have been impossible. Sister Ethna told me of an instance in her time when a field worker, a woman, had been mauled by a tiger. The animal had been shot, and then the woman and the dead tiger had been brought to the hospital by the entire village, several hundred people—the woman for treatment, the tiger for examination for rabies. Seeing the vast crowd, the sisters realized they would be unable to do anything in the midst of such clamor and commotion. So they sent word to the gate that unless everyone went away they would not treat the woman at all. This did the trick. The villagers withdrew to a respectful distance, the woman was taken into the hospital, though about ten in the crowd insisted on going along to watch. She regained full health.

I was shown the children's quarters, where some four hundred children are kept in a hostel, and the school, where one thousand day scholars come for class. It is Tamil medium, where English is also taught after third standard. The two puppies from the Kodai convent were there too, having grown a surprising amount since I had seen them first, a month before. They were to be trained as watchdogs for the convent grounds.

Sister Evangelist had not slept, after all. After a short time in her room, she had resumed her wandering habits; she awakened all the other napping sisters on her floor, and again insisted on packing. At dinner the sisters again reminded her that packing was a very simple matter, done in five minutes' time, since she would not require her white habit at Kodai, where she would wear black wool because of the chilly air, and she pondered this while she finished her simple supper. I took her for a short walk and we sat for a while afterward on the veranda, until driven indoors by large, black flying ants, which had a disconcerting manner of landing on the neck and crawling around in the hair. The veils and habits of the nuns prevented an invasion of exposed skin, but during chapel I had to restrain myself from reaching forward and removing them from the white habit of the nun kneeling in front of me.

"Wouldn't screens help?" I asked an Indian sister.

"They'd get in anyway, because of the rain," she said mildly. "This is the tropics, you know."

After reciting simple night prayers in chapel with the sisters, and feeling suddenly as though I had indeed joined the order, I wandered back to the hospital with Sister Xavier, and with some magazines to read before I finally went to bed.

The bell rang at five-fifteen. I quickly arose, bathed, dressed and found my way with a flashlight back to chapel for morning prayers. The bugs, I noted happily, had disappeared. After office there was a quiet period of meditation; I refused the tea offered me, and at around six the sisters began preparing the candles for Mass. I closed my eyes for a few moments of silent prayer, and when I opened them again, found that the entire front of the chapel was filled with women in beautiful saris. They had come in so silently, on their bare feet, that I had not heard a sound! India is a very restful country in this regard. These were the teachers and hospital workers. It was a Tamil Mass. The women sang in strong, alien voices, and I could follow dimly only by watching the priest. The readings were in Tamil too; I drifted off in a reverie of my own, watching the dawn find its way through the open windows and the bright flowers become visible in the growing light.

At Communion the sisters went up first; since I was kneeling with them, I joined in the line too. Two places up, Sister Evangelist had a bit of trouble with her woolen shawl, which she always kept wound around her middle. It came undone and was dragging along behind her. Quick hands from all sides came to hitch it up again.

A fat little wall lizard came down from behind the Stations of the Cross, and I reflected that he must have had a great feed on flying ants. Sister Theresa, one of the nurses, had told me an interesting bit about these "fly catchers." She said that patients often said when they would be talking to their doctor or the nurse, if the conversation would be interrupted by the distinctive "click-click" of the wall lizard, "Now the truth has been spoken—hear the lizard?" When one of these creatures lost its footing on the wall and fell from it, great stress was placed on the manner of its fall. If it fell on the head of someone in the room, great bad fortune would befall that person. If it hit on the left side, other catastrophes would ensue, and each part of the body was staked out for a different fate, depending on the portion that had been thus struck by the falling lizard.

The morning air at Thani is cool and pleasant. Sister Pius and I walked out to the gateway to watch the town come to life in the cool sunshine under the tamarind trees. Bullock carts went lumbering by, in processions of five or six together, laden with bales of cotton bound for the gin. A stream of farm workers strolled past, greeting the sister and curiously gazing at the foreign lady. School children came in at the gate from their farm huts, wearing the green shorts or skirts of the school uniform and folding their hands in namaste to us before running into the school compound.

Sister told me of the time she had been attacked by a robber, long ago at Presentation Convent, Kodai. She was a very young nun, and the intruder had entered her room through the second-story window. When she attemped to cry out, he held a harsh hand over her throat and attempted to smother her with a pillow. She had thrashed about, and banged her fist on the wall near the bed. The noise awakened the nun in the next room, who ran in and saved her life; the man realized he was outnumbered, and fled. So frightened had been this poor little sister that she was taken down to Thani after that, and it was a long time before the horror of that experience left her.

We walked back to the convent, across the compound, where the early scholars were peacefully sitting in the shade of lovely trees, studying their lessons for the day. One little girl, who looked about four years old (she was seven) held up her slate, where she had written her arithmetic homework: tiny little columns of numbers neatly drifting down the slate. I marveled at the exactness of the work. The children assembled outside the school veranda, facing their teachers in respectful silence, while the teachers, standing a little above in the shade, awaited the full attention of the thousand assembled kids before a whistle blew and the little black heads all bowed in prayer. Bright hair ribbons stuck out at angles as the various classes in various heights and sizes said aloud their morning prayers. Not a muscle moved in that entire crowd; with eyes shut tight, their little hands earnestly clasped before them, they begged a blessing on the work of the day. A Tamil hymn, led by one of the teachers, followed, and then, as the Sign of the Cross was made, they yelled, as with one voice, "Good morning, Sister. Good morning, madam!" I bowed to acknowledge their greeting. A phonograph on a small table struck up a lively Indian march, and they gracefully flowed past me into the cool schoolrooms to the work at hand. I could hardly believe that such discipline had been accomplished by this small group of women, whose gentle voices and quiet manners must have concealed tremendous talent. These children were not boarders, but the children of the rural poor. I realized that the town of Thani had learned to appreciate the blessing God had given them in the Presentation Sisters and their hospital and school. I afterward learned that only about thirty of these one thousand kids were Catholic. The rest were either Hindu or Muslim!

Sister Evangelist was tenderly packed into the back seat of the car like precious cargo, while the entire staff of the hospital and school came over to bid her good-bye. They had jokes to make her laugh, and the love with which she was surrounded was evident in their eyes. The doctor even got into the car beside her and pretended to take her pulse one more time. He pronounced her very well indeed. Sister Xavier sat on one side of her pillow and I on the other side. Sister Ethna and the driver got in, and we slowly pulled away, to the accompaniment of waves and smiles.

"I'll never see Thani again," said Sister Evangelist.

"You say that every year, darling," said Sister Ethna.

We drove back to the lovely hills again.

CHAPTER 17

St. Patrick's Day

Sure, and you've never lived until you've been a part of St. Patrick's Day in India! At Presentation Convent the little girls arose at four-thirty and began singing Irish songs under the windows of the Irish nuns. At Mass, the altars groaned under a burden of magnificent white and green lilies from the convent garden. The school trooped in, wearing their suddenly appropriate green uniforms and filling the entire chapel, including the tiny balcony. All the sisters wore green badges or harps on their white habits. Father Montaud celebrated High Mass in white and gold vestments, as the little Hindu and Muslim and Catholic girls sang "All Hail to St. Patrick" and yearned in song for "Sweet Erin, Land of My Birth!"

Father Montaud, in a Maurice Chevalier accent, based his sermon on the virtues of Patrick, stressing the humility he had learned as a slave in Ireland in his youth, and his surpassing love for Christ when he came as bishop to the heathen Irish and traveled the length and breadth of the country converting Ireland in so marvelous and complete a manner that she became the foremost daughter of the Church, sending her youthful men and women to every land to share the joy and bounty of Christ. I glanced around at the solemn little Hindu faces around me, their braids gleaming in the gentle chapel light, as they listened to his exhortation to go forth themselves and bring Christ to the world in which they lived.

The organ pealed out its lovely songs, played by Mrs. Gibson, a Protestant English gentlewoman, who taught music at the convent and always played the organ for Sunday Mass. And the Indian sisters, with their beautiful faces lit in smiles and sparkling eyes, prayed most fervently for the grace of St. Patrick to enliven their vocations and their love for Jesus.

At breakfast there were colorful cards done by the children to greet the glorious feast, and the poster in the dayroom hoped that the wind would always be at your back. A phonograph provided the proper music for the day, and Sister Ethna's eyes misted as she remembered one hornpipe as it was lilting into the room. She had danced this as a child, and recalled tenderly her happiness when her father had lifted her down from the prizewinning performance and praised her. The memory was still green.

I told them all about the St. Patrick's Day parade in Chicago, when, under Mayor Daley, of blessed memory, all the ethnic groups were represented; of the green-dye coloring of the Chicago River, and the glorious music of pipes along State Street. And I remembered, too, that Al had loved John McCormack above all other singers, and how he had delighted in that mellow voice singing, "I Hear You Calling Me" and "The Garden Where the Praties Grow." It was my eldest daughter, Ann's, birthday—Ann Patricia she was—and I felt a stab at the miles between us, and wished I could suddenly be transported home for her party. For years, Ann had believed that all the green decorations and song were exclusively because of her birthday. For our family at least, it always was! I felt a glow of pride in the wonderful woman our little Ann had become: her home one of the finest I have ever seen, where she and Paul had lavished such loving care on the smallest detail of its furnishing and decoration, and the wonder of their children, so that in spite of modest means, they had made it magnificent. Peter, my companion of a previous trip to India, now tall and handsome and graduating from grammar school in the spring; Mark, with his intuitive, creative mind, busy with a thousand projects and accompanying Peter's French horn with his shining trombone; and Miss Laura, the only girl among the precious brood, with a charm doubly appreciated because of this fact, and delighting in her ballet slippers, her doll collection and her friend "Daven," who had been baptized David but had obligingly changed his name to suit Miss Laura's preferred pronunciation. How I missed them all! How wonderful if I could suddenly wave a wand and transport them all to these hills! I wondered if my daughters might let me steal them, one at a time, to come back for sojourns here: Mark first, then Sean of the blue eyes, Dan of the golden smile, Miss Laura with her chatter, my beloved Joe, a brain surgeon in the making, and then Kevin, that stout-hearted giant of three years. I could see myself living in a little house near Kodai Lake and sending them off to school in the mornings, wearing the proper green uniforms, to the convent, and spending my evenings with them by the fireside, reading stories and correcting homework. Nice dream. But Laurie and Ann would never part with them for long, I knew. Two weeks, perhaps. Longer than that? Nothing doing. I couldn't blame them. I was the same with my own.

I went to sleep that night wondering why I had never traveled to Ireland. It was an error I hoped to correct one day.

CHAPTER 18

An Interview with
M. S. Kalyana Sundaram

Several people at the American School had suggested that I meet and speak with a scholar who worked at the school, M. S. Kalyana Sundaram, since his knowledge was deep and his range of interests very wide. One afternoon, I found him at his little classroom. He was a small man, wearing a very old Nehru jacket. His gray hair was cropped short, giving him a military air. He made me welcome and plunged at once into his story.

He had been born at Madurai, since there had been no hospital at Kodai in those days; his father had been an official at the observatory. His early schooling was at Madurai; he had come up to Kodai only on vacations. He recalled those adventurous early journeys with great enthusiasm. The coolie ghat road, the only access to the hills in those days, was reached by train. The station is still there but is called Kodai Road Station. In those days, it was called Ammayanayakkanur, after the chieftain of that place, who collected revenue. From the train, they proceeded by bullock carts to Periaculum, a distance of twenty-five miles, the carts taking seven or eight hours to go that distance. At Periaculum they slept at a friend's house, and in the morning took another small cart for four or five miles to the coolie ghat road to prepare for the ascent.

One could go up on a conveyance called a chair, carried on the shoulders, but first one had to awaken the coolies waiting there in the dark. Once on the road up, the coolies formed a caravan, led by a lantern, with plenty of noisemaking to scare away wild animals. Cheetahs were common in the hills in those days, as were tigers.

I inquired about the Jesuits at Shembaganur. Kalyana Sundaram remembered them in the early years. He recalled that the population of Kodai was about three or four thousand and that the hospital was a poor little place, where the doctor had few facilities, little medicine, and no one trusted it. The British Army had one Doctor Thomas, who traced everything to stomach-ache. The people called him "Stomach-ache Doctor."

Indian medicine was used by most of the population. Most women knew the combination of herbs for ordinary illnesses. Barefoot children who cut their feet were cured with a combination of garlic, lime and calcium, applied to the wound. Today, at the Madras Medical College there is a section on Indian medicine, which preserves this folk wisdom. One bitter medicine that grows in the hills, called *nilavembu* in Tamil, and in Hindi *chirata*, is more effective for malaria than quinine, because it has no side effects, such as giddiness or deafness. Sundaram also told me of a leaf, with five longitudinal veins, called *angianayambulai*. This leaf, smeared with vegetable oil and warmed over a slight fire and applied on boils, will cure them. Today, however, he admitted that most people want Terramycin instead of the old remedies. I told him that much of Western medicine was based on herbs, and he sighed and said, "Yes, yes. But we use them only when they go to the West and come back to us. It's a weakness of our character."

As a boy, he drank from the mountain streams, with no fear of contamination. He laughed recalling this, and told me of the boiled water of the school, and their disregard of his advice to "let the boys develop antibodies." Without this chance, Westerners are more susceptible to diseases. Few, however, will risk the chance of becoming ill; water is routinely boiled and filtered in India for foreigners' use.

Sundaram's most outstanding teacher was Mr. Slatham, of Oxford, who was principal at Madurai College. He had a broad mind and was in sympathy with the nationalistic ambitions of India. Later on, he was advanced to director of public instruction. He was active in student dramas, and was greatly loved by his students.

Gandhi's rise in India around 1920, was heralded eagerly by young students like Sundaram, who saw in him the hoped-for liberation from English rule. His noncooperation policies were quickly taken up by the students. Sundaram was by this time at Kumbakonam College, and he recalls vividly the visit Gandhi made to the school. He immediately began to practice the disciplines advised by Gandhi to free himself from the use of English cloth. He obtained a charkha and began to spin and wear khadi cloth. He wore his suit of khadi even when he worked for the government service as a telegraph man, though he had been advised not to do so. At the end of 1930 he resigned from the department and went to Gandhi's ashram at Sabarmati.

"Where was that?" I asked him.

"Near Ahmedabad—four miles away. Now it has become a Harijan center. I had to get letters of introduction; they doubted, thinking I might be a spy for the government—the police side; so I had letters."

Young Sundaram remained at the ashram for some time. He made up his mind not to marry, in order to be able to live on very little. Then Gandhi told him to go and take up Hindi work, teaching others to read and write the language, and to spin khadi. He returned to the South, to Periaculum, in the foothills of Kodai. There he began to learn Hindi, teaching others daily what he had learned himself the night before. Together with his students, he appeared for the Hindi examinations, and passed them. By the time he had gathered his second batch of students, he was an expert at the language. He read continually in Hindi, so he could make the work easier for them.

I asked how he was able to support himself. He had resigned his job, having saved a bit of money. He lived on the interest from that. But he had learned the lessons of frugality well. He needed only nine rupees per month for food, and five or six more for coffee and other luxuries. He did all his own cooking in the small hut provided by the school. There he taught, slept, washed and cooked. By 1935 the school was well established, and when he had secured his own students as teachers and was paying them, Gandhi's example was so ingrained that he took no salary at all. He passed it on to his assistants. His memory of that small school was still bright. "It was more like a club than a school," he said. "We gave them conversation, dramatization, dialogue. In the second or third year of that school we staged a full five-act play at Periaculum. It was considered so good that people asked us to go to Madurai and do the same thing. We gained a few hundred rupees, which was good for the school. We came to Kodaikanal with those boys; there are Hindi songs in those plays, and we gave a show in Hindi. The Maharaja of Nebha, whom the government didn't like and who was interned here in Kodai with his family, said, "I can't believe that these are South Indian boys who are doing this, their pronunciation is so good."

"Is Hindi easier than Tamil?"

"Yes, much easier. The words are two, three or four letters long, not like in Tamil, where you don't know where to stop, the words are so long."

"How many languages do you now teach?"

"Here, as required, I can teach Hindi, Urdu, Sanskrit, Bengali, Gujarati, Marathi, Kannada, Telugu, Tamil and German. Next week I will start on Malayalam for a boy who used to speak Malayalam. I do not speak it. But he wants help only in being able to read and write it."

After his experience in Periaculum, he went to Lahore and founded a school for Madrasi children of some sixty or seventy families who worked in government offices there. He spent the next six years running that school; an article he wrote, "Happy School," was published in *The Hindu*. His method was simplicity itself. Gathering some of his former pupils who were not working, he encouraged them to learn typing and shorthand, and pushed them into local firms as telegraphers. With the aid of their combined salaries, they set up the school, living a communal life as before, sharing all the housework along with the teaching. Tuition was kept to a bare minimum. They lived on a monthly expenditure of twelve rupees and were thus free of government help and interference.

Gandhi's advice to him, written from a prison cell, was: "Don't go to jail. That's for a certain class of people who can't do anything else. Those who can do constructive work, must work." And work he did.

He returned to Kodai with the idea of founding a public school with reasonable prices. He investigated the first public grade school of India, which was spending a large sum of money. He knew this plan was wrong. He visited the private schools in Dehra Dun, thinking: "I won't do this, I won't do that; here is a good idea, and so on."

But World War II interrupted this plan. Japanese suicide squads devastated two big ships in Singapore by diving into their smokestacks, and bursting them. People began to wonder whether they should concentrate on English education or go in for Japanese education. In Madras bombs fell, and the city merchants moved their goods to different storehouses. Those planning to send their sons to school did not pursue the correspondence. He had to abandon his attempt.

Maria Montessori was in India when the war started, and so became an internee. The government of India gave her a lot of freedom to teach, as long as she kept within certain municipal limits. She had a teaching center at Madras, at the Theosophical Society Headquarters, and then for health and climatic conditions she came to Kodai, to Rosebank. There she conducted three-month child-psychology courses. So, in 1943, young Sundaram entered one of these courses, not as a tuition-paying student but only as an observer. Determined to learn all he could for the sake of the poor, and not a candidate for a certificate, he was admitted free of charge. In the class were forty students; three or four of them Catholic nuns, others hill people: Indians, from Bengal, Delhi, and so on.

I asked him how Montessori taught without knowing the language. The answer was simple: she spoke, and her words were translated by a gentleman Sundaram thought was her brother's son, Dr. Montessori, but who was in reality, I later learned, her own son. And her attitude toward the child, and her loving and warm manner of treating this subject, remained always with the eager young observer.

"Whenever she spoke about a child, she was simply embracing that child in her spirit," he said. "Her love for children was not like that of these fashionable people who love a well-brought-up child in a park, but hers was for real children. She said, for example, 'A poor child, uncared for and left in the street, is probably more fit for a full and rich life than a well-brought-up child at the bottom of a perambulator, who can see only 45 degrees of the sky; whereas that child in the street, near the dust bin and all that, can see 180 degrees of the sky.' Beautiful, is it not?

"It is also very true that many die of dysentery, diarrhea, typhoid, and so on; but if the child survives all those things, he has more experience of people. At four or five years, such a child can take care of poultry, keep an eye on crafts and know more about life, more about people, and see through the trickery of adult thinking."

He recalled too her attitude about fairy tales. She developed that subject for about twenty minutes, stating that though fairy tales satisfy certain temperaments, the child educated through the activity-educational materials of the Montessori Method, in which the child has full play for the working of his imagination in a constructive, educative way, does not need fairy tales—he is making discoveries all the time. He was greatly impressed by this.

I asked about the success of the Montessori Method in India. He is not impressed by what he sees today. He is convinced that many of the wealthy send their children to these schools at an early age to get them out of their way, so that they will not interfere with the adults' pleasures. He says Delhi is mad over Montessori today, and that if he wished to earn money he could go there today and make bundles of it. He contrasts the amount people spend on children today with his own, simple youth.

"When I was a child, I didn't cost my family anything until I was some fifteen or eighteen months old. I didn't need milk, my mother took care of me. Now, as soon as a child is born, a child costs more than an adult in a family . . . all the tinned stuff and all that. Add to this the advice given by the doctors, about what vitamins to give, and so on."

"But surely," I said, "most of the people cannot afford special baby foods."

"It makes no difference. They see that the rich have these things, and so they have to do it too. Except for the fuel collectors, the coolie women, who breast-feed the child, the women want these modern things."

I told him of the trend in America back to natural childbirth and breast-feeding, and he sighed and said that it would take time before this fashion returned to India. I believe he is correct in this. India is about forty years behind us in fads—and the canned-baby-food craze is just hitting the cities of the subcontinent with the same fervor we experienced about forty years ago.

We spoke of religion in India when I asked what he believed was the greatest need of his country today. "More honesty and more character at the grass-roots level. These things must have a religious basis."

But when I objected that India had a deep religious tradition, he replied that it is being lost. Certain reflexes remain, he said, such as the response to Krishna when he is depicted on the movie screen, but he believes that these gestures of piety are purely surface reactions and have no deep meaning any longer. He himself is a Hindu, a Brahmin. He considers that his is a more intellectual and rational approach. Contrasted to that is the typical Hindu, who is told to face east and wash his hands ten times after, say, coming from the lavatory, and who will perform this faithfully as a kind of ritual. But if he had been told to "observe hygienic principles," he would do nothing.

Times are changing greatly in modern India. Pop music, the Beatles, long hair, and the generation gap are realities, spawned by the movies and the radio threaten the old order without replacing it with anything of value for the youth to cling to. From the West come the tales of graft, of Watergates, of union troubles, of all the ills of mankind. India had a stable way of life for a few thousand years, in spite of invasion and wars, and has survived. Sundaram wonders if it will survive the present ills. He believes change must come slowly to be good. The use of chemical fertilizers to push up production and rob the land, making plants subject to attacks by unknown diseases, is one of the evils India must now cope with.

He views Christianity as a very good thing. The Bible, he realizes, is not to be taken literally, particularly Genesis. But he considers Jesus a great man, who was born many times on earth in the course of time and in various parts of the world. Hindus sense that reincarnation is a reality; Buddha was the ninth reincarnation of the Being that was also Jesus.

"In other words, He was the same Being being reincarnated all the time?"

"It was the Godhead with limited qualities and limited scope; some of them conscious of what they were, and some not. Rama treated himself as a man. Krishna, at the back of his mind, knew that he had gotten a spark from God."

"Was Krishna a real person? Historical?"

"Krishna was a real person; all the incidents need not be taken literally; he was a person who came to set right certain things. Now, in all these cases, they were all reactions. Something was wrong, and had to be set right."

"Do you believe man has an obligation to his neighbor to try to improve the world?"

"Yes. We are talking about incarnation and all that. My personal belief is that every one of us is reincarnated from a previous stage in the in-between world somewhere; after one death we wish to be born somewhere and do some good work as far as possible."

"In Hindu belief there comes a time when you escape this?"

"That is true, but it takes a very long period of time."

"What is that term again?"

"It is called Moksha, salvation condition; I am not so keen on Moksha, because I believe a lot more has to be done, and then as critics of the Buddhist religion question about Nirvana, what is this, and so on."

"Nothingness."

"But this nilness which has nothing of no-ness about it, must be described as very, very yes-ness. But the critics take it as a no-ness, and that is where the mistake lies. It all requires a lot of sympathetic understanding and also taking some things on trust. The inside of the egg—the yolk and albumen—are they living or doing anything or not?"

He did not wait for my answer.

"They are doing something. Everything is doing something. With our present knowledge of physics, in an atom an electron is moving at the rate of thirty thousand miles per second; and we'll not know anything about it. We take this as a firm table, we are sitting in a firm chair with a feeling of confidence. But, really, this is like millions of insects going around and round very fast, and it is the statistical average of it that gives stability to this chair, the statistical average of the large numbers and the large velocity which gives essence of solidarity. The place which one insect has vacated, another insect has come and taken up. You note how insects go around a lamp; large enough in number, and fast enough in speed, you could go and sit on them. That is what we are sitting on. That's what we are writing on."

He was deep into the subject now, and shared with me a moment when he had been asked to address a class on Hindu philosophy and answer questions. He had spoken for some time, and then the questioning began. One boy asked, "Sir, there is a translation here, and it is like this: 'That is wholeness, and wholeness is taken out of wholeness, and wholeness is left': does it make any sense to you, honestly?" And Sundaram had answered that if he understood it immediately he would appear to be a genius, which he was not. But he added: "To make you understand that such a thing is possible: wholeness taken out of wholeness, with wholeness left, I can give you an example from mathematics. It may help you, not to understand it but to think that such a thing is possible. If you take 1, 2, 3, 4, 5, I have not given you the whole thing: that is infinite. The odd numbers, 1, 3, 5, 7, and so forth, that, again, is infinite. If you put away the odd numbers and are left with only the even numbers, 2, 4, 6, 8, they are, again, infinite. You have infinity, you have pulled out infinity, and infinity is left there. We can question it with our present ideas about mathematics and things like that, and we learn that infinity plus infinity is not two infinities, it is only one infinity. Half of it taken away is, again, infinity."

We spoke for some time about the various theories of the earth's creation—from Einstein to Hoyle, but I was soon out of my depth. It was clear from his exposition of the various theories, however, that Sundaram was in solid command of all that was presently being discussed, and that he could explain these things in simple terms so that even one uneducated in physics, like me, could comprehend them.

He does not believe in horoscopes, or in the influence of the planets, explaining it this way: "In the olden days, when Delhi was three days from Madras, with the slow trains and so on, a man could write a letter from Madras to his son in Delhi on the first day of the month and die on the night of the second day, the letter reaching the son on the third. The son would be thinking, 'My father *has* written, he would not be thinking, 'My father *had* written.' This is the way we must understand the light coming from far away. Five thousand years ago the whole Polaris group might have vanished, but I still might think Polaris is directing me. It seems unreasonable. Or, some say, 'If the light is coming, the influence is also coming.' But the question is, light travels at 186,000 miles per second. What is the velocity for influence? Who knows?"

"But," I reminded him, "look at the influence of Christ, from two thousand years ago, which still lives today."

"I believe," he said, "that the Spirit was, before 1978 years ago, is now, and will be here. That His Spirit works with the Spirit of other people, Mohammedans, and other people."

"Do you follow a discipline of life?" I asked him.

"Yes, but it is mostly mental. I don't use water, and materials, and things like that. I do it mentally, anywhere. Suppose I have to walk a long distance to go home. I repeat certain things."

"Prayers?"

"There are certain things to be repeated. I repeat those things while walking along."

"Do you mind my asking what they are?"

"As words, it doesn't mean much; it means something like: just as we have the sun as the great luminant, there is a huge group of intelligences, not as in mathematics, but knowing, and guarding by personal courage and so on, and we pray to the Keeper of that globe or body to give us that so we will be able to face life's problems with wisdom, supported by courage. It is supposed to be a secret mantra."

"Given to you by someone?"

"Yes, yes. It has come down for the last five thousand to eight thousand years."

"In other words, many people could use it?"

"It goes from father to son, with the help of the Purohit (priest), when the boy is between seven and ten, when the sacred thread is put on. Then he is given the mantra."

"Do you wear the sacred thread?"

"Yes, I have it. The thread is put on and the father repeats that mantra in the boy's ears. Nowadays, many fathers have forgotten it; we have not been doing it properly. Only worthy people can hear it, and so on. Those days are now passed. Anyone eager to hear it is a worthy person."

"So, if you had a son, you would pass this on to him?"

"Yes, yes."

"So it's like the passing on of wisdom to the child."

"Yes. The meaning is not given in all cases, but my father was a great Sanskrit scholar, and he told me the meaning also; he was so liberal-minded as to say, 'You may not say the words, but keep the thought in your head.' But saying the words is more helpful in keeping the thought in the mind."

"So, when you are alone and have a task to do that may be monotonous, you can fill your mind with this."

"Yes; then sometimes we can say it and it is soothing. Some of us say it to fill the world bank of spiritual power. It spreads to Australia, Eskimo land, Lapland; it helps all people."

As the dusk gathered in the little tutoring room and shadows filled the corners, we talked on and on. We spoke of truth, and the difficulties in straining it out of the courts of law and their quandaries, and the relative values of sight, sound and testimony. I found myself greatly drawn to this saintly man, whose love and concern for the poor and selfless life of service to his people were so like that of the missionaries I had met in India. I asked him what leadership was.

"To take the responsibility to show a better way of doing things; responsibility, and the necessary skill for it. It is said, 'Yoga is skill in action.' Yoga is not just sitting like an anthill, but skill in action." Kalyana Sundaram had indeed mastered the art of Yoga.

CHAPTER 19

A Social Flurry

One quiet morning, a tap at the door announced an Indian gentleman with a note for madam. It was an invitation to a buffet luncheon at the Tubros', the nice Danish couple on the hill above me. I was delighted; I liked them very much, and their home was a gracious and hospitable place, one that spoke of the gentility of former days. I answered at once by telling the bearer that I would be delighted to come. It was only afterward, when the Tubro car pulled up alongside me as I walked in the bazaar, that I discovered they were still in the dark as to my acceptance of their invitation; the bearer either did not speak English or had forgotten to convey my message to them.

On the day of the luncheon, I dressed carefully, thankful that I had brought suitable clothes. I also carried my umbrella, against the midday heat, and slowly ascended the hill to the Tubros'. Their house is on a high precipice, accessible only by a complicated route upward; I remembered the name of their estate, Abernyte, and when at length I found the sign, I left the outside rim of the hill and again ascended via a very high buttressed wall, the gray rock looking very much like that of a fortress. This road led past a number of other houses, some very poor and others quite comfortable, reflecting Kodai's pattern of poverty and wealth living side by side in harmony. Servants' homes are small huts behind the homes of the well-to-do; flowers and trees and a kindly sky cover this plan with grace and bounty. All along every roadside, kids play, most of them the children of the poor. Their sunny smiles and attempts at English phrases lightened every walk; their requests for sweets and money lightened my purse as well.

As I ascended the clay path that led to the Tubros' gate, a car went past me; I recognized Mrs. Gibson and the Harts, who waved. Evidently, many had been invited to luncheon. I passed the beautiful beds of roses, hydrangeas, and many plants I could not recognize, and came to the veranda of Abernyte. It was filled with guests, and at the doorway on one side stood Mr. and Mrs. Tubro, graciously receiving them, while on the other side stood their daughter, Mehta, her husband and the two children who were temporarily attending Presentation Convent during this visit to Kodai. I was struck again by the quaint manner of the children: the little girl curtsied, while Hans Christian, at seven, bowed over the hand like a small knight. All of the elite of Kodai seemed to have gathered for this event. Major Mohan Lal and his wife and daughter were there, the two women in beautiful saris; the principal of Kodai school and his wife; the owners of the Carlton, a beautiful Parsee couple; Mr. and Mrs. Engineer, who lived near Presentation Convent; a great many people I had met at the prayer meeting but whose names had escaped me; a journalist, a doctor, and many retired people who had wisely chosen Kodai to live out their days in beauty and harmony. In the lovely hall of Abernyte, with its dark wood staircase and balconies, a replica of an English manor house it was said, there were oil paintings and Indian art pieces of great taste and refinement; I was struck again by the dignity and exquisite gentility that pervaded the old house.

In the drawing room a fire was burning, and before it, standing with his hands clasped behind him, a perfect picture of an English gentleman, the Reverend Bagshaw radiated kindliness and cheer. He was wearing a woolen suit, and a woolen vest underneath, but though I was quite comfortable in my printed cotton tea dress, he said he was feeling the cold and that the fire felt good to him. On the mantel behind him, two bronze birds from Hindu mythology, which I had also found in the antique shop run by a Kashmiri in town, had been polished from their ancient black to a high luster of bright brass and had been fitted into small wooden stands. A lovely oil painting of a street scene in Copenhagen and some bowls of flowers made the wide mantel a shrine of beauty. Very large comfortable chairs, originally from their home in Bombay, had been covered with embroidered cotton cloth in white and blue. A wonderful old oriental rug covered the entire length of the room, and a wide bay window fitted with cushioned seats opened the room to the garden, the trees, and the purple hills beyond. At a side window, two

strands of fuchsia bougainvillea made a pattern against the panes
that no fabric or art outside of nature herself could have achieved.
The walls were high and the ceiling dark; the paintings, brass rub-
bings, and priceless art in the room were so soothing and attractive
that I found it hard to concentrate on conversation, wanting only to
wander around, touching the tables and gazing at the paintings and
hangings.

But the conversation was great fun. One of the guests, slim and
handsome, having delegated himself official walnut cracker for a
group of ladies chatting in the bay window seats, came over many
times with a handful of cracked nuts for us, with mock complaints
about our laziness and dependence on man for this difficult task.
The Parsee couple who ran the Carlton told me a little about the
Parsee religion, and promised to lend me a book about it. One of the
ladies, a diminutive blue-eyed lady from Australia, chatted about her
planned rental of a house near Kodai Lake, where the lease would
soon run out, making it possible for her to acquire this house, where
she preferred to be. Her present dwelling, it seemed, was woefully
short on water supply. Together we agreed that rental was best,
because of the difficulties of reclaiming the purchase price on a
house once it had been sold. Turbaned waiters wound in and out of
the groups, dispensing drinks and appetizers.

At length, after all the guests had been served cocktails and had
reached the proper pitch of hunger, the huge doors separating the
drawing room from the dining room were slid open by the servants
to reveal a room nearly as large on the other side, where another fire
blazed in a wide hearth and where a table covered with a white cloth
groaned under a burden of smörgåsbord in the true Danish tradition. At a huge carved buffet, Mr. Tubro took his stand, handing the
guests white Copenhagen plates decorated with blue flowers, nap-
kins and silverware. Across the room, another antique and highly
polished sideboard extended about seven feet long and six feet high,
with mirrors and shelves and drawers. This held a large cut-glass
bowl containing fruit compote and glass dessert dishes. I had not
seen such an array of food since coming to India: Danish ham, roast
beef, pâté, potato salad, various vegetables, pumpernickel bread, and
all the relishes and pickled wonders to garnish and add color were
spread in bewildering array on the table. The guests filled their
plates, retired to the drawing room to eat in small groups, and re-

turn again and again to the dining room. Later, I was to pay the pen-
alty for indulging so enthusiastically in the rich repast; for the moment, disregarding the insult to my innards, which had become
accustomed to rice and vegetables and fruit only, I munched away
happily and chatted with Mehta's husband. He was a tall, handsome
Dane, an employee of SAS, and he related his experiences while a
student at Purdue University as he held one arm around his young
son, Hans Christian. The child had run a fever earlier but, true to
form, was unable to remain in bed with the prospect of a party and
had recovered sufficiently to be with the guests.

It was with regret that I finally bid good-bye to my hosts and accepted a ride down to Snyder "B" with my landlord, Major Mohan
Lal.

On the following day I had been invited to the home of Mrs.
Ghose, a beautiful, slender woman I had met at Presentation Convent on the evening of the tenth-standard entertainment. She was a
professional classical dancer of note, and I hoped to be privileged to
witness one of her recitals before leaving Kodai, so when the invitation came, I most eagerly accepted it. The cab took me higher and
higher in the hills beyond the convent and dropped me at a spot
overlooking a lovely valley, where I could see a low, spacious stone
building stretching along a surprisingly large area and set into the
side of the hill. I descended, met a young girl who was picking
flowers in the garden, and she led me into the fastness of the Ghose
estate. I entered by a low doorway into a reception room, and was
at once struck by the exotic atmosphere of the place. Beautiful old
carved friezes decorated the walls of the small room as well as the
massive doors. After a moment or two, another servant led me up a
small flight of stairs into a drawing room lit at one end by a bank of
windows overlooking the valley and Perumal Peak. The room was
dark and cool, and I was invited to sit down. Presently the son of the
family appeared, said his mother would be there in a moment and
offered to show me around the house. And so began a tour of the
most extraordinary Indian home I had ever seen. The exterior was all
of the most solid construction: stone and brick, with lovely architectural feaures such as rounded doorways and wall niches built as
part of the construction. We began the tour on the second floor,
where Prasanna Sindar opened the door onto a library containing
what seemed many hundreds of books. He explained that his father,

Dr. Ghose, had founded a society dedicated to the education and eventual employment of young Indians. This portion of the house was intended to serve them as a cultural center and meeting place, where they could gather for meetings, discussion groups, or lectures. From this library, he brought me onto an open terrace, where again the view of the hills dominated the scene. We went down a semifinished corridor into a very large area where he showed me a vast manorial hall, still unfinished, which would eventually be a lecture hall. It was the size of a football field, with windows very high up and with walls that seemed about forty feet high—not unlike the proportions of the great hall at Hampton Court in England. From this portion of the house we retraced our steps and entered upon a staircase that led to underground tunnels connecting all portions of the house. We found ourselves in a subterranean area, all of brick or stone, built into the hillside. I had heard constant pounding sounds, and now understood their source, when we came through an opening in the tunnel and found ourselves in a threshing shed held up by huge pillars, where a group of workers were threshing the golden grain by a primitive method, no machinery in evidence.

From this chamber we reentered the tunnels, which led to what Prasanna called "the factory." It was an amazing size. There was to be a modern bakery installed there; huge mixing machines were already in place, and I could see the brick ovens down below, where the bread would be kiln-baked. Dr. Ghose had a plan to bake nutritious whole wheat bread there, using their own wheat, and packaging and preparing it for market—all in this vast chamber. In one spot, two gargantuan generators lay already there, rich in potential but still not working, awaiting the completion of the other portions of this master plan.

In still another room, a distillery for the oil of geranium leaves was being prepared, complete with a laboratory. Prasanna explained that when all was in readiness, this processing of oils would run three months for geranium and then for eucalyptus oil for the balance of the time. They would grow the geraniums on the estate on the side of the hill.

I realized that the mind that had conceived and created this vast structure was a genius, and was eager to meet him and speak to him. This was not possible, however; he was in Bombay, practicing medicine.

Back in the drawing room, Mrs. Ghose and I had an opportunity to get acquainted. She sat, regal and slim amid her priceless antiques and talked of the Hindu pantheon of the gods. She was born a Parsee, but when she married Dr. Ghose, took up his religion with wholehearted enthusiasm. She was totally ecumenical in her approach to God; amid the statues of Krishna and Rama were crucifixes, lithographs of the Sacred Heart, buddhas, and many photographs of her favorite holy people: Sri Aurobindo and the Holy Mother, and many whose names were unknown to me. Tucked into the crevices of the dark wood carvings of Krishna, Vishnu, Ganesh and Christ were beautiful fresh flowers, glowing against the polished wood. Many old wall hangings depicting the gods in various reincarnations decorated the high walls, while on a ledge above hovered more of the pantheon, interspersed with bronze oil lamps and two winged Hindu carvings that looked very much like angels. I realized, finally, that everything in the decoration of this home was symbolic of the faith of its owner and his beautiful wife. There were three elaborate shrines in the room and one in the next. At twelve noon, Mrs. Ghose interrupted the conversation with the question: "Will you excuse me for a small ritual? I always do this, and if you do not mind?"

Of course, I did not, but I was totally unprepared for the pageant that followed.

First she brought a candle and lit the small lamps at all three shrines, some twenty of them, then disappeared into the next room, where, I presume, she did the same. Then she returned and lit incense sticks at all the shrines, pausing to pray on her knees when this was completed. This was followed by the bringing in by the servant, Jesu, of a kind of powder and a bowl of glowing coals. The powder was kept in one hand, while Mrs. Ghose gracefully glided slowly through the room, feeding powder to the coals, permitting the smoke to swirl up from the small brazier to all the shrines, including the doorway figures and all the corners of the room. It was like watching a beautiful ballet. The servant then brought a tray containing water and milk, and these were placed before one of the shrines and blessed. She told me later that all the food consumed in the house was first offered to God, and only when thus blessed was it considered proper to eat. The water and milk were symbols of the breakfast food. A small bell was rung now at each of the shrines, and the tinkling bell, the strong scent of the incense, the rhythmic pounding of the threshers below, and the mighty crest of Perumal, now half covered in clouds, gave me an unearthly feeling. Could there really be a busy world outside this peaceful place? It did not seem possible. Mrs. Ghose now knelt down in adoration before her God; I knew that it was the same God I worshiped, though under a different name, and together we prayed, each in her own way. I found myself whispering the Jesus Prayer; I don't know what invocation she was making. When her prayer was completed, she came and sat again in the chair opposite me, her beige and olive and purple sari swirling around her bare feet and her lovely eyes closed in meditation. At length she opened them, and our conversation resumed.

She told me of her husband, whom she considers an authentic genius. His plan for the welfare of the poor will be put into action one day, she is convinced. All the money they do not need for their living expenses is funneled into the building of this factory plan, clustered around their living quarters and underneath their feet. She sees it coming into actuality when God decides the time is right and sends the proper people to aid Dr. Ghose in making it a reality. For the factory as planned is a complete cycle, each portion feeding another; the unused fuel of one pressed into service in another, thus forming a complete circle of productivity. The total absence of a profit motive is a unique thing in India; it is difficult to find similar-minded people, who would understand what he is trying to do. But, she smiled, when it is actually in the works and running as he planned it, he will already be far ahead, making innovations and working on the next portion of his master plan for the poor. I wondered where they would find the necessary experts. God sends them at the right time, she is convinced. Perhaps they will be Americans.

We had lunch in the next room, which I saw for the first time. It turned out to be a bedroom, essentially, with beds placed so that the occupants had a full view of the peak and the valley below. In a corridor leading from the bedroom was a long table set into the wall, with chairs on one side only. This was the dining area. We sat facing the wall, where ancient wall hangings of embroidery hung in their old frames. The two children joined us, and I ate sparingly, explaining the reason: my foolish overindulgence at the party the day before. We had a delicious soup, made with leeks and what seemed like caraway seeds, though the word meant nothing to Mrs. Ghose. I ate appapalum and a little white rice and curds, and had mint tea. This proved the correct thing as far as my stomach was concerned. At lunch I became acquainted with Meenakshi, the thirteen-year-old daughter, who attended Presentation Convent. She was dressed in the white Sunday uniform of the school, in preparation for the Good Friday services, which we all planned to attend later in the day. A very ladylike little girl, she plays the piano and thinks she would like to be a doctor, though her father has encouraged her to study art.

After lunch, Mrs. Ghose played the tape that accompanies one of her dance programs. The music was beautifully recorded and made more interesting by an English commentary in cultivated male tones describing the dance intended to go with it. The recordings had been made to eliminate the necessity of orchestral accompaniment for her dance recital. Since it was Good Friday, Mrs. Ghose had decided to postpone the dancing for another time, and invited me to come again to witness a performance. I accepted most eagerly.

Noting that I seemed rather tired and under the weather, she offered me a nap in one of the quiet rooms of her house, and I was delighted. Thus it was that I lay down with the Holy Mother of Aurobindo Ashram gazing down upon my slumbers, and I slept for two full hours before a rustling in the corridor caused me to awaken and prepare myself for the trip back to Presentation Chapel for the services. We drove back in their 1947 Austin; I thought how my grandson Peter would have loved to see that car, considered vintage and priceless in the States and here simply a useful conveyance, lovingly shined and tuned up for a daily round of the hills by the family chauffeur.

The Good Friday services had attracted not only the servants but many people who lived nearby, so the chapel was filled to overflowing. Father Montaud conducted the solemn rites, his rich French accent interspersed with the crisp English voice of Brother James, who had come up for Easter from Batalagunda and did the readings. These were answered by the students, mostly Hindus, who shouted out, "Crucify Him," portraying the Jewish throngs on that fateful day. We venerated the wood of the Cross, received Communion, and prayed for the entire world. Mrs. Ghose and her son and daughter, reverently wrapped in prayer beside me, took part in the entire service, excepting only the Communion.

At the convent, Sister Ethna had a cup of arrowroot prepared for me to drink, for the sake of my still tender stomach; then I bid them all good evening and rode back down to Snyder "B," where Regina had supper waiting for me. I had to tell her to put it back again, and retired early.

I awoke the following morning completely myself again, and managed to extract from Regina two soft-boiled eggs instead of her usual, seven-minute variety. At around 10 A.M. a knock at the door announced the car from Sacred Heart Seminary, loaded with wood for the fireplace. Also in the car were two tourists who were seeing Kodai, a Jesuit from Cleveland originally, now a citizen of Nepal, and Sister Rosalia of the Medical Missionaries. I hitched a ride with them out to Pillar Rock and cheerfully pointed out landmarks on the way, feeling very much the Kodai resident instructing the neophytes. Father Leo asked me to come to Nepal, and I thought I just might do that, one day.

Easter began before midnight, in pitch-black darkness, outside Presentation Chapel. An overcast sky hid the moon, and all the convent girls were hovering around the chapel door, their green-blazered shoulders hunched up against the chilly air and their white Sunday uniform skirts and sox gleaming in the darkness. The unofficial congregation were also there, mingled with the white-clad nuns: the dentist, his wife and two children, Mrs. Ghose and her son, Mrs. Gibson (the organist who also played the services at St. Peter's Protestant Church), Brother James of Boys' Village, the teachers in their beautiful saris, some men who worked at the convent, and myself. Only the church was lit, and through the open door the light gleamed out the gothic arch, lighting a small space around us. Father Montaud arrived, entered the chapel, and returned, vested, a short time later, followed by the driver (who often served as acolyte) bearing the paschal candle. All the lights of the chapel were extinguished. The lighting of the paschal candle was dramatic, marred only slightly when someone stepped on the convent cat, which let out a very unliturgical yowl. One by one, we passed Father Montaud, who stood at the church door, igniting our candles from the new and holy fire.

The Mass was a glory of beautiful hymns (the result of extra hours of practice by Sister Cecilia and her choir). Brother James did the long readings. Father Montaud's allelujas were delivered with perfect pitch and joyous conviction. We shared, that nighttime Vigil

Mass, a mutual hope and thanksgiving for yet another Easter. My thoughts centered around my loved ones at home. I knew there would be baskets of candy eggs for all the children, a paschal-lamb cake on the table, and that all of them would be together except for Bill and me. Bill was backpacking in a wilderness area of Arizona, and I mentioned his name rather anxiously to the Risen Lord. We came out of the chapel to find the host of a full moon sailing over the forest trees in a velvet blue heaven.

After tea in the convent and a little music and a joyful exchange of gifts and hugs to celebrate the end of the Lenten season, the nuns handed me a key and told Brother James to guide me to the place where I was to be their guest for the night. We walked out into the darkness again, with only the moon for a light. I had a small torch in my purse, having been in India long enough to know that nights are very dark and that I have not the Indian gift for seeing in the dark. Aided by the torch, we found a long flight of stairs, and then another, and then still another. I had to stop for breath. At the top of this climb was a lighted door, which the key opened. We entered Sinclair House, part of the Presentation property and now used to house their lay teachers. They reserved here, as well, two guest rooms in the wide and beautiful ranch house: I was to have one, and Brother James the other. The rooms were immaculately furnished, the red tile floors polished brightly, and everywhere the air of sweet cleanliness that only nuns can accomplish. Brother James showed me my room, acquainted me with the light switches, and saying good night, went to his own quarters. My room was a marvel. It was, by rough estimate, about thirty-five or forty feet square, and just as high in one spot, where the ceiling slanted up to the rooftree. There was a fireplace with nice paneling over it, some dressers and wardrobes, a narrow bed, and several desks. There was still room enough in the place to hold a dance, if one wished. Adjoining this was a bathroom. When I turned out the lights and lay down to sleep, the bright moon found a skylight high up on the wall and sent a beautiful ray down to the polished floor. There is one thing about high ceilings: one has the feeling there is plenty of air to breathe. I reflected that it must be hard to heat in the colder months, however—probably the reason for the fireplace.

I had stayed at the convent once before, in another guesthouse, where I had heard jackals at night, so when the howling began, I was not worried. "Jackals," I said to myself and turned over and went to sleep. It was just as well, because promptly at 5 A.M. an unbelievably loud racket of Indian music blasted me from my slumbers. I thought at first someone had put a transistor radio under my bed; it sounded as though it was coming from quite close. A little investigation (I opened the window to see if someone was outside with a sound truck) proved that it was coming from a loudspeaker in the hills nearby. One horrendous selection followed another. There was no returning to sleep. I decided to put on my robe and slippers and explore the house. Padding around that huge house was rather exciting, the music lending a carnival atmosphere to the adventure. I found the light switches and discovered a dining room fully fifty feet long, another huge room with chairs set around as in a sitting room, and in back of that a little room with a table containing a large Bible. The window in this room framed a beautiful sunrise just beginning its spectacular Easter show, so I sat down and greeted the day by watching the dawn. The sun accomplished its daily marvel, but the music was nowhere near finished. I washed and dressed, and slipped outside in the cool morning air to discover that the house had a terrace all around it, entirely surrounded by a curving, ancient wall. Below the wall were terraced fruit trees, and some flowers, bordered by yet another, higher wall. With a practiced real estate agent's eye, I went over the exterior of the house from front to back. It was of gray stone, with pleasant lines, low and spacious. The roof had two levels, the top one permitting the insertion of high windows, which admitted extra light to the interior rooms. The usual roof of metal sheeting covered with tiles was punctuated by three chimneys, so I knew I had missed some fireplaces inside. Off to one side was a garage, joined to the house by a glassed-in areaway. There was an open door there, so I stepped through it and out to the back of the property, where there were more terracing and garden possibilities. The house sat on a very high hill, making possible a full 360-degree view of the hills all around. Presentation Convent roof could be seen far below, near the front. I wondered if the house might be for sale. The sisters had told me it had been a gift to them by the Kelly family, and I decided to ask to see the rest of the house after breakfast.

Brother James appeared, waved good morning to me, and went down to Mass. I locked up and followed him down, the music still blasting so loudly the very birds had stopped singing, and the leaves seemed to quiver in protest at this cultural insult. The chapel was quiet, except for the noise nuisance, which was mercifully muffled somewhat there. The Mass began at seven-thirty, and again the girls sang beautifully, their Hindu, Muslim and Christian voices mingling in joy and praise.

After breakfast, Sister Xavier sent Mickey up with me, armed with keys, and he opened the house for my admiration and inspection. There were seven bedrooms, most of them large, and four bathrooms. A very nice kitchen and butler's pantry and a long service hallway rounded out the information I had gleaned earlier: it was a fine house, and admirably suited for a large family. I knew the Kellys must have been happy there. The building at the back of the garage also had been turned into a four room apartment, so that one could house a servant or guest there as well. Sister Ethna, however, when I broached the subject of sale, smiled and said no, it was not for sale. I had some fun renaming the place Anton Hall and mentally fixing up a room for mother (lower the ceiling there and get a large rug for her floor) where she could also have a servant sleeping in the adjoining room. All through a very pleasant Easter Day I joked with the sisters about it, and they with me. Actually, what I would do with a house that large, I don't know, though the thought of just having a bedroom and study like the one I was housed in was very intriguing. I lay there in the window bay, where a daybed was thoughtfully placed, and tried to read but constantly found myself musing about Sinclair—no—Anton Hall, and its possibilities. A tap at the front door announced one of the servants from the convent: Sister wanted me in the parlor I combed my hair and went down to find the Jesuits visiting, and had tea with them, exchanging Easter greetings all around, before retiring again up the hill. Regina was at her home for the day, and the nuns had thoughtfully invited me to remain there and dine with them. I was only too glad to accept.

Dinner was at noon, with all the sisters at table, in a festive mood occasioned by the feast and the fact that most of the girls were away for vacation. Those who were still in residence had been allowed to go off for the day to amuse themselves on a picnic, or go rowing on the lake. Each girl had been given money to spend, and they had taken off like a shot; it was hard to say who was happier about the picnic, the kids or the nuns. I told them all about Mrs. Ghose's interesting theory about Mother Teresa of Calcutta, the saintly foundress of The Missionaries of Charity. She believes that this Teresa is a reincarnation of the great Teresa of Ávila, who said in one of her journals that she had regretted that during her life she had been unable to love Christ through His poor. It is a very intriguing possibility, I think. The conversation centered around this for a time, and then on the working conditions of the poor, their difficulties in keeping out of the hands of the moneylenders, and their childlike habit of hand-to-mouth existence rather than cultivating the habits of thrift. In this, and indeed in every conversation about the poor, one fact stood out above all others: these nuns care deeply about the plight of the people, and have done an enormous amount to aid them in every way possible, from medical care to education.

After a short nap, I found Brother James writing letters, and we had a chance for a good conversation about his work at Boys' Village. His newest project, that of creating village industries for the villages he is reconstructing, has him completely enthralled. As soon as a new brother arrives, who will eventually take complete charge of the boys, Brother James will be off on this new scheme, in the hope of creating weaving and pottery cottage industries, which will give his people financial aid and dignity. He has seventy-five lepers under his care, and he told me of the difficulties to be faced in their treatment. Since the community would not permit a leper colony to be built in this, the largest concentration of lepers in the country, he has now purchased a bit of land for each of them, built them houses, and sends food and medicine to them. After they have been treated for six months, he says, their disease enters a negative phase in which it is no longer contagious. In all his work, he consults with the village headmen, who form a committee. Their complete cooperation and involvement in the work ensure that long after he is dead, this committee can carry on. I was struck anew by the total dedication to the poor and the helpless this De La Salle Brother radiates. He told me of his plan for the aged in his village: he builds them a small house near the center of town (old people, he said, hate to be removed from the life of the village) and gives them a weekly allowance of grain and money to keep them content and happy. He said, "It's so nice to see them sitting there, talking together, free from want and worry after their long, hard lives."

After still another tea with the nuns, Father Montaud, and

Brother James, and greeting again the ever-welcome Father de Mello, who had come back with the Holy Oils to administer the Sacrament of the Sick to old Sister Evangelist, I came back to Snyder "B." Regina was not yet back from her holiday; I walked around Kodai Lake in the early dusk and met some of the convent kids with their parents. Three carloads of them all stretched out and waved at me as they passed back up the hill en route to Presentation.

It was a happy Easter.

CHAPTER 20

All Around the Town

A soft rain clothes the hills; I don my raincoat, and armed with my little coral umbrella, start out the front door. Regina, alarmed, cries out, "But madam, raining, raining."

"I love the rain," I tell her. "I'll be back in an hour." Down the path I go, toward my favorite lakeside walk. Once there, I make my way around the puddles and piles of horse dung, delighting in the fresh, rain-washed air and the circlets on the lake where the drops alight. Under a tree huddle a morose little party: a pretty lady in a silken sari and two gentlemen, one of whom appears to be her bridegroom, the other a photographer. The camera is slung, open, around his neck, quite unprotected from the rain. As I approach, the photographer comes up smiling, and I sense the usual request to take their photo all together. But I am wrong. He reaches for my umbrella, and gestures toward the lady. He desires to photograph her holding my coral umbrella. I hand it over, and stand there in the drizzle, while he poses her with the green lake as background, the coral umbrella tilted over the black, flower-bedecked head. She looks very pretty indeed. I hope the camera will work in spite of the dim light. The bridegroom is overjoyed. The photo is taken, and I am about to receive my umbrella again. But no. They also want my photo with the pretty little bride. So I stand holding the umbrella over both our heads and thus become an unwitting portrait in some family album. There are fervent namastes all around; I take the umbrella and continue my walk around the lake.

Farther on, a very large eucalyptus tree has come loose from its mooring, high on a bank, and hangs suspended over the road like a swaying bridge, its uprooted feet on the high bank at the far side, while the top rests on the electric wires on the other. The straining wires are bent ominously by the tremendous weight. The structure moves in the breeze, and I note the trembling as cabs zoom underneath the natural bridge. One day the wires will snap, electrocuting several cows and perhaps some locals, and plunge the entire lake district into darkness for weeks. In the meantime, it hangs like the sword of Damocles, awaiting the moment of fate.

All the roads of India are literally handmade. In Kodai the process goes like this: High up in the hills, workers chip away huge slabs of the granite that forms the mountains. Bullock carts haul the slabs downhill, the loads often forcing the poor beasts to run, making the procedure hazardous. The slabs are dumped at certain spots where road repair is needed. Teams of women and children squat on these spots in the hot sun, and chip and pound the stone until it is reduced to walnut-sized pieces. Thousands of woman-and-child-hours are required to make one heap of this gravel. It is then spread in the prepared roadbed, and when all is in readiness, hot tar is smoothed on top. This is done by barefoot men with lots of burns on their legs and feet. An antique steamroller stamps the whole thing down. The road is finished. Well, not quite. Thousands of cattle and horses add their droppings, which provide top dressing, and in Kodai, hundreds of toads and frogs choose to immortalize themselves in the hot tar; these can be seen forever preserved, in perfectly neat pressed condition, like the prints of movie stars on Hollywood Boulevard.

* * *

The cabs and lorries of Kodai have an evil game they play. They overtake a pedestrian, who, eschewing annihilation, moves to the side of the road. As the vehicle pulls abreast of the poor sap, it emits an earth-shattering blast on the horn calculated to frighten him out of a year's growth. All the occupants of the vehicle observe carefully to see if the slightest twinge or nervous twitch can be detected. They make a count of these on any journey; some days are better than others. I have refused to play. When a cab approaches me from behind, I step smartly into the ditch, turn and face it with implacable features, and do not turn a hair when the blast goes off. They think I am completely deaf, and have begun to tire of it. It is wise, when engaged in this pastime, to make certain that one is standing on the side away from the cab's tailpipe. They burn old rags as fuel and send forth a smoke screen that can blight the brightest day. I now note which side the smoke is coming from, and leap to the opposite side of the road. It keeps me in condition.

*   *   *

I go to the bank to cash my traveler's checks. The bank opens at 10 A.M. I am there, with my passport, traveler's checks, and a deliberate load of patience. I enter the bank among the first customers and proceed to the desk where the sign says, AMERICAN TRAVELER'S CHECKS CASHED HERE. An oiled head is busy over some homework. I cough delicately to let him know he has a customer. He suggests I be seated and relax a bit. I have had a sound night's sleep, and a morning of shopping to do, and turn down this offer. More people line up behind me. The head does not rise for ten minutes. When it does, I hand over my passport with the check and say in distinct, polite tones: "May I please cash this check?"

"Certainly, madam. One moment, please." He goes back to his arithmetic. The other clerks behind the counter carry on a lively Tamil conversation, joshing each other, slapping one another on the back, while huge trunks (painted green, appropriately enough) are carried out of the open vault. It is an amiable crew, who obviously enjoy their work, their comrades-in-arms, and life in general. All are wearing neat, clean cotton shirts, and some have obviously spent some time with their hair, which is carefully coiled in nice black waves.

Finally, in a desperate effort to win the scribe's attention again, I say, "What is the rate of exchange this morning?" This often proves a grave mistake. It means he has to abandon his multiplication tables, and open numerous drawers next to him, to find a book wherein the code for this mysterious information lies. He begins a new series of calculations on a separate piece of paper. The pen moves with dreamlike languor. Long minutes pass.

Finally he says, "Eight rupees, twenty paise, madam." I am ready for this, and with lightning speed grab a pen from my purse, multiply 40×8.20 and come up with a product, which I announce triumphantly to him. He doesn't believe me. He computes it himself. Noting a similarity in our answers, he smiles congratulations to me, and then removes from his desk a book containing forms and carbons. Painstakingly he writes on this form my passport number, my name, my address, my birthday, my mother's name, and nationality. Then he adds to these data the figure we have agreed upon: 328 rupees.

He not only prints it, he writes it out. Ever so carefully removing the original document from his book, he hands it to me and requests that I sign its back. I do so. He also wants my address. I add that. He scrutinizes my signature, makes comparisons with that of the passport and that of the traveler's check and records the transaction in a large, tattered ledger, which must then be restored to its place in the bottom drawer of his desk. At length he promotes me to the next grade. I am given a round copper tag with a number on it. He also returns my passport. I take the round copper tag and cross the bank to another window, where an affable gentleman is deeply interested in how I like Kodai, how long I intend to remain, and how I spend my time here. I tell him all of this, and add that I would like three hundred and twenty-eight rupees. He raises his hands helplessly. This cannot be done until all the proper paper arrives from the other side of the bank. So we chat awhile about this and that as the bank fills up with customers and the merry camaraderie of the office force continues unabated. A sign on a post draws my attention to the fact that if the customer is caused any delay, the bank officials want to know about it. I decide that it will not be news to them anyway, and decline to play. Meanwhile, the mysterious paper I have countersigned sits on the desk of the assistant manager, who has several would-be customers clustered around his desk in abject petition. He manages to tear himself away from them long enough to initial the paper, which is then placed in a book and given to a bearer. This gentleman ankles over to the teller's window and places the crucial paper in a slot. My interlocutor pauses in a lengthy tale to glance at it, somewhat annoyed at this interruption. I clutch at the bars and whisper desperately, "I would like three one-hundred-rupee notes, and the balance in tens, fives and singles." This has the desired effect. He cuts off his story and opens his cash drawer. Bundles of currency are stacked therein. But do they contain the proper number of rupees in each bundle? This man is no fool. He will count them first to make certain. I stand on one foot while he makes the count one way, and then the other. Satisfied, finally, that no one is playing tricks on him, he counts out three one-hundred-rupee notes with amazing dexterity, and then from another bundle whips out the required tens. The fives will have to be counted first, before I get mine; the maneuver of the final three rupees is completed, and I bid him good day. Forty-five minutes have been consumed of a morning that contained such bright promise. I sigh and promise myself not to do this again for several weeks.

* * *

While Regina is at Shembaganur on family business, I go down to the Kashmiri shop near Spencer's to buy some gifts to send to America. There is a glorious profusion of papier-mâché boxes, trays, walnut pieces, and crewel-worked cushions, all wonderful in design and execution. I am busily selecting next Christmas's gifts when Regina comes in, beaming.

"How did you find me?" I ask her. Foolish question.

"Man in bazaar tell me, 'Your madam, she is buying at Kashmiri shop.'" The grapevine works very well in Kodai.

* * *

It also operates so that all the beggars in town know when one is making purchases costing more than five rupees. These worthies line up outside the shop as one emerges, and before the purse is closed, extract their share of the purchase, pulling long faces and whining, "Amah, amah," as one comes down the steps. One of them tried to bleed me twice in one shopping morning. I balked at that, particularly since I had been generous with her the first time and thought she'd give up for the day and buy the rice she said she desperately needed.

The man with the horse, who had taxed me ten rupees with his tale of someone having impounded his horse just because it was eating some grass, and who faithfully promised to return these rupees on the following Monday, met me again in the bazaar with another tale about the horse. This time, I asked him about the ten rupees he had promised to repay. "Oh, yes, madam. You just give me ten more rupees and on next Monday I will bring you twenty rupees." I did not fall for that one. When I repeated this adventure to the nuns, they laughed and laughed. Everyone knew the man with the horse. He has been using this story for years.

* * *

Father Ignatius, of Shembag, came with a request for help that had been sent to him by a nun whose sister needed aid very badly. Since Ted had sent money with me just for this purpose, I had it to give, and I was very happy to help. In the ensuing conversation, we spoke of the plight of the coolies who go for firewood daily. He, too, is at a loss as to how to help them. It turns out they are really stealing this wood, having bribed the forestry men daily so that they will be allowed to take the saplings. We talked about the rich in India, who do nothing to aid the poor. He feels that the very rich will never help; there is nothing in their culture or religion that encourages them to do so. I suggest that perhaps giving them permission to declare income-tax deductions would be the proper method to encourage helping, but he says they all cheat on their income taxes anyway and need no further deductions. What to do?

*   *   *

At the archives in Shembag I find the records of the years in which Father Nevett was there as a novice, and read these with tremendous interest. Occasionally I find the note: "Brother Nevett goes to Trichi to see the doctor" or interesting stories about panthers killing the college cows. I mention to Father Ignatius how wonderful these diaries are. He tells me that the custom has now been abandoned; no one wants to take the trouble to make these notes anymore. Even the large cyclone in November is not recorded in the annals of the house. This is a tremendous loss to the future. A tradition of record-keeping that dates back to the founding of the Madurai Province, in the seventeenth century, has thus been allowed to die. So even among these highly educated men the slow erosion of a sense of history and tradition has done its damage.

*   *   *

The kitchen supplies being low, Regina and I went marketing one bright sunny morning. I needed extra supplies, since I planned to bake a cake and make some party sandwiches for a tea. The following grocery purchases might be of interest for comparison with costs in the States:

1 kilo of sugar	Rs. 3.75	½ kilo peas (fresh)	Rs. 3.00
½ kilo of dal	2.15	½ kilo onions	.20
1 box soap powder	9.53	1 bunch leeks	1.00
Vim (scouring powder)	3.00	½ kilo tomatoes	.70
Amul (dried milk powder)	13.05	½ kilo brinjal	.20
1 bar kitchen soap	1.38	(eggplant)	
1 kilo walnuts (shells)	10.00	1 doz. eggs	4.50

1 kilo margarine	Rs. 15.00	1 doz. oranges	Rs. 6.00
1 kilo flour	2.12	1 papaya	1.50
1 can cheese powder	18.70	1 bunch plantains	2.50
1 can brass polish	12.55	½ kilo fresh carrots	.70
1 pkg. dry yeast	3.75	handful of peppers	.30
1 can sausages	9.20	1 cucumber	.50

This comes to a total of 125.28 rupees, or approximately $15.28 American; slightly less than that, actually. The soap and polishes would last me a month. So would the cheese powder and milk powder. The other items would go in about one week's time, and we would return to the bazaar for more fruit and vegetables on the following Monday. So I was feeding two people very well on around $12 per week. No meat, of course. No fish. The rice diet with vegetables and nuts suited me so well I decided not to tamper with it anymore. The sausages I splurged on would find themselves blanketed in small rolls and offered at my tea party. And unless my memory of the supermarket in America was defective, the above list of groceries would have cost at least three times that amount at home. Some items in India are very high, however. Toilet paper, for example, costs the equivalent of sixty cents per roll, and this roll is half the size of ours at home, making it well over a dollar a roll. Of course, no one but foreigners ever purchases it.

I came to the conclusion that I could live in Kodai for years and never need a car again. If I arranged for Raja to come to my house three days a week at fixed times, I could have contracted on a price for this service that would have taken me everywhere I wished to go —grocery shopping, visiting, or Mass—and all for the equivalent of about $2.50 per week. My lovely little Datsun cost me much more than that for insurance, initial investment, upkeep, tires, gas, etc. I never quite figured it out, but probably just sitting in the garage all day it was costing me far more than $2.50 per day.

From my very elementary grasp of math, I estimated that the cost of living in India, even at a resort like Kodai, was roughly one fifth that of the U.S.A. The plains would be much cheaper, but the climate was so torrid I could never have borne it for long. On an income of five hundred dollars per month, one would be very wealthy here, because it translates on today's exchange at about four thousand rupees. One could also live very well on two hundred dollars per month, minus the servant. In my case, I knew, the clothing already in my closets at home would last half a lifetime here.

*   *   *

Pleasant diversion interrupted the usual routine. Regina's sister-in-law brought her little son, Robert, and Regina's two first communicants, Philomena and Joseph, to pay a call. Philomena and Joseph were resplendent in their First Communion whites, with scapulars and medals around their necks, barefoot, and bearing a bouquet of pretty flowers for me. I was quite overcome, as I always am when anyone kneels before me. I hastily blessed their foreheads and made them sit down to lemonade and cookies. Only Regina spoke English, so she had to translate all the excited conversation between us. I had purchased, a few days before, a collection of small brass animals, very old, in the bazaar, and got these down for the children. They moved them along the coffee table and had a little parade, much as our Joe and Kevin would create. Then I thought of the tape recorder, and brought it out for them to hear music. They were much impressed with Vladimir Horowitz on the piano, Joseph's intelligent eyes gleaming at the pearly runs up and down the scale. When Regina said Joseph would sing a little song for me, I turned the Sony to RE-CORD and let him go. He has an amazing voice for such a young child, full and rich, and with marvelous expression. I had no idea what he was singing; he did a whole recital of Tamil songs, and at one point Philomena raised a timid little monotone to join him. At the conclusion, I rewound the tape and let them hear themselves in song. Their expressions of surprise were wonderful! Philomena collapsed in a girlish bundle of giggles and embarrassment, while Joseph sat very straight, smiling a wide and beautiful smile, as his lips silently formed the words to accompany himself as he listened. Once this source of entertainment had been exhausted, and the children had excused themselves mysteriously to go outside (I finally figured out they were going to the toilet, and knew the neighbors wouldn't mind), Regina broached the topic I now realize had prompted this visit: Would madam take photos? It was a good idea, of course, and I got out my small camera and posed them before the fireplace, Regina having fitted a Communion veil on Philomena's black curls. The camera has a flash, so we took many indoor shots from every possible angle. I warned Regina it would take three months before she had the proof of my efforts, and she understood.

I also learned that the new child of the family, a little girl born recently to Regina's brother and his wife, had been named Rita, and, as Regina pointed out to me, in case I had missed it, that is also my name. This family came to call when the mother was strong enough, and I made the expected gesture of recognition of the honor I had been thus paid, in the form of an appropriate gift for little Rita.

One day, walking up to the bazaar, I passed the dispensary of High Clerc School and noticed a large group of children there. Inquiry revealed they were all getting rabies shots. When I had an opportunity to talk to the school authorities, I found that the little pet dog of one of the teachers, which had been too young for rabies shots, developed excessive vomiting. The pet was taken to the local vet, who said it was nothing, just an upset stomach. When the vomiting persisted, the teacher took her little dog back to the vet again, with the same result. In the meantime, the dog was much fondled by the children of the school, who were fond of it; it also visited the house where the Kesslers had another dog of the same litter. Jon Kessler became suspicious when he saw how the dog was behaving, and later his suspicions were justified; the little dog went into the classic symptoms, and died. The brain was sent to a hospital in the plains for examination, and rabies was confirmed. The same car that brought the news back to Kodai also brought back some serum to begin inoculations for the children of the school. More of this was obtained, and a master plan was put into effect so that no possibility of rabies would remain untreated; all animals that might have come into contact with the dog were disposed of. Three general classifications were identified: those which had been either bitten or scratched by the dog, those which had been in actual physical contact with it where open sores on the body might become entries for the deadly saliva of the poor animal, and those which had had contact without open sores. The only one in the first category was the owner, who had a few scratches on her hand. She was being given the most potent and longest series of shots. The others were taking two cubic centimeters daily for either seven or ten days, depending on exposure, age, weight, etc. The remarkable organizational ability and complete calm with which this widespread treatment was being undertaken was admirable, I thought. As I watched the children in the infirmary cheering one another, peering under the curtain on the door to see who was administering the shots today, and the kindness of the doctor and nurse, I was impressed by the outstanding work done under trying circumstances.

The rabies scare gave rise to all kinds of new information, which came as a surprise to me. I had had no idea that rabies was so deadly a disease, nor did I know about the virulent aspects of the saliva of an afflicted animal. I was told about a case several years before in which a boy had been bitten on the leg by a mad dog. He was immediately given treatment and survived. But his mother, mending the torn trouser, pricked her finger with the needle and died of rabies! Mrs. Ghose told me of a case in her village in the North where a woman was bitten by a mad animal, and knowing that hydrophobia was one of the first indications of the disease, deliberately went to seven wells, mentally forcing herself near water, before going off for the treatment. The effects of the virus can remain in the system for months before reaching the brain, so that it was difficult to trace how the little pet had gotten infected. It had been in Madurai at Christmastime two months before, and it was thought it might have contacted a mad animal there. Apparently it is possible for the virus to remain in the human system for as long as two years, particularly if the entry spot was at the foot or hand. The farther from the head, the longer it will take to show up.

India has a great many rabies cases each year, it seems. There are wild jackals in the hills which often come down at night and attack local animals, and this could be one means of infection. But I found the lame excuse of the vet the worst case I ever heard: he later stated that he knew all along that the dog had rabies, but, since its owner was a single lady, he hated to give her the bad news. How much of this was genuine ignorance and how much a lame attempt to excuse poor judgment is problematic. At any rate, the vet and all his assistants had to take the shots too. Hating to come to the hospital for them, they asked if the High Clerc doctors could come to the clinic and administer them privately.

The coolies who run down the road in their bare feet often have cracks in the skin, and even they are susceptible should they step on some of the saliva of a rabid animal. Many have thus contracted the disease and died. This virus, and the danger of tetanus, I should think, are the best arguments for wearing shoes, even if only sandals.

When I came back to the house from the school, I found a little family group awaiting madam. Regina's sister had brought the new baby, Miss Rita, as well as Regina's little son, Edward, and the sister-in-law. We all admired the baby extravagantly on the front lawn, and then went in for tea. I had baked the day before, so I had something to offer with the tea, little muffins with berries in them, and my walnut banana cake with chocolate frosting.

Little Rita was a very pretty baby. I held her for a while, and was amazed at the utter calm and peace with which she surveyed her new surroundings. She was then about six weeks old. There was a baby bed in my house, and we placed her there to kick her small feet in the sunshine streaming in through the windows and to wave her chubby little fists in the air while we had tea and attempted to communicate in a strange blend of Tamil, English and sign language.

I remembered the recording we had made of Joseph and Philomena, and put the tape on for the family to enjoy. How they giggled and laughed! When Joseph's last song was completed, I asked Edward if he would like to sing a song. At fifteen, he is leaving soon for Bangalore, where Father d'Silva has found him a job as a houseboy for a Tamil-speaking family. Regina has given her consent, and Edward is now a potential earning member of the clan. Confronted with the tape recorder, he was a bit shy, so I started the tape and went back to admire the baby. At the whispered urging of his mother and aunts, he began to sing, very nicely indeed. Music seems to run in the family. I let him hear it, and again, the results were most gratifying to all concerned. I asked what the song was about. "From the films, madam," said Regina. I reflected that he must have seen the film many times to learn so long a song; it seemed to have many verses.

Regina showed me the "formal" portrait of the first communicants taken at Doveton Studio. It showed a frozen Philomena, cheerful Robert and grinning Joseph, all arrayed in their finery, and looking very grand. Father d'Silva again.

I read a great many books in bed in the evenings, among them John Moffitt's *Journey to Gorakhpur* and three on the life of Dr. Ida Scudder, an American woman missionary who founded the first Indian hospital to train women doctors, at Vellore. She had been a Kodai resident too, according to the books, and I determined to find out where her house was. But though it was certain that India's greatest need was medical assistance, I knew that I would be of little use in that field. Education was more my line, the Nevett Fund having been founded to help children obtain technical education. More and more, however, I found myself becoming interested in the field of communications, and was genuinely puzzled to learn that the Indian Government had banned American films, posters and audiovisual materials. No one seemed to know exactly why. It seemed obvious to me that a good sound projector in every educational center was needed, and that some kind of plan should be set up with the American Library Association to ship films to India. Certainly not only education but also medicine would be thereby furthered, since through the medium of films the people could be shown more in one hour and by a more acceptable means, than they could be taught in a year. Not only a cultural exchange but a genuine service could thereby be provided, so that the necessary work of hygienic instruction, food preparation, infant care and good health habits could be given to the village people. Preventive medicine would thereby be given a tremendous boost in India. And I had always believed that if the apostle Paul were alive today, he would have been on TV, using the airwaves to spread his message of love and salvation.

I inquired at the convent about the possibility of more adequate projection equipment. The first problem seemed to be the haphazard nature of the electrical supply in the hills. So a good generator was the first requirement. After that, many kinds of electronic improvements could follow, including television and the possibility of videocassettes. But TV is a very long way off. It would have to come to Madurai first and then be beamed up to Kodai. And with the ruined nature of western TV before me, I wondered if it would ever in India be more than the toy it had degenerated into in America. No, it would have to be films, and the order seemed to be: first a good generator, then a good projector, and then the possibility of rental of good films. I decided to question the Jesuits about communications in India; I knew they had someone in either Delhi or Calcutta who was a specialist in this field.

En route back home one sunny afternoon, burdened with some books from the High Clerc Library—Graham Greene's *Travels with My Aunt* and V. S. Naipual's *A House for Mr. Biswas*—I hailed one of the local taxis and rode back. Since I had arisen at five forty-five in the morning, it was easy for me to excuse my laziness, since I had

had no nap that day. I was a bit annoyed when I got no answer to my knock but thought Regina would be sitting out in the back, gossiping as usual. But she was not there. The back door was open, so I went in and put some water on the electric plate to make tea, and settled down with my book. Some time later, she came in, plainly flustered at finding me home early; apparently she had underestimated my ability to return so soon.

"Where were you, Regina?" I asked.

"Just sitting out in the back, madam," she lied. I told her I had looked for her, that the back door had been left open. She knew that I was annoyed.

Later, drinking my tea and thinking for the hundredth time how boring this job must be for her, I resolved to try again to readjust our schedule. She really cooked only one meal a day, and that at noon. The small amount of laundry took very little time, and the cleaning required was minimal. From 2 P.M. on, she had nothing at all to do, since my evening meal was fresh fruit and tea. She would wander disconsolately around, flicking at flies and rereading old movie magazines while I worked at the desk or read. I put my teacup down and went to the kitchen to talk to her about it.

"Regina," I said, "I will be going to Madras next week and won't be back until Friday. On the following week, we will try a new schedule: you will work from nine until 2 P.M., and then go home. You can take the afternoon bus, and have the evening and night with your family. Come back on the early bus in the morning."

She was greatly agitated. Any upset in the regular routine was difficult for her to accept. "But, madam, why?"

"There just is not enough here for you to do, Regina. Besides, Philomena and Susai really should have you at home with them at night. This will work out fine, you will see." I left the kitchen, thinking that at last I might have a shred of privacy under the new arrangement. She and I found it hard to avoid one another in the small house; privacy was a value unknown to India.

My supper was served in complete silence. The papaya and pineapple, oranges, bananas and curd were all in their separate bowls, the tea in its pot, covered, and everything as usual. But I was aware of the strain in the air, and noticed that she held a corner of her sari in her mouth as she served the food.

At seven-thirty, as usual, I said good night and retired to my room, where I washed out a few things, got ready for bed, adjusted the pillows and lamp for reading, and became absorbed in the hilarious adventures of Mr. Biswas. A low, ominous buzzing interrupted the peace, however, and I located a large bee flying around the room, smacking into the rafters above and crashing against the blinds at the windows. I spent some time standing on the bed, wielding a damp towel, and finally brought him to the ground. Another good thing about Regina's new schedule, I reflected, would be a lessening of flies and bugs in the house: she often left the screen door ajar, having removed the spring, which would have slammed it shut. The result was a constant need of spraying and fly catching.

Settling down with my book again in bed, I had just succumbed to the entrancing Naipaul descriptions of Mr. Biswas and his marital adventures when a timid knock came at the bedroom door.

"Yes," I called out.

"Madam, I must talk to you." And with that Regina came in and flung herself on her knees beside the bed. I was astonished, but even more so to see that she was crying.

"What's wrong, Regina?" I asked, already sensing the cause.

"Oh, madam, I sorry. I make big mistake today. I not do this again," and here she burst into a fresh flood of tears. I was horrified. I tried to get her up off her knees, but it is a difficult maneuver when one is supine on a bed.

"There's nothing to cry over, Regina," I said. "I'm not angry with you."

But she wept on, wiping her nose on the towel she had draped over her head. "Madam no send me away. I here two months. When Madam go, I go. I not going home now."

"Regina," I said, drawing the quilt up to my chin and trying to sit up. "It will be much better for your family if you are there with them. There is not enough for you to do here; it's too boring here all afternoon and evening. I plan to pay you the same wages—just shorten the hours, that's all."

But she was now vigorously wiping her nose again, her gold nose ornament catching on the turkish towel as she rubbed. "I not go, madam. I stay here with you. Muthusamy say bad men in Poombari. Not safe alone. I stay."

I couldn't believe this at all. She was obviously using the local potato workers' strike to make me fear to be alone at night. "I'm not afraid of anything, Regina," I said. "Good locks are on the doors. I'll be fine."

But by now the tears had stopped, and a determined glare had come into the red-rimmed eyes. "Madam not be alone. Me stay. When madam go, I go." And putting her head down to my hands, she again repeated her apology and sorrow at her "mistake." "I not do that again, madam," she said.

There was no way I could convince her that my decision was not a punishment. And the thought of going back to that one-room hovel was in no way intriguing to her. I thought of the home at Shembag. Philomena and Susai were not really deserted: grandmothers and aunts lived in rooms adjacent. The emotional scene was very tiring for me. "All right, Regina," I said finally. "You stay here."

She tried to kiss my hand, but I got it back on my book. "Good night, madam. Thank you, madam," said Regina, getting up from the floor.

"Goodnight, Regina," I said.

CHAPTER 21

Ordination in Madras

Basking in the cool ghats, I heard the faint echoes of visitors from the plains complaining of the ferocious heat that now engulfed the country there. Some said "120 degrees . . . scorching . . . impossible," and I made frequent trips to my little wall thermometer, which seldom changed from 70 to 75 degrees. The ordination of Kanikairaj, which I had planned to attend when it was first set for possible February, and then March, was finally moved to April; I had simply put it out of my mind as a possibility. My health was stable; I had still one month of my visit remaining, and did not want to jeopardize it with possible illness brought on by heat stroke. I sent Kanikairaj a letter explaining all of this, and had already sent his gift, the embroidered vestments, and a check for fifty dollars from the Fund.

But he wrote back: "I have written to Father Nevett also to come for the ordination. I hope to have him here. Kindly, you also come. The way you have expressed yourself in your letter, it seems to me that you say, if weather is bad, be saying excuse. But I kindly request you to make it a point to come by all means for the ordination."

I knew Father Nevett was not able to come nearly two thousand miles to Madras, and began to despair of getting my point across to Kanikairaj. In the days before the event, I found myself slowly changing my mind. Examining the invitation again, I found that the ordination would be held in the evening, hopefully after the sun had gone down, with the First Mass fixed at six-thirty the following morning. I thought of the tremendous importance of this day in the life of the slim young man, and his earnest desire to become a very good priest. I thought of the Connemara and the air conditioning there. I thought of the long ride down the ghat road and the uncertainty of train travel, particularly overnight in India. I honestly

believed Kanikairaj must be praying for me to come; I also wondered
how to spell his name. His invitation spelled it S. Kanikkai Raj, and
he himself spelled it without the extra *k*. About two weeks before
the event, I decided to go.

I went down to the train office in Kodai, stepped across the piles
of gravel and sand optimistically awaiting some building project, and
made my way into the dim interior. I said to the man behind the
bars: "I would like to book a ticket for Madras, first class." I told
him the date of my journey, and inquired about costs and details. I
was given the usual form to fill out, with my name, address, require-
ments (ladies' section, first class, lower berth), when I found that no
private compartments were available. The cost of the train ticket included the bus transport down to the train in the plains. "We will
send a wire to Kodai Road and make your reservation, madam. You
come in two days."

But when I mentioned my plan to others in town, they said I
should have requested an air-conditioned compartment. I had not,
since this undreamed-of luxury had not been waved before me.
When I returned to the railroad office, stepping over still more piles
of gravel and sand, I mentioned this new whimsy to the man behind
the bars.

"I will wire them again, madam. You come back in two days."
Two days, and several large piles of gravel later, I found that they
could not fulfill my request for air conditioning, because there were a
limited number of these tickets available and all had been booked by
the Lions or the Moose or some such organization. I inquired about
the sleeping arrangements. There were none; one either arranged the
rental of a bedroll from the authorities at Kodai Road or brought appropriate bedding along. I decided in favor of the latter. Ann had
made me a beautiful little patch-work pillow, and I had a nice cotton throw, gift of Brother Paranjothi, which could cover the seat as
well as me.

Thus it was that on the day before the ordination I had my bags
packed with clothing to see me through the next few days, including
my travel iron and hair dryer, as well as bedding, pillow, a parcel to
be delivered to the Presentation Convent at Madras, and my movie
camera and film. We had taken the precaution of using up all the
vegetables in the house before I left, so the larder was empty; Regina
was to decamp for Shembaganur on the same bus. I would continue

on down to catch the 8 P.M. train for Madras. I left my passport and most of my money at the house, all locked up, and brought about four hundred rupees with me in a little bag around my neck. Clearly before my mind was the memory of travelers' tales in which night-time robberies had been so successfully carried out that the victim slept through a thoroughly clean sweep of all his possessions. It would certainly be an adventure! Winnie had been alerted, and wrote saying she would visit me in the air-conditioned hotel; Kani-kairaj responded that he was overjoyed, and that his parents would want me to come to their house too. He inquired again if Father Nevett was going to be there.

The bus ride down the ghat road was never pleasant. This one was further tainted by the additional charges slapped on my two small bags. "For the weight of the luggage, madam." The luggage, includ-ing the camera, weighed sixteen kilograms. The train permitted sixty kilograms with no additional charge, but one had to take this bus to the train. I paid, grinding my teeth in fury. My anger was not mollified by the discovery that no one else had been thus taxed, though they struggled aboard with mammoth bags of potatoes, and three men ahead of me had two huge suitcases each. The rule seemed to apply to foreigners only.

Having selected my seat, about three back on the side opposite the driver, where only one vacancy was left next to me, I settled down to ruminate, avoid the bus-stop beggars, and ponder my sanity. Long minutes passed as passengers changed seats, rearranged sacks of comestibles, got off, got on, called Tamil messages to family members still in the road, and opened lunches. A lady behind me hummed a pretty tune, plainly pleased at the prospect of travel. Regina was still outside the bus, awaiting the permission of the driver to board, a permission that could only be granted after all the "reserved seats" had been occupied. A ritual bottle of water was poured into the radiator. The driver eased the bus slowly from the depot. Regina waved. The bus was half empty.

"Next bus in one hour, madam; I take that one," she called to me.

Ten minutes later, at Mungigal, the village farther down the road, we stopped and admitted some forty-five men and women. These clambered aboard with loud cries, wielding baskets, gunnysacks and children riding on hips. When the scramble for the few seats con-cluded and about twenty persons were straddling the sacks in the aisle, a very loud fight erupted. Ladies in the seat across the aisle from me shouted imprecations at other ladies farther back in the bus. Tamil may be a musical language. Tamil screamed from throats corded and fierce, sounds like the cry of strange and exotic seabirds. The driver, pinned in the cockpit, was a noncombatant, nonchalant. The conductor, at the rear door, struggling to eject the excess passengers, bore the full brunt of the battle. One of the contestants, a young woman in a scarlet sari, wearing beautiful golden earrings, knelt in the seat facing her tormentors and gave full vent to her vocabulary of what I assume was less than ladylike invective. The din arose to a pitch that threatened my eardrums. I turned and surprised myself by shouting, "For God's sake, sit down and shut up!" It had no effect whatever, except on the frightened gentleman behind me, who raised a cautionary finger to his lips and his eyes heavenward. I withdrew from the conflict. Fifteen minutes later, the bus lunged forward again, minus the excess hopefuls.

But, five minutes later, we stopped again. It was time for the ritual head count and cross-check. The conductor leaped across baskets and hardware, calling out figures to the driver, who tallied them with a stubby pencil in his dog-eared log. The bus lurched forward again.

The young lady in red draped her body gracefully across the aisle and placed her head in the lap of the toothless granny next to me, a difficult feat, since granny was already holding a baby. Room was made, however, as I pressed myself against the side of the bus. I inquired what the difficulty was.

"Stomach pains," said the toothless one. A veteran of car sickness myself, I speculated on the possibility of heavy vomiting, and moved my luggage out of range. It proved to be a prudent gesture. The lady in red was violently sick all over saris, baskets, the small baby and a sack of potatoes. Helping hands, so recently raised in fists, now carried her bodily over four persons to a seat next to a window, where she continued the illness in more suitable fashion, her upper half draped outside. Ten miles farther down the ghat, a sympathetic woman in a yellow sari also joined in, at the next window. The double bill delighted the passengers, providing exactly the restorative they needed after the fight; general laughter greeted each new heave. The bus bumped along, honking merrily at each turn, the red and yellow saris rose and fell rhythmically, former enemies chatted amiably with one another, alarmingly naked babies were lifted back and forth over the seats to be fed, petted and jiggled out of their usual placidity. Thus misfortune makes all men brothers.

The infant next to me placed a tiny, braceleted foot in my lap, companionably, and nodded off to sleep. The last rays of daylight, touching with gold the thatched huts and terraced hills, switched off like the familiar power failures. There is no twilight in India. The sun plunges to the horizon with the alacrity of a shopkeeper closing his stall in the bazaar for tea. Sufficient unto the day, says the sun, and departs for more promising climes.

At Uttu everyone but me got out to shop. Jackfruits, obscene and bile green, bulged in the poisonous neon light of the bazaar and proved the favorite item on the supper menu. The shoppers returned to their seats, laden with food wrapped in plantain leaves and juggling glasses of coffee. The picnic began in earnest. The crone next to me, deftly wielding a finger containing some pink paste, dipped this onto what looked like violet leaves, rolled them into a compact ball, and popped them into her mouth, chewing ecstatically. I discovered it was a confection wrapped in betel leaves. The baby slept on, undisturbed.

Plantain leaves were unrolled next. These contained the jackfruit's interior, which looked like jasmine flowers, though sticky and moist. The fruit had to be freed from white pods with the fingers. The crone was an expert, I noted; she held the pink-pasted finger aloft and worked deftly with the other nine. Having operated on several pods, she offered them around the bus. I declined; the lady in red, having recovered sufficiently to sit up and take nourishment, ingested an alarming quantity of these. Small black hands shoved additional supplies through the bus window. I passed it on to the excited picnickers. A vendor boarded the bus, closely followed by the inevitable depot beggar, and hawked his minuscule oranges. No one bought.

A goat came alongside, shrewdly awaiting the rain of plantain leaves that would shortly fall to him. The timid soul poked me in the back. I turned to find an orange being offered. My appetite, however, seemed gone, perhaps forever. I thanked him anyway. Three horses paused for a small conference outside on the road. One bore on his back the terrible sores caused by saddles and indolent owners. The other two seemed to be offering condolences, nodding their heads and venturing philosophical opinions on reincarnational possibilities next time around. The engine coughed to life, and the horses moved prudently to the side of the road and gazed at the passengers scrambling back to their seats with something like pity. The horn blared a warning. We were off again.

The train depot at Kodai Road boasted a FIRST CLASS WAITING ROOM, and there I found two American ladies. We chatted awhile, swatting mosquitoes and comparing notes. They were, however, traveling second class. "There is no first class in India," they informed me.

I found my compartment, where a small Anglo-Indian woman awaited me. The railroad had issued two lower berth tickets for this compartment. She eyed me speculatively, to determine if I would give in and climb to the perilous perch above. I was not in a generous mood and was on the point of summoning the conductor to see what could be done about it when she said quite cheerfully, "No problem. I'll sleep on the floor." It seemed a drastic solution, since she had a ticket, but she assured me that she would be quite comfortable. It developed that what she had was a free pass, due to her husband's former job with the railroad. She was dizzy in high places, she said, and preferred the floor anyway. With no further ado, she spread a cloth on the floor, and arranged herself on it. I spread my cloth on the lower berth, got out my pillow and flashlight and removed my shoes. The conductor appeared at the door to instruct me to close and lock both windows.

"But why?" I asked. "It's terribly warm in here." But he was gone.

The Anglo-Indian lady supplied the reason from her long experience with the railroads. "Rogues come near the train at night, when we are at stations, and steal." I closed and locked the windows. The ride was very bumpy, the closed-up room very warm and the night of record length. At four-thirty I was peering out into the dim passing landscape, surprising men in their early eliminations and householders sweeping their thresholds. We pulled into Tambaram, and out again. In a little grove of trees entire families were awaking from the night's rest. The cooking pots, already blazing, lit the scene as we passed. In a river two men washed buffalos. On a station platform white-clad Brahmins with sandalwood-pasted foreheads awaited mysterious events. We passed Mambalam Station. Housewives in small huts tossed water aloft on the red dust before their doorways. Closer to Madras, commuter trains pulled alongside, with hundreds of neatly dressed city workers standing in the open doorways. Kodambakkam Station. Man milking cow in front yard. Chetpat Station. Madras at 6:30 A.M. Found a cab and entered the Connemara with the hushed gratitude of a pilgrim entering Mecca.

Mr. Thip Thop was pleased to see madam again. He had personally delivered my note of instruction to the office of Pan Am, and expressed great pleasure at the news that my bags had finally arrived in Kodai. I found my room huge, handsome, cool and clean. I bathed, breakfasted and went to see Sister Stella again, in her lovely workroom at the School for the Deaf and Blind. The girls all made their mute signs of welcome, and bent again over the looms of exquisite embroidery.

Sister Stella shared with me her own favorite travel tip: Tie a string to the suitcase at one end, and the ankle at the other. Anyone tampering with the suitcase in the dark will cause a telltale tug on the string, which will awaken the traveler. She told me of one nun who did not follow that excellent advice, and arrived at Delhi to find that she had been robbed of her suitcase, purse and shoes.

"How could that have been done without awakening her?" I asked.

"They sprinkle a powder near the face. Sister said it was a drug— she had a hard time awakening at Delhi," said Sister Stella. I was glad the rogues had not found me during the night.

Returning to the Connemara via rickshaw, I saw the Victoria Institute, on Mount Road, and paused there for some purchases. Coat racks of elephant trunks, elegantly carved and quite inexpensive, were added to my Christmas purchases, as well as some rosewood paperweights, an Indian doll in a lovely sari for Miss Laura's collection, and two sandalwood fans I planned to use at the ordination. Most of the purchases went directly to America.

Sister Fredericka came to the hotel to visit me and to receive her parcel from the nuns at the Presentation Convent. She was a dear lady, Indian from Goa but with an Irish accent from the years of association with the brogue. Winnie arrived; the two were old friends. We had tea together; then Sister departed, and Winnie and I, armed with our fans, took off for the ordination. En route Winnie told me of her early train rides, third class, when she first came to India. She would enter the third-class compartment with about forty women, and climb immediately up to the luggage rack near the ceiling, where she could have a bit of cramped privacy. On the first experience, however, her shoes were stolen. She had thoughtlessly removed them before ascending to her little wire perch.

St. Francis Xavier Church, scene of the ordination, is situated on a very large, sand-covered plaza. The steeple of the church had lines of flags affixed, which fluttered down in graceful arcs to lampposts many hundreds of feet distant. The blackened statue of the great Xavier himself, arms extended over the scene, dominated the entire plaza from his perch, high up on the steeple. Before the church doors, an outdoor altar had been erected, with a platform large enough to hold several hundred people. In front of this and fanning out to each side, rows of chairs had been placed on the sand. These were already filled as we alighted from the cab. In one section, about one hundred priests were seated, dressed in identical golden vestments. The white-robed Salesian sisters, all native-born Indians, occupied another section of the outdoor church, while all around them the bright and festive saris of the family and friends of the two ordinands fluttered in the evening breeze.

Schoolchildren in uniforms and many observers from the town crowded in the aisles and watched the solemn event with awe. Archbishop Arulappa, seated before the altar, conducted the ceremony in Tamil. A choir sang lovely hymns. The sky turned from azure to a deeper blue, and some pink wisps of clouds arose behind the steeple as the night breeze from the Bay of Bengal softly rippled over the assembly, lifting veil edges and wafting incense from the altar down to the people. Two lone, white-clad figures knelt before the Archbishop. Kanikairaj and his classmate were blessed, anointed and ordained priests together, and given the tremendous responsibility and charge to live holy lives and to be men of God for all time.

The words of the ceremony, I could only guess at, though everyone else could understand Tamil. I was thus free to marvel at the magnificent scene before me, and to mark the huge crows that came, first in small numbers, fluttering and gliding high overhead. As the choir sang, the busy crows flew off to tell their friends about the free concert, and returned with hundreds. These perched on every available ledge of the church and lampposts, their black silhouettes inky against the darkening blue. High atop a neighboring building, a small crowd of onlookers stood to watch the pageantry below.

A young man found me in the crowd and handed me a tray containing the neatly folded vestments that were my gift to Kanikairaj.

I had no time to wonder how he had found me, for he was telling me that I must offer them at the altar.

"When?" I asked. But he was gone.

One of the sisters turned toward me and smiled. "During the Offertory Procession," she said.

So, during the Offertory, I stepped across the countless saris on the sand, and made my way through the crowd up to the altar. I mounted the stairs with my gift, and placed it in the hands of the Archbishop, bowed, and made my way back again. Many others did the same, though I was unable to see what they had brought in their hands. Doubtless the gifts were rice, and plantains, in addition to the bread and wine to be used at the Mass.

The choir sang again, Kanikairaj and the other young man were clothed in dazzling golden vestments, and the Mass proceeded through the prayers of the Preface and the Consecration. At Communion time the huge crowd were all participants, being offered the Host by the multitude of priests, each standing at various points around the altar. By now the sky was black, lit only by the early stars.

The heat of the day remained in the sand underfoot. The final prayers of the Mass were sung, and the ceremony concluded. The Archbishop left the altar, but the two new priests, now divested of their chasubles, sat with solemnity in chairs facing the crowd, while numerous speeches in Tamil were given by important members of the parish community. Winnie and I were led across the plaza to a spot where we would be eventually brought in to dinner. A crowd of small boys followed us around, trying out their English and reveling in the general festivities.

Dinner in the parish hall was served by the ladies of the parish, who had planned and cooked it as well. Large plantain leaves formed the dishes for most of the guests, though Winnie and I were given porcelain plates. Rice, curry, fruit and soft drinks were served. Kanikairaj and the other new priest flanked the Archbishop at the head table. Winnie and I chatted awhile with the other guests, all priests of the diocese. We were the only women guests.

We made our way outdoors again, where Kanikairaj detached himself from the crowd and came to greet me. I offered my sincere congratulations. He brought me to meet the Archbishop, who proved a charming man. We spoke for a moment or two and had our photos taken together with Kanikairaj and his parents. Winnie and I scuffed across the sand to the road again, found a rickshaw and departed, she for her house in Rosary Church Lane and I for the Connemara and bed.

The first Solemn Mass was at six-fifteen the following morning, so I arranged for an early cab. We found Fatima Church, Kanikairaj's home parish, near Loyola College. I was ushered in with great ceremony by a young man in white who seemed to be waiting for me. He brought me to the first pew, thereby dashing any hopes that I might slip outdoors in case the heat became too oppressive. A little choir group consisting of a violin, organ, two tablas and four singers tuned up near the altar and softly turned pages in earnest conference. The Mass began at six-thirty, with a procession from the rear of the church led by acolytes, a cross-bearer, eight priests in gold vestments among whom I recognized my good friend Father Varaprasadam, and finally, wearing my gift of vestments, Kanikairaj.

He came to the altar of God, and it was plain that God had given joy to his youth. The dark head bowed in fervent prayer as he turned to face his new life. His voice rose in confident, steady tones as he began the Tamil prayers of this, his First Mass. For the remainder of his natural life, Kanikairaj will begin each day with the same sacrifice. I prayed it will be with the same fervor and joy as on this day of days. The lovely white silk vestments, given stability only by the wide red velvet strip down the front and back, and bearing on the velvet the golden embroidered symbols of the Mass and of Christ fitted the slim frame very well. I made a mental note to thank Sister Stella again for her excellent taste in selecting these splendid vestments for the new priest.

The sermon was delivered in Tamil by the former pastor of Fatima Church, who claimed the honor of having sent Kanikairaj to the seminary. He spoke for forty-five minutes (by my watch). Apparently his sermon held tremendous interest for the congregation, who leaned forward in eagerness to catch each word. I experimented with various devices to discipline my facial muscles, continually fighting a tremendous desire to yawn. Beads of perspiration trickled down from my hair and gathered on my neck. I mastered the impulse to disturb the spell of the speaker with anything as crude as a facial mop-up. My yoga training came to the fore and won for me the necessary control.

Across the aisle from me, I could sense the tremendous emotion of the family. His mother, a tiny woman with a red sari, knelt nearest the aisle. She trembled, clasping her dark hands tightly to steady herself. Kanikairaj was her Benjamin, youngest of five children. At Communion time, the sacred words of consecration having been pronounced for the first time, she was led to the altar by an acolyte to receive Christ at the hands of her son. She knelt to receive Him, and my heart turned over in the shared glory of that moment. The rest of us stood, as is the custom now, but our hearts were prostrated before the mystery of God made man.

At the conclusion of the Mass, before the final blessing, Kanikairaj gave a short message, again in Tamil. He pointed to the former pastor, to Father Varaprasadam, and to me, during this speech, and I heard the word "benefactor" linked with my name. Afterward, in the bright sunlight of the churchyard, several priests came up to shake my hand as the "benefactor" of their friend Kanikairaj. The pastor, a hospitable Jesuit named J. S. Jeyapathi, invited me to breakfast with the newly ordained, so I dismissed the cab that had been waiting for two hours. As I turned to join the breakfast group, my foot betrayed me in the confusion of sun and uneven ground, and down I went in a heap. Gentle hands lifted me up as I cursed my clumsy fall and viewed the skinned knee. One priest, genuinely concerned, asked, "How old are you, madam?" It restored my humor.

"Father," I told him, "you should never ask a woman her age." But I told him, all the same, since it was fresh in my mind. My birthday had been just the day before. The nuns put some antiseptic and a Band-Aid on my knee. The stocking with its gaping hole was mercifully covered by my skirt. Breakfast was very nice. I was seated across from Kanikairaj this time, and told him how beautiful had been the Mass and the ordination ceremony. His happiness was so transparent and infectious, it filled the room. The Salesian sisters served the breakfast, pausing often to hover over the new priest in happy anticipation of his needs.

I inquired about a cab, but Father Jeyapathi said the school had planned an entertainment for Kanikairaj and invited me to remain for this function. The day was growing much warmer, my knee was stinging, and I longed for the cool Connemara, but I stayed. I'm glad I did, for the children's entertainment was charming and inventive and added much to the spirit of this day. Four youngsters, dressed to the teeth, enacted the parable of the ten talents. When the man who had buried his talent came forward to present it to his master, he was dismissed with a passionate wave of the hand. The effect was electrifying since the hand also swatted the mike, which suddenly gained an electronic whistle. Everyone clapped wildly.

Kanikairaj and I were garlanded with beautiful pink roses, presented by a tiny boy who was scared out of his mind by the enormity of this role. Kanikairaj whipped his off immediately, and placed it over my head. Tremendous cheers. Thus, buried in flowers, their fragrant petals falling down my skirt and into my shoes, I sat on display for a time, and then, quietly, during a subsequent dance number, removed the lovely garlands and carefully placed them at my side.

One of the teachers spoke, pointing out a fact I had not realized: Kanikairaj was the first boy from that school to be ordained a priest. Kanikairaj responded with a crisp talk, tailored to the schoolchildren, on the new life he had embraced, and asked for prayers that he would be a good priest, faithful to his calling throughout a lifetime. He asked how many of the little boys were planning to become priests. Every hand shot upward. A mighty harvest indeed, it appeared. I was asked to say a few words, which I did, abandoning the performing mike entirely. I thanked the children for the wonderful entertainment, told of my joy in the ordination and First Mass, and descended back to the audience. The event closed with a solemn singing of the Papal Anthem.

Tea in the rectory followed. I asked about a cab again. Kanikairaj had arranged for one that would bring us to Pushpanagar to greet his parents and family in their home and then take me to the hotel.

Pushpanagar had changed little since my last visit. Cattle, dogs, children and crows still choked the narrow areaways between the small huts. Naked babies played in the dust as our cab threaded its way, honking constantly, to the home of Kanikairaj. From every doorway, people rushed out to wave to the new priest, and many children ran along behind the cab. We drew up before a canopy that had been stretched across two huts, thereby creating a pleasant, shaded space about fifteen feet wide and some thirty feet long. We entered this corridor and made our way along ranks of smiling relatives and children amid the clamor of excited voices. Before the door of Kanikairaj's home, we stopped. Chairs were fetched, dusted and graciously offered. The dim light around us was lit with shining eyes and beautiful smiles. All the cousins, nieces, uncles, aunts, and neighbors gathered around Kanikairaj, touching his hands shyly and beaming their joy and happiness. It was truly a wonderful moment. I am happy I did not miss it.

Kanikairaj's mother came through the doorway, and bowed in my direction to greet me. I overcame the desire to put my arms around her, and contented myself with touching her in greeting. His father, too, was there, hands clasped in Indian courtesy and grace. It was beautiful to see their joy. Someone—an uncle, I think—called me "second mother" and posed me with the parents for historic photographs. The sun, thwarted by the canopy, had not penetrated the festive corridor, and I wondered if the photo would be successful.

One of the relatives gave me a brief sketch of the family history, which was not Tamil, I discovered, but Telegu. They had migrated to Madras years before, attracted by opportunities for employment.

A timid hand touched my shoulder, and when I turned, I recognized two widows whom Ted Huebsch had been aiding for years with his monthly checks. They told me, through an interpreter, that Stella was working now, and Arokiamary and Santimal expressed their gratitude for all the help they had received. I told them I would tell their benefactor in the States.

How things come full circle! I had first visited Pushpanagar in 1971, with Father Nevett. And seven years later, because of Father Nevett's tremendous love and interest, these many lives had been transformed and lifted up; this happy day was the culmination of long years of loving effort. Kanikairaj was the first priest ever in that community of people. He would be leading them from this day forward toward untold vistas of new life and hope.

I was handed a coconut with a straw stuck in the middle, which I sipped gratefully. It was cool and pleasant, this coconut drink. I thought of my beloved Al, whose entire working life had been bound up in the importing of coconut from the Philippines. All the edges of the circle had thus been drawn together. The cab awaited me. I bid them all good-bye and left with the happy cries of the children of Pushpanagar in my ears and a tremendous gratitude to God in my heart for all I had been privileged to witness that day.

The train ride back promised to be peaceful. I found, upon examination of the printed list in Egmore Station that I had been assigned a two-person compartment, lower berth, and that the upper berth was vacant. It would be great, I thought, to relax in privacy for a night's ride back to Kodai Road. But it was not to be. As I sat in solitary splendor, my bags at my feet, a sister poked her head in the doorway with an anxious smile. Behind her I could see the conductor and a small girl with long pigtails. "I wonder," the nun began uncertainly, "would you mind very much sharing this section with a child? We did not have time to get a reservation for her, and must bring her with us." I closed my book and said I did not mind. The child entered.

"She is Elisabeth Rani, and she will sleep in the upper berth," said the sister in a heavy German accent. The conductor, beaming in the doorway, assured the nun she had made a wise choice, as I was a very nice lady. I was moved to inquire how he had come by the information but refrained in time, realizing suddenly that my "niceness" consisted in not making a fuss when I had been thus robbed of privacy. The sister moved Elisabeth Rani's suitcase in, appraised me a bit anxiously again, and finally left for her compartment forward.

Elisabeth Rani sat down next to me, having arranged her two oranges and a small kit containing toothbrush and towel neatly on the folding table near the window. "I am an adopted daughter of the sisters," she told me, leaning a bit toward me to identify herself. "They brought me from Tuticorin when I was a small baby."

I found this interesting, and we chatted about her life in the convent, where she had many "mothers" but one in particular, Mother Elisabeth, who was a superior of the Sisters of St. Ann. They were a Swiss order, I discovered. Elisabeth Rani, at fifteen, was a wonderful blend of innocence and character. Her speech was refined and soft, with unexpected twists and turns that could only have been echoes of the sisters. We were passing a desolate village at the time, and I turned from the depressing poverty of the mud huts and squalor to express my sadness at the sight of so much destitution.

Elisabeth Rani demurred, "But the little huts are really very cozy and homely. The people love them."

She herself, however, had a room of her own. She had completed tenth standard, was very good at science, English and history, though a bit weak in maths. (Indians always pluralize math.) Her plans included college, and then a course in nursing and midwifery. I asked if the sisters would find her a husband.

"Yes, I suppose so," she said, but added, "when I complete my education."

I told her of my children and grandchildren, and she extracted the details of my homeland and visit to India. Finally, at a loss for further items of interest, she inquired, "Would you care to see my hobby?" I said I would. She removed from the neat suitcase a metal candy box from Switzerland, large and decorated with flowers. The contents proved to be many colored pencils and pens, some writing pads, and at the very bottom, a pile of clippings from magazines. These clippings were lovingly placed in my hands.

"My hobby is wineglasses," she said seriously. And wineglasses there were—hundreds of them—all neatly scissored from Swiss magazines, held aloft by manicured hands or grasped by male fists while messages proclaiming the virtues of Cutty Sark and exotic cordials streamed under the colored pictures. Elisabeth Rani leaned forward to receive from my hands each precious picture, as I commented, exclaimed, and otherwise expressed appreciation of the shining glassware.

"Have you seen Waterford crystal?" I asked her. She had not. I told her of the wonders of that cut glass and wondered if I could send her some *New Yorker* clippings of their ads when I got back to America.

She was pleased by my interest, and excited at the prospect of fresh examples of wineglasses. "You know, my friends call me the class poet," she ventured shyly. I asked if she wrote poetry. No, but she loved nature. And from another fold in the candy box came forth many lovely photographs of sunsets, sunrises, birds, flowers and landscapes. Also shiny cars, wristwatches, engagement rings, boats on blue lakes, and perfume bottles.

"I am mad for perfume," she explained. I gave her a small vial I happened to have with me. She was charmed.

"At home I have to go to bed at eight each night," she confided, "but I could stay up until midnight!"

"Not tonight," I said firmly. "I am very tired, and need my rest. I've had a very busy day."

She accepted this with good grace, and climbed aloft with a little book to read. There was a light up there, and I fully expected her to read until midnight, but after I had spread out my cotton quilt on the seat, adjusted my pillow and wound my watch, her light was already off, and a gentle noise suggested slumber. I left the windows open, defying all rogues. It was too hot to close them. But I failed to fall asleep. The train bumped along over the rocky roadbed, my sore knee made it impossible for me to get comfortable on the hard berth, and I passed another long night counting my blessings and watching the stars hang low over the palm trees.

At three, four, and four-thirty I consulted my watch. And at five, as I finally dozed a bit, a small warm body perched alongside me on the berth. I opened one eye. It was Elisabeth Rani.

"I believe," said she sleepily, "if we wash our faces we shall then feel quite fresh." There was definitely an echo of Mother Elisabeth in this sensible statement. I surrendered, and went to the lavatory to wash my face.

The train lavatory was innocent of toilet paper but boasted an innovation never before seen in facilities I had traveled: there was a shower. It sprouted from the ceiling of the room, serving two purposes. The traveler could bathe completely, and wash the floor all in one operation. The damp floor suggested I was not the first to enter that morning. I rolled up the cuffs of my slacks to prevent them from getting wet, and gingerly washed my face at the sink. With water from my thermos, I also brushed my teeth. Glancing at the Indian-style toilet, I promised my kidneys relief at some future date, and plodded back to the compartment.

Back in the cabin I watched Elisabeth Rani unbraid her long black hair. She combed it carefully, one side at a time, measuring its length across her small chest and stomach. Finishing up the ends with rubber bands, she departed with her wash cloth to the lavatory. She returned, also quite fresh.

Then there was the question of her two oranges. "I can eat one, but shall have to give the other one away," she said. "To whom can I give it?" I didn't know at the moment. We split the peeled orange, and she shoved the peelings through the window bars. Trichy Station hove into view, and we stopped there for a full twenty-five minutes. A boy came alongside, selling glasses of hot coffee. Elisabeth Rani pressed the orange into his surprised hand.

"I suppose I shall be quite bored in Kodai," she said, quite unconvincingly.

"But you can hike, sketch, ride horses and visit me," I said. She made careful notes on how to reach Snyder "B." The sister popped her head in again, plainly relieved to find Elisabeth Rani still safe and happily chatting with me. She hovered over her ewe lamb, instructing her in the exit procedure, now imminent. The train paused at Kodai Road for only three minutes, she said, and we must be ready to hop off quickly.

A short time later, on the platform, we bid one another good-bye. I found a cab, pointed the driver in the direction of the hills and ascended into the cool air. It had been a worthwhile journey.

CHAPTER 22

The Water Diviner

Water divining, or dousing, had always been, in my lexicon, classified in the same dubious category as bilocation, fortune-telling and astral projection. I had read *Malabar Farm*, by Louis Bromfield, and knew of his experience in that field, but this evidence had been filed in a remote corner of my mind, under phone numbers and birthday data. Had I been asked point-blank, I would have replied that I put no credence in the possibility of finding water in that exotic manner, particularly when the water tap was so conveniently placed in my home. But I soon found that in India, where wells were founts of life for entire villages, the pinpointing of underground springs was of paramount importance. This process was usually placed in the hands of an experienced douser.

So when Father Montaud announced one morning that he had been asked to find a well in the hills, I questioned him closely. I found that he had discovered over one thousand wells in his time and that he enjoyed a reputation for water divining among the people. I immediately changed a luncheon date to join him in the expedition, in order to see how it was done.

A car arrived for me at 9:30 A.M., and Father Montaud and the prospective well owner drove me to a section, some miles from the bazaar, that had been British headquarters during the Second World War and that was now Holiday Home Resort. It consisted of a large number of low whitewashed bungalows nestled in a lush valley and surrounded by huge trees. A small river bisected the property. In all, it seemed to contain about thirty or forty acres. They already had water, of course, but because of the present use as a hotel, needed more for the guests as well as for the potato fields and orchard.

We entered through an iron gate and began walking toward a

grassy knoll under some fruit trees. Father Montaud was carrying a small metal box containing his materials, "witnesses" he called them. He removed a pendulum suspended from a copper chain and walked ahead alone. The owner and I followed at a respectful distance. Suddenly Father assumed a strange position, body bent slightly forward, the left arm raised before him, with the hand relaxed. The right arm, bent at the elbow to permit the pendulum to hang freely from his fingers, formed a right angle with his body. He might have been advancing toward a dancing partner. His step was deliberate, one shoe placed exactly in front of the other, his white cassock flapping in the wind. A black felt hat shaded his eyes, but I could see that he was concentrating intensely as he walked in this queer position. He changed direction several times, and then registered disappointment.

"There is nothing here," he said to the owner, turning his open palm expressively from side to side slowly. There were plenty of other places to try, however, and he moved silently along, up and down little hills, the pendulum swaying in a forward and backward direction as he went.

In a little open clearing, some one hundred feet from the first spot, he suddenly noted a different reaction from the pendulum. With a smile he turned, deliberately noted the exact location, and slowly advanced on this spot again. Sure enough, before my startled eyes, the pendulum changed from a back-and-forth motion and assumed a swift clockwise spin, very fast. I was about to comment when I noticed Father was now counting: "one, two, three, four," and so on up to twenty.

"There is water here, at twenty feet," he announced. A farm worker drove a stake into the ground at this point, while Father opened the small box to remove his "witnesses."

The witnesses turned out to be small glass vials containing earth, sand, mica, rock, gravel, lime and water. Protruding from each cork was a small wire. Father now selected the earth-filled vial and held it in his right hand, grasping the wire between his thumb and fingers as he again held the pendulum over the spot. I noticed he was very careful to face a particular direction as he did so. The pendulum turned quickly in a clockwise direction as he counted. "There is about eight feet of earth here, first," he said. Then grasping the lime vial, he determined the amount of lime that would be encountered. Then the amount of hard rock. The owner happily made notations

on a bit of paper, carefully noting the number of feet to be exca-
vated through twenty feet of material before the water would be
reached.

Now Father began walking away from the stake in a certain direction, measuring with his shoes the number of feet as he walked and
holding out the pendulum before him over the ground. It continued
to sway as he walked. When it began to spin again, he stopped and
made a calculation. Traversing the ground in the opposite direction
from the stake, he repeated the maneuver. Finally he pushed back
his hat and said to the owner, "The well will yield one hundred fifty
gallons per hour." I wanted to applaud, so marvelous did I find this
feat. But the owner had seen Father in action many times before
and took it in stride.

"Just come over here, Father; there are two more places where I
need wells. Will you look at them, too?" Father was willing, and we
returned to the car and drove to another section of Holiday Home,
near the river. Potatoes were being cultivated there. Father discovered a well fed by three springs, which would be able to irrigate the
potato fields already planted and provide fresh water for the hotel
guests.

Higher up, where the pear trees grew in soft clay, he found a third
well, this one fed by two springs. It was all in a day's work. The digging would begin in a week. The owner shook his hand, and we
drove back to my little house for lunch.

We sat before the fireplace in Snyder "B." Regina clattered pots
and pans in the kitchen, preparing our rice and curry. My mind was
buzzing with questions.

"How long have you been water divining?" I asked him eagerly.

"I began in 1930, when I took up the Kallers' reclamation. We
had been asked to help by the government, and of course they meant
educationally, economically, by all possible means. I took up water
divining to help those people."

I remembered that the Kallers were the robber caste he had
worked among for seventeen years. They were a lazy people, having
relied for so long on thieving for their livelihood that their land,
though fertile, was quite barren.

"But there was plenty of water there, underground. The ground is
calcareous, filled with lime. Drinking it gives urinary trouble. But
they needed water for farming, so I began. From 1930 to 1947, in

those seventeen years, I found five or six hundred wells for them, practically all of them successful." He leaned back in his chair, unzipped his tan jacket and looked around my little house with appreciation. "This is a very nice house," he said. "It seems quite warm, too. My room is very, very cold."

La Providence, I knew, was on the cliff side of Kodai, subjected to all the fog and mists that arise out of that two-mile canyon from the plains below. But I pressed him to continue about his wonderful talent.

"After a while, my reputation grew among the people. They called me from all over Madurai District. I was continually invited to come and find wells in many villages. That brought my total to more than one thousand two hundred wells."

I was about to inquire whether or not he charged for this service, when he answered the question for me.

"I was building a church at Attur, twelve miles from Dindigul, so I would say to them: 'For myself I am not asking anything. But I ask something for my church.' I managed to build a church from that money. The cost of the church came to one lakh. Not all from water divining, of course, but a great deal of the building fund came from that." He stroked his gray beard in happy recollection of the successful building project.

"Who taught you to douse?" I asked him.

"It's a family affair; my father was doing it with a rod. There is in France a special tree. The branches are very flexible. You take a branch like this"—and here he described a branch with a right angle —"and you place the ends of the branch in your palms like this." He lifted three fingers over an imaginary branch, with the thumb and little finger under it. "You keep it straight out before you, and you go over the ground. When you come to water, it dips."

"You mean, it actually goes down by itself?"

"Yes," he said, "by itself. Of course, it's more difficult to count, using the branch. I use the pendulum; for me it is better."

He described the method he used to train himself. I could picture the scene; a young Jesuit in a small village hut, with a table before him cleared of all except the thing he was training himself to find, water. Slowly, with the pendulum before him, he walks around the table, noting any small change in the action of the pendulum. Hour after hour, day after day, week after week, until each slight movement of the pendulum speaks to him as clearly as a voice: "See that swing now? Which direction does it go? Slow? Fast? How long will it spin? Count now, one, two, three. Now let us try again. Same place, aha, same reaction. Try from this direction: nothing. Where was the difference?" And so on, patiently, carefully, in the dark, lonely room, the experiment continued. "Is there water here? Where is it? How deep to dig? Through rock? Through lime? Through earth? Will there be enough water to make the digging worthwhile? How much will there be? One spring? Two? Three?" Water for the fields and men. Water for the cows and bullocks; water for a parched and barren land.

Not content with giving his entire life to India, this young man from rural France, far from the loving family and tender vineyards, living among alien tribes, must give them more than the Living Water; he must give them fresh springs. Turn them from robbers into farmers. And he did it. One thousand two hundred living springs of water, brought up from the secret hidden underground rivers to the brass pots of the village women.

"Do any of the Indians know how to douse?" I asked Father Montaud. Luncheon was nearly ready, but my questions were still unsatisfied.

"Usually the Indians call in the sorcerer. First of all, he must be given a hen. He must kill the fowl, and spread the blood, and make all kinds of incantations and so on. Then he will go around and point. Finally he says, 'Oh, we will find water here.' But many of the cases are false. That is one reason why I was happy to take it up for the Kallers: to try to help them in this way.

"Once, I had a very interesting case: a very important, rich man dug a well. Twenty by about twenty-two feet; a regular tank. So they first built the well, but then found no water. He had been relying on the local sorcerer. So he called me. I went and began going around the well. He wanted to know, of course, if water was anywhere near the well. But after I went around once, nothing. So I began a second round. On the second round I was followed by a man. I thought, I wonder what does he want? After I went about twenty feet, he tells me, 'Father.' 'What?' I ask him. 'Say that there is water here.' I said, 'Why should I say there is water here, where there is no water?' 'But I have told them that there was water here!' I said, 'No, I cannot say there is water. How can I damage my reputation and say that there is water?' I refused."

"Your talent is of tremendous use in India," I told him. "Water is so crucial . . . they need it so badly." But Father was not yielding to praise.

"Of course," he said, "once you know the direction of the water, it is easy. There are many underground rivers, and you must know where they are. You cannot see them, but the pendulum will tell you. When I go to Brother James's, he has remarked this, that I always start on the same side. I tell him, 'The water comes from there!' Why? I just *know* that."

Father mentioned that the pendulum worked even over a map of a given area. This I found very difficult to understand. "I can understand that this electric current can flow from the underground water through your body to the pendulum. But how can this happen over a map?"

"With a map, I always insist I be given exactly the four corners of the compass, so as to be able to transport myself in my imagination to the spot which I am to examine."

"Have you been successful at this?"

"I have tried it several times, and have been successful several times. Of course, I am not going to proclaim that everywhere I have always had a success, but thus far I can say: I have succeeded. I can say to them, 'For the time being, you will get your water from this side. When you dig down, you have rock here, and lime here.' I follow the same process, once I know the place exactly. More or less I must also know the configuration of the place; but, having north, south, east and west, it's all right."

Regina brought the lunch from the kitchen. We walked over to the table, and Father crossed himself briefly. It was our usual lunch: rice, curry and apappalams; Regina had fixed a more pungent curry for Father, in a separate dish. There were also sliced cucumbers, whole wheat bread and peanut butter, fruit cup for dessert: papaya, banana and pineapple. As we ate, we continued our conversation.

"The best example of map use is that of a certain Swiss father whose name I've forgotten. He was asked by a planter from South America to come there. He was going to pay all the expenses, if the Father would just come and find water. He had an eleven thousand-acre plantation and said, 'I can't find water on my plantation any-where.' So the Swiss father told him, 'Look here. Send me a map with all the measurements and the four corners of the compass. No need of paying my expenses, just send me the map.' After some time, the map came, and the Father studied it and wrote to that man, 'Try here, in this place. At exactly so many feet, you will find water enough for your eleven thousand acres.' And he did!"

"Could you find water in the desert?" I asked him.

"Why not?" said Father Montaud, shrugging. "If there is water there, I can find it. It is possible to find anything: oil, minerals, any-thing under the surface, providing you take the trouble to teach yourself."

"Could you find gold?"

"Gold I did not try; I have had no gold in my hand. But other metals, certainly. And oil, for example, is very difficult. There is a compound reaction to be studied there. The first and most impor-tant thing in finding water is this, I must concentrate very hard on water. I must put my mind in such a way as to say, 'I want water. Where is water?' And the direction in which I face is also important. For myself, though each has his own method, for myself I put myself in a northwesterly direction to find hard rock. When so placed, if I get a positive reaction, I know there is hard rock there. If in this same direction I get a negative reaction, there is no hard rock there."

"It must be northwest?"

"For rock, northwest. For lime, it must be east. And the reaction must be negative. Then I know there is lime. Then I begin to count the circles to get the depth or number of feet."

I had heard that it was sometimes possible, with a pendulum, to elicit from one's subconscious the positive or negative answers to questions, and asked him about this. He had no interest in it. But then he said, surprisingly, "Diseases can sometimes be detected in this way. We are not supposed to do this, though. But there was a priest who went to see the Pope after this prohibition was given [that the Fathers should not busy themselves with things like that]. Pius X knew him, so, in the conversation, the priest said, 'Your Holiness, would you allow me to douse you for your disease?' At first the Pope said no, but finally the priest was permitted to try. And he found the correct disease. The Pope was very surprised, and asked, 'But how do you know this?' The priest told him, 'It is the saying of the pendulum.'

"Another father had stomach ulcers. He knew precisely the number of ulcers he had. He was a pendulum man. The doctor asked, 'How did that man find out that he had this many ulcers?' He had put the pendulum over his stomach, and counted out. So many."

I had been reading *The Light Within Us*, in which Albert Schweitzer says, "A great deal of water is flowing underground which never comes up as a spring. In that thought we may find comfort. But we ourselves must try to be the water which does find its way up; we must become a spring at which men can quench their thirst for gratitude."

I looked at my guest. Fifty-six years in India. Indeed, not only had he found springs, he was himself a spring of refreshment for the people of India.

CHAPTER 23

A Village Called Pattiveeranpatti

One day, an interesting letter arrived via the postman:

Dear Madam,
I would like to inform you that I have consulted our good Rev. Brother Paranjothi, S.J., as desired by you. He has inform me when you will visit him, and on receipt of your reply, I shall send my car for your journey. I also request you to kindly visit our house at Pattiveeranpatti to dine with us, after your visit to St. Mary's Estate and oblige. Thanking you, Yours sincerely, P. R. K. Joseph, Planter.

I recognized this name: it was Pajus, the pleasant young man I had met at Manalur the previous month. The prospect of an invitation to an Indian home was most exciting; I was eager to respond at once and fix a date. I replied that I would be free April 13, and hoped that date would be convenient for the visit. This brought an immediate and courteous response:

Dear Madam,
This I beg to acknowledge receipt of your goodself's kind letter dated 29.3.78, with thanks.
I am very glad for you have agreed to honour us by visiting our place on April 13th. I shall send my car to your goodself on 13th April to be there at about 8:30 A.M. This is for favour of your kind information. Thanking you, Yours Sincerely, P. R. K. Joseph, Planter.

Two days later, two more letters arrived, one from P. R. K. Joseph and one from Brother Paranjothi. The Joseph missive read:

Dear Madam,

This has further reference to my previous letter dated 1.4.78. I would like to inform your goodself that Rev. Br. Paranjothi, S.J., has written to me that himself and Rev. Fr. S. A. Rayappar, S.J., Manager, St. Mary's Estate, will be going over to Pattiveeranpatti on the 13th instant to meet your goodself.

Hence, I request your goodself to kindly go over here straight from Kodaikanal by my car, which I shall send there at about 9 A.M. on the 13th instant, as confirmed in my previous letter. Thanking you. . . .

Paranjothi's letter confirmed this plan. The visit was taking on the proportions of a royal visitation, I thought with some dismay. I hoped I would prove worth all the postage.

On the morning of the thirteenth, promptly at eight-fifteen, a gentle tap on the door revealed P. R. K. Joseph's driver. He handed me a little note:

Madam,

As per your goodselves kind wish, we are sending our Car TMX 3737 there, through our driver, B. R. Genasan, for your trip to St. Mary's Estate and then to our place. We are all very happy to see your goodself. We request you to kindly pay a visit to our home in our above car. With kind regards, Yours Sincerely, P. R. K. Joseph.

I gave Regina a few instructions and set out for Pattiveeranpatti. It was one of the clear, glorious days, when the cool air lifted the heart, and the flowering shrubs and singing birds gave the soul a smile. B. R. Genasan, who confided he was a Brahmin but no other facts, drove with great skill and care. The Ambassador was black and shiny, obviously cared for like a pet elephant. The hood ornament was a little silver statue of St. Christopher carrying the child Jesus. In deference to the saint, B. R. Genasan threaded his way down the narrow ghat road with caution, in and out of herds of cattle and goats and sidestepping the lumbering lorries and buses that snarled up around every turn. By now I had been up and down so often I knew the various landmarks: the sudden glory of poinsettias high as a house, the monkeys that haunted a particular bend, the Silver Cascade, whose water was, in this season, too scant to qualify as a cascade, though silver it indubitably was. We did not stop at any of the squalid roadside villages for coffee. This driver scorned the low-caste handling of his food. We found Manalur and Brother Paranjothi in about two and one half hours.

A pleasant-faced, elderly Jesuit came out with Brother. This was the other Father Montaud, Peter, brother of my water-divining friend. He had a white beard and a youthful smile. Laugh lines around the blue eyes spoke of a joyous and peaceful spirit. In seconds I felt I had known him a lifetime, and we had an opportunity to speak of his brother Clement as we had tea in St. Mary's dining room. Father Peter Montaud is also a water diviner, he told me.

"But not as good," he said, "as my brother. He is justly famous in southern India. Everyone knows of his ability." I had time to reflect on this generous appraisal by the big brother, delighted with his younger brother's fame. Father Clement Montaud, when I spoke to him later on, remarked on the tremendous work of his elder brother.

"He was sent to a parish once," said Father Clement, "where there was an unfinished church. His room was the stable. The floor flooded with water during the rains, through holes in the roof, so that the only dry spot was the bed, because it was a bit raised up. When the superior came and saw how he was living, in such terrible poverty, he said to him, 'Now, forget the church for the moment and build yourself a small house, before you fall sick.' But my brother, like David, could not rest until his eyes had seen the glory of the temple of the Lord. He finished the church first. That year, his hair and beard went completely white." Father Peter Montaud, at eighty-nine, is completing his seventy-third year in the Society of Jesus.

Together, Brother Paranjothi, Father Peter and I were again seated in the Ambassador and pointed down the mountain to Pattiveeranpatti. En route I got some details concerning this family we were about to visit. It seemed that, about sixty years ago, the father of the family worked on the Jesuits' estate growing coffee. The man was very poor but a very honorable and loyal man, hard-working and dedicated to his employers. The Jesuits, on their part, were so delighted with him that they set him up in business, lending him the funds and offering the considerable resources of the Society to enable him to make a start for himself. So successful was the venture that his four sons are today multimillionaires. Their coffee plantation adjoins that of the Jesuits, and their two coffee-curing plants are enormous industries, employing hundreds of people in the hills.

And it is nice to report, the gratitude of this family is such that, for them, the very name of Jesuit is synonymous with all that is fine, cultured, and noble. They named all the children in the family after the Jesuit fathers, so that P.R.K. is Pajus, named for a Father Pajus who was at St. Mary's Estate during the years before P.R.K. was born. In the same manner, all the sons bear the names of their benefactors. I had noted, in our previous meeting, the profound reverence of Pajus as he knelt before each Jesuit for a blessing. I thought he was a seminarian. Later I was to witness the same genuflection on the part of every family member, down to the smallest child. The family are devout Hindus, of the Nadar caste. They have, in addition to their reputation for great wealth, an equal one for hospitality and a love for the gracious art of welcoming guests. The wedding, still spoken of in Kodai, was one I was sorry to have missed, when ten thousand guests had gathered for a two-day festival and where one hundred priests, bishops and archbishops had been invited. All had been transported to the village at the family's expense, and had each been given a beautiful cashmere shawl.

As the village arose in the distance, I saw an enormous white factory shining in the hazy heat like a mirage. We drove through the gates and found ourselves at one of the two coffee-curing works. There the coffee of their plantation is graded and sorted for quality before being taken to auction. The inner court was vast, and completely surrounded by either buildings or walls; it seemed to cover the space of about two city blocks. A raised platform in the center contained some coffee spread in the sun, but my attention was captivated by the long white veranda of stone and cement that dominated the far end of the courtyard. All along its expanse, as far as the eye could see, were women seated on the floor with triangular baskets before them and open sacks of coffee beans. When I found I could not count them, I inquired how many there were. One hundred and fifty women! It seemed to be pleasant enough work: clean, and shaded as they were from the hot sun. They were removing all the darkened or discolored beans from the sacks before them, their fingers deftly plucking rejected beans and disposing of them with swift precision. There was no talking. I discovered that bonus payments rewarded them for good work, though the basic rate of pay seemed low.

We inspected the grading room where metal screens with holes sifted the smaller beans out and made it possible to separate the quality beans for the auctioneer's hammer. A visit to the offices followed. There several clerks worked on huge account books. They offered these to me for inspection. The accounts were done in Tamil, in copperplate, as perfect as it is possible to imagine. Everywhere, the air of modern efficiency, scrupulous cleanliness and the highest degree of maintenance made me feel for a moment that I was in Glenview, viewing the plant of Sara Lee. But, smiling down from the ceiling picture gallery was photographic evidence of the Joseph family: the father and mother, brothers, archbishops, Jesuits and local dignitaries. This was modern India at its finest. That family, it was obvious, had learned the Western system and was disciplined enough to re-create it there.

It was with great anticipation and excitement that I entered the house of Pajus, a very clean white building in a corner of the little village. He was at the door, all smiling and happy, asking if the journey was hard and if the driver had given satisfaction. We entered a cool entrance hall, and beyond it a central room that seemed to be a reception hall for guests. The ceiling was very high, and a fan there moved the air about. All along the top of the walls was a picture rack, where a gallery of photographs reposed, the household gods of this family. In the place of honor were the patriarch and the mother of the family, the Sacred Heart, a whole college of cardinals and bishops, many Indian gentlemen whose imposing dignity suggested their rank, and enough Jesuits to gladden the heart of Father Arrupe, who was, himself, also represented. There were garlands and little festoons gracing these, which moved in the breeze of the fan. The furnishings of the room were simple and quiet, and I could see, through a doorway, many women and children who were hovering there in great excitement, all smiles. Pajus drew them into the room, one by one, beginning with his wife, a very pretty girl in a lovely sari, who was carrying a small girl in her arms. Then the sisters-in-law were introduced, each shy and small. Several children came forward as well. All knelt to the Jesuits for the blessing, and greeted me cordially. But no one spoke English except Pajus, which limited the conversation. Father Peter and Brother Paranjothi, however, were engaged in rapid-fire Tamil that soon revealed that the family was concerned about one of the children, who had a sore throat and had been taken to Dindigul to the hospital for a throat culture. They feared diphtheria. The word had just come, via the phone, that it was not that dreaded disease but just a bad cold. I noted the interesting fact that this family had a phone that worked. It was the only one I saw like that in the entire visit to Kodai.

Pajus, one of the few people I ever met who could smile while speaking, suggested after a time that we go to the house of his brother Joseph, who was awaiting our visit. We walked across the road, rounded the corner, and found this house, not twenty feet away. The house was larger, as was fitting, since Joseph was the patriarch of the family, following the father's death. Again, we found the room cool and dim, the terrazzo floors shiny and probably a help against the scorching heat outdoors. We again sat in a large reception room, where two couches faced one another across a coffee table, and where lovely dark, wooden doors led to other rooms. The saintly gallery smiled down from above, this time graced with the Holy Father in addition to the family-with-Jesuits. When I expressed an interest, the identity of each honored friend was explained in great detail. It was obvious that the remembrance of kindness would be held in that family's bosom for all the generations to come. The women had come in by another entrance, and now appeared carrying cups of hot soup. It was gently spiced with curry. I found it delicious.

Joseph, my host in this house, explained that the dinner we would be served was not prepared by servants but by all of the women of the family. This is a very great honor, and I expressed my gratitude, though I thought with dismay of the hard work my visit had imposed on these little ladies, who must have preferred other pursuits in that heat. The Jesuits assured me that this was their delight, however, and that they worked very well together. The children danced in and out of the room with the unselfconscious charm of children everywhere. I noted that most of them were girls. Only one boy has been born thus far within this joint family, a heavy cross for them all, I am sure, since they depend so completely on the male to carry the line.

As we spoke, another brother, Augustine, arrived, and made his profound reverence to the Jesuits. Then a third Jesuit entered, whose name I have unfortunately forgotten. He was apparently a great favorite, for at his entrance all the children and women came out from the nether regions of the house to kneel at his feet. He chatted pleasantly with them all in Tamil, chucked the little girls under the chin, and sat back with the air of one who has an honored place in the home.

When dinner was announced, Joseph led us through the doorway into a skylit hall, where a dark staircase ascended to the second floor. In this room, like the water fountain at the entrance of a Japanese tea garden, a tiny sink, towels and soap were provided, and the guests were requested to cleanse their hands before entering the dining room beyond.

In the dining room I was given the place of honor, with the other Jesuit at the opposite end and Brother Paranjothi and Father Peter on my left side. No members of the family sat down with us. Instead, Joseph, serving as a kind of maitre d', strode back and forth directing the traffic as the women began serving the delicacies they had prepared for us. The Indian Jesuits had huge green plantain leaves for plates, while Father Peter and I had porcelain. Many tiny servings of mysterious and delicious foods were served, while Joseph stood guarding the honor of his home and table and urging more on everyone. He reminded me of Al, who so loved to see his guests eat and enjoy his hospitality. Nothing had been heavily spiced, in deference to me, I was told, so that the flavor of each food was both distinctive and delightful. There were about twelve or thirteen different dishes prepared, many unfamiliar; a noble feast indeed, and worthy of such a house and clan.

During the meal, as we ate and chatted under Joseph's watchful eye, his wife arrived from Dindigul with the ailing grandchild. The formalities of greeting over, she conveyed in Tamil her fears and relief that the illness had not proven serious. Certainly it didn't look serious: the child was romping around the house with her cousins as though she had never been sick a day in her life, probably revived by all the attention of the family and doctors.

Coffee was served in the reception room. A delicious ice with fruit was also served, and I realized they must have refrigeration, a tremendous luxury anywhere in India but unheard of in the villages.

Thinking that the children would enjoy the tape recorder, I put it on the table with a Horowitz tape playing, and everyone was lost in admiration at the small size and tremendous fidelity possible in that tiny box. A discussion of music followed, the veena being mentioned by Brother Paranjothi with great affection. I told them of my family at home, about the grandchildren, about our family business, which was also in food: the importing of coconut for the baking and confectionary industry. The brothers stood under the picture gallery, so attentive and so obviously united that I thought suddenly of Al and his brothers, who had loved one another so much. The eldest brother of Al was also Joseph. A wave of memory swept over me, as it so often does, and I was back in a happier time, my dear ones around me, entertaining in our home as we loved to do.

Augustine expressed the desire to have us all come to his home, and we took leave of Joseph and family after I photographed them all. As the car approached a point about two blocks away, I saw a magnificent house of blue cement surrounded by a spotless white wall. We entered this driveway and were in the courtyard before the home of Augustine.

Before entering the house, however, I was led through a gate in the wall to the compound adjoining. Graceful ornamental trees and coconut palms swayed in the leaden air, meeting high over two pillared shrines. These were constructed in marble, and the crucifix over each immediately suggested their use. "My mother and father are buried here," said Augustine. The Jesuits and I knelt and prayed for the parents of this gracious household. I was impressed by the power that made it possible for them to eschew the usual regulations covering burial and thus to keep the family together. Farther on, I saw a smaller platform, similarly adorned, where the babies of the family were interred. The use of the crucifix interested me greatly, since I knew the family was Hindu.

As we approached the house again, Augustine waved to the area beyond his compound, where another compound was entirely enclosed by a high white wall. "Pajus will have a house there. We begin building next month." So Pajus, the youngest, who was living for the present in the old family house, would also have a fine mansion for his wife and children, next door to Augustine and down the street from Joseph. A fourth brother, whom I did not meet, was away from the village. He, too, lives nearby with his family.

Now we entered the home of Augustine, through an open veranda where bamboo chairs and a table rested in the deep shade. The rooms were spacious by American standards, at least half again as large in every instance as those of the homes I knew. The floors throughout were terrazzo, making maintenance completely carefree.

The woodwork was a warm brown, the walls pale plaster. In one corner of the drawing room, a saint was enshrined. I asked who it was, though I should have known: St. Augustine. The gallery of family saints smiled down on the simple furnishing, and the sun was thwarted, in its attempt to heat the house, by wide overhangs all around. Ornamental bars graced the windows in Indian geometric designs.

Augustine took me through the first floor. A dining room, and a very large kitchen that contained food-preparation counters and a refrigerator on a stand suggested that this home, too, would be geared for hospitality on a large scale. An adjoining room contained the stove, which was run on gas. I inquired about it and discovered that they used cow-dung gas. Through an open window, Augustine pointed to a red tank about 150 feet away, behind a high wall. A pipe led from there to the stove in the kitchen. He said it was quite efficient.

There was a large bedroom and bath on the first floor and, I presume, many more upstairs, though I did not go up. In a little room under the staircase I was shown the prayer room. It was cozy and intimate and contained a lovely shrine created entirely from penicillin bottles, which had been stacked up and glued together in a tiered effect to create little niches for the statues of the gods, the Sacred Heart, Ganesh (the elephant-headed god) and a Christmas crib. It was a most ingenious use of scrap material and could be lit to pretty effect. Incense sticks and various brass and copper lamps suggested the *puja* that was daily performed there.

We were served a rather mysterious iced drink that was saffron-yellow, and chatted awhile about business, the new house Pajus would build, and my next visit. Pajus invited me to halt with his family (which means remain for several days, breaking the journey) when I came again. I promised I would at least visit. There was so much warmth and friendship there I would be happy to renew the acquaintance when I returned again. It reminded me in many ways of my own family at home.

Our departure was rich with blessings, promises of swift return, and gratitude for a most pleasant sojourn. The faithful Brahmin driver, who must have been weary after his six-hour journey up and down, took the wheel again and drove us back to St. Mary's Estate, up in the hills, where we dropped Brother Paranjothi and Father

Peter and, after tea, began the climb back to Kodai. The trip was uneventful, save for several occasions when the driver swore in Tamil at the bullying lorries and at a recalcitrant water buffalo that refused to yield the right of way. At four thousand feet I put my jacket on again, and at seven thousand had to button it around my neck. The hills were chilly in the evening air. Regina was waiting with the outdoor light on, and gave the Brahmin coffee before he retraced his route back down again. He had spent twelve hours driving madam around, that day.

On the following morning I wrote a little note of sincere appreciation to Pajus. I was very grateful for this glimpse at an Indian family at home. One week later, the following letter arrived:

Dear Madam,
This I write to acknowledge receipt of your goodself's kind letter dated 14.4.78, with thanks. Kindly accept my sincere thanks for having visited our house and for your goodself's good wishes and prayerful blessings on our family for a great joy and happiness, which I most heartily reciprocate to your goodself and your family. My wife and my brothers join me in sending their kind regards to your goodself and to your family members.

Kindly remember all of us in your daily prayers. You are always welcome to our House. Kindly make it convenient to visit us often whenever your goodself returns to Kodaikanal positively.

I hope this will find your goodself in the best of health and fine spirits. With kind regards. Yours Sincerely, P. R. K. Joseph, Planter.

I certainly shall return to visit them again.

CHAPTER 24

The Nuns' Tales

Sister Ethna and I were standing in the convent parlor after breakfast one morning, leafing through an anniversary book that described the work of the Salesians. The photo of a nurse and child suddenly sparked a memory, and Sister Ethna smiled and said, "I remember Santosh."

"Who is Santosh?" I asked her.

"Santosh was a little child at Thani," she said, her eyes lighting at the recollection. "She had a tiny little body, and was in terrible rags. But she had enormous, beautiful big eyes. I sometimes had a bit of candy and used to keep it in my pocket for when I'd meet her." She laughed gently. "I can still see her coming toward me, looking at my pocket, to see if I would have candy for her."

I remembered Father Nevett's letter of long ago, when I asked if he could use some Halloween candy: He'd written back, "Sure, send it along—the kids love it."

Sister Ethna fingered the crucifix on her white starched habit. "Anyway, we became great friends. She stayed in our school up until the fifth standard, and I was so happy; then suddenly she was taken from the school. They needed her at home, of course, and that was the end of her education. Five years went by, and then one day a little person came walking into the hospital. She was looking terrible, so thin and emaciated. I thought it was another poor patient looking for treatment. Then she said to me, 'Don't you remember me, Sister? Santosh?' I was dumbfounded. Santosh, you know, means 'happiness' and this poor girl looked so ill, mistreated, and destitute, I could hardly keep from crying.

"'Santosh! What has happened to you? Are you ill?' Then she told me she was married. Imagine! At 14! She was two months pregnant. I examined her, and realized she would need very careful nursing if she was to have a healthy baby, or survive the pregnancy herself. I told her that she must stay with her mother, who lived at Thani, and come to the hospital each week for treatment until the child was born. But she said she could not. She had to return to her village. I sent for her mother and explained the situation to her. There was nothing the mother could do at all. The husband was sent for. He never came. For a long time I did not see the girl at all.

"Then, one day, her mother came to me at the hospital in terrible distress. She was weeping so much she could hardly speak. I discovered that the baby had been stillborn and that Santosh herself was dying. I was the only sister on duty at the hospital and could not leave. But I told the mother to bring Santosh to me, as quickly as she could.

"She did. I looked at the tiny little child on the stretcher and could not recognize her at all, except for the eyes. She clung to my hand and wept. Then she told me she must speak to me, and that I must send the mother out of the room. I asked the mother to step outside.

"Santosh was clearly dying. But she had one thing on her mind only. She wanted baptism. She was frightened that she would die without it, and I didn't know what to do. I had no way of knowing if she really knew what baptism meant, so I began to ask her. Yes, she told me, she knew there was One God. She loved Him. She wanted to be with Him. I told her I would send for the priest, but she grabbed my arm and told me I must not do that. She was terrified that her mother would find out. No one must know. It would have to be between the two of us, and God. A daughter turned Christian would mean the mother would have been turned out of her house, and Santosh didn't want that calamity to befall her poor mother. Could she be buried in the Hindu way?"

Sister told her she could. And so, with trembling hands, Sister Ethna poured the water of life over the small head of Santosh, giving her the name she requested, that of God's mother, Mary. "She died that night," said Sister Ethna, looking at me through tear-dimmed eyes.

"We washed the poor little wasted body, put on a white skirt and sari, and prepared her for her burial. And in the long years since then, even if I did nothing else in all my lifetime, I feel I would have come to India just for that moment. And all because of a bit of candy!"

Irrepressible Sister Carmel, whose jokes and teasing kept Presentation Convent constantly in good humor, regaled me with her Kerryman jokes. The Kerryman is closely related to the Pole in this regard.

"Did you hear about the old Kerrywoman who went to the doctor about her sore right leg?" she would ask unnecessarily. "Well, the doctor told her there was nothing he could do for it. 'It's just old age,' he said. 'Sure, that's nonsense,' replies the Kerrywoman promptly. 'Both me legs are the same age!'"

Another of this genre has the Kerryman perusing the obituaries in the daily paper and remarking pensively, "Isn't it amazing the way people always seem to be dying in alphabetical order!"

In return I related the news, from Barbara's letter, about Kevin shoving grapefruit seeds up his nose, and showed them a picture Joe had drawn and mailed to me.

And Sister Ethna related the tale of the dhobi who came tearfully to their door to beg money with which to bury his mother. The nuns had been very sympathetic and had given him the necessary rupees. The following week, the dhobi's mother herself arrived to pick up the laundry, undaunted by her own miraculous resurrection.

Dhobi tales, I found, have a charm all their own: witness the nun who sent her habits out for laundering and encountered a woman wearing her best habit in the bazaar the following week. The dhobi, sensing an unusual garment, had rented it out. This, I was informed, is in no way uncommon; any wedding in town is outfitted to a large extent thanks to the rentals of the garments given for laundering to the dhobi by richer members of the town. Amusing as all of this was, I was privately happy that I had brought wash-and-wear garments and was able to oversee their care myself. Snyder "B" created something of a sensation in the neighborhood, with the clothesline in the rear. Everyone else in Kodai, it seemed, used the ground and any low bushes to hang wet wash on. Muthusamy had a hard time finding a piece of rope for this purpose, and even more difficulty trying to figure out what I needed it for. But finally we had a permanent clothesline, attached to water pipes at one end and a window handle at the other.

It was Mrs. Lord who first brought up the topic of witchcraft.

Somehow I had never associated it with India; it was a topic that belonged in the tabloid section of the Sunday paper, more of a curiosity than a fact.

So when an elderly woman doctor, visiting the convent, mentioned the limes, I did not immediately make the connection.

"But of course you know," she said in answer to my question, "Limes are used in Tamil witchcraft!"

"Witchcraft? In India?" The others laughed at my incredulity, and the conversation burst forth in a cornucopia of tales. I discovered, for example, that in the villages limes are placed under the four wheels of a vehicle that is being used to carry a corpse. The reason? The wheels, in crushing the limes, chase away the spirit of the corpse, who would otherwise take possesion of the engine, causing terrible accidents. Why limes? No one seemed to know. But definitely limes must be carefully placed under the wheels. And if it is discovered that one lime did not burst, the vehicle does not move from that spot until another lime is deposited under that wheel, and crushed in the forward motion of the car.

I was fascinated. Not just because the tale was interesting but because this group of educated women—a skilled doctor and a group of dedicated nuns—obviously believed that witchcraft had power. Sister Cecilia, the music nun, whose lovely voice rang out at Mass in the chapel in the quiet mornings with clear tones of praise and joy, smiled and said quietly, "A spell was placed on me, once, by a witch."

The others knew the story, and urged her to repeat it for me.

"It was at Madras," she said, "when I was a very young sister. One of the people we had hired there was angry with me and placed an evil spell on me."

"What kind of a spell?" I asked her.

"They had obtained some of my hair, and it had been nailed to a tamarind tree on our compound, with a little red spot under it. On the ground before the tree, he had placed four limes in a little square, with red and white powder on the ground. That was all. But one of our servants, who knew about it, came to me and warned me not to pass that way. I would have been in great trouble if I had. So I went by another route, and saw the thing from a distance; it was between two of our buildings. At first I laughed, but the others told me it could be very serious for me, so I called the priest. He came immediately, wearing his surplice and stole, and he brought holy water with him. I remember, he also had a heavy log in his hand. I had to stand at some distance and watch."

"Watch what?" I asked impatiently. "What did he do?"

"It was an exorcism," explained Sister Cecilia. "First he prayed for a time. Then he leaned over the limes on the ground and disturbed the red and white powder. Taking the log, he crushed the limes. Then he threw the log at the tree, and the hair and nail fell to the ground. He used the holy water on the whole area, and then on me. I had to pray too. That was it."

My eyes must have revealed my complete surprise and shock. Sister Cecilia related the tale as though she were telling of an incident that happened every day. Then she remembered an additional fact. She had spoken to the priest sometime later, and he had told her that for three nights following that event he had been forcibly thrown from his bed and his sleep greatly disturbed. This, too, was evidently not an unusual reprisal following an exorcism.

Later that evening, I mentioned this to Sister Ethna. I noticed an inner struggle as she recalled an instance in her own life and pondered whether or not to reveal it. Finally she spoke. "Once, when I was on night duty at the hospital," she said, "we had a gypsy woman admitted who had an aura of horror about her. I can't explain it, but I recall saying to another nurse when she was admitted, 'If I ever saw the devil incarnate, that woman is it!' But she was in a coma, very ill, and needed help, so we nursed her, of course. But she grew worse, and we knew she was dying. It would just be a question of time. Meantime, a baby was having trouble being born elsewhere, and I had to go to the delivery room. The baby was safely born and the mother all right, and I knew I should go back to the dying woman. Another sister and I came to the door of the room where she was and opened it. A very swift, black, flying thing came right at us, and flew over our heads, hitting my veil. I yelped and ducked, thinking it was a bat. But the sister with me, when we recovered, said, "It was much too large to be a bat." There was no sign of anything in the corridor at all. I grew frightened, and approached the bed. The evil-looking old gypsy woman was still alive, though in a coma, and the feeling of horror and despair in that room was overpowering. We left again when we saw there was nothing to be done for her. I prayed very hard in the presence of that strange and mysterious atmosphere of untold dread.

"An hour or two later, making the rounds again, I opened the door. This time the Thing, whatever it was, hit me squarely on the forehead. I saw nothing, but I distinctly *felt* it. It gave me quite a blow. Then, nothing. When I approached the bed, I saw that the woman was dead."

Sister Ethna's face reflected clearly the memory of that night; I, too, was silenced in the contemplation of the unknown. Finally she aroused herself again. "I spoke to Father about it the next day," she said. "He brought holy water and blessed the room. He said it was an evil spirit."

I decided to ask Father Montaud about witchcraft, to see if he had encountered it in India. He devoted an hour to the topic, and told me many interesting things about sorcery and the superstitions of the Hindus.

He told me of the "auspicious signs" that the Hindus watch for to help them make decisions. Birds are often studied. Wall lizards, as Sister Theresa had told me, are very important to them in this regard. The side of the room in which it begins to cry at night is regarded as the clue to the nature of the message. If on the west wall, the meaning is different from when it's on the north wall. The time, date and day on which the sound is heard is also reputed to have a particular meaning. The red eagle, with a white neck, is an auspicious sign for many. Hindus go at certain times of the morning to a tree where these eagles habitually roost, and watch for the manner in which the eagle approaches the tree. If it circles the tree thrice before settling down, this is taken as a good sign, and one may safely proceed on the project at hand. If, however, the eagle does not come at all, one may as well stop everything for the day. Nothing will have success on such a day, according to the superstition. Father Montaud told me of a joke his driver once played on a Hindu who came each day to their garden where a red eagle had a nest in one of their fig trees. This Hindu would come each morning at a certain time, and stand and watch. The driver took a sling shot, before the Hindu arrived, and drove the eagle away. The Hindu went home, blaming all in his household for the bad omen. It went on for several days, until the Hindu happened to catch the driver with the sling-shot.

Superstition is deeply ingrained in the minds of these people. The Kallers, for example, the robber caste among whom Father worked for seventeen years, would, on the day of a robbery, go first to a shrine of the local god to pray for success. But if, coming from that shrine, a crow should fly toward them, the robbery attempt would be abandoned, since this was an omen of bad luck. They really believed that animals of all kinds had a "feeling" about the events to come. Jackals, panthers, tigers, dogs, or birds might convey to these ignorant people clues as to the future. Father Montaud believes it is an actual slavery for them, since they can do nothing without consulting these auguries.

Astrology rules all the important events of the Hindu's life. No event—birth, marriage, or any important decision—can be completed without consultation with the astrologer, who maps the horoscope from the birth dates and times of the people involved, and who then announces the auspicious time for the event. Even intellectuals cannot celebrate a marriage without the astrologer. Friday is considered a bad day, unlucky. I asked if he thought it was because it was the day of Christ's crucifixion, but Father said they do not think of Christ at all.

Palm reading, said Father Montaud, is very common throughout the country. Those who read palms are very clever, using facts learned beforehand about the person, and psychology, to make their readings. Father told me of a priest who consulted a famous palm reader without revealing he was a priest. The reading went on at length about his "unhappy marriage, and his children," both of which were nonexistent. My own belief, however, which I had no time to expound to Father, is that there is some possibility that the body contains clues as to the inner being, and that patterns of thought may be as clearly etched on the palm as they are, we are told, on the brain itself. How many there are who are gifted in actually discerning these patterns is another question.

Certain extraordinary events that take place in India are mysterious and unexplainable except as possible manifestations of the devil's power. Father Montaud next spoke of having once witnessed, together with two other priests, actual tongues of fire. The villagers had told him that at a certain time of night, strange fires arose from a Hindu shrine under a tree, and passed through the air to another tree. He was skeptical, and took the other two priests along as witnesses. At the precise hour mentioned, a long tongue of fire arose quite high in the air from the shrine. It could not have been the will-o'-the-wisp, a form of swamp gas sometimes seen, because of the height to which it arose. Will-o'-the-wisp remains close to the ground. This tongue of fire ascended, and then crossed through the air directly to the second tree, where the other shrine was, and rested on the branches. Before their astonished eyes, it broke into thousands of tongues of flame. Father believes it to be a manifestation of Satan. It happened at 9 P.M.

Similarly in a village, the people were greatly disturbed by tongues of fire passing over their heads and going straight to the hut of a woman who was believed to be possessed by the devil. The priest was summoned and saw this himself. On the following morning the entire roof of the hut was covered with flowers that had not been there previously. The people asked the priest to bless the village, which he did. The tongues of fire ceased from that moment.

There is a feast in one of the villages, in which the people go in procession around and around, each one accompanied by a tongue of fire at his side. This has been seen by Father Montaud. And one of the Christians told him that, once, when he had to pass this village at night, a tongue of fire arose before him and preceded him on the path for some time. When he came to a torrent, when he attempted to wade through, the tongue of fire stopped, as if refusing to allow him to go ahead. At the sign of the cross, the fire disappeared.

The devil is very powerful. In pagan lands, where Christ is all but unknown, these mysterious powers of evil make themselves known to the people, to gain their souls. There is evidence of this all over South India. In one place on the road from Kamudi to Madurai, this fire can be seen every night.

Witchcraft is apparently practiced all over India, according to Father Montaud. Some sorcerers are well intended; some are malevolent. They are capable of making mysterious preparations, using fire, camphor and so on, called *pillisuliam*, or magical material. This is wrapped up and thrown into the house of the enemy. It must be done in such a way that it rolls to a place where it will not be detected. But when such a pillisuliam enters a house, terrible things begin to happen there. The people look throughout the house to find this magical material and get rid of it. As Father told me of this, I recalled a nun from Mangalore telling me of the method used there to detect such a pillisuliam when it was secretly buried in front of a house. An egg is rolled on the ground, starting at the door of the house. Wherever the egg stops rolling, there the householder digs, and will find the evil material that causes his misfortune.

In the town of Tanjore a pillisuliam had been thrown into a house, whereupon endless troubles of demonic origin began for the family. There was a young girl in the house, of whom poltergeists took possession. The priests were called and the pillisuliam was found and destroyed, but the troubles continued until the spirit was exorcised. Another instance, in which a girl working for a convent was attacked by a poltergeist and had burning coals fall from her mouth, all the sisters' clothing was burned up, and the food on the table turned into disgusting things, until she was blessed by the priest. Then peace was restored to the place.

Father Montaud converted a sorcerer once, long ago. He was teaching in a boys' school where two of the sorcerer's children were studying. A prize had been offered, a medal, to the first who could learn certain prayers. The two sons of the sorcerer, who were very bright, were the first to learn the prayers, and came to the priest to receive their prize. He, realizing who their father was, at first tried to give them something else instead, but the boys insisted on the medals. They wore them around their necks and went home. That night, their mother had a nightmare, during which, she said, Satan had tried to strangle her. In the morning, she tried to get her sons to give up the medals, which she feared had caused the devil's anger and might result in her own death. But the sons refused. Instead, they said, they would sleep in the mother's bed, one on each side, and should the devil try his murderous assault again, the medals would save her. That night, they retired as they planned, the woman with one son on each side. The evil one appeared as before, and as he grabbed her by the throat, she reached out and clasped the blessed medals on the necks of her sons. The evil one disappeared immediately.

The sorcerer, seeing that happen to his wife and seeing the steadfastness of his children, knew there was a power there stronger than his own. He sought instruction from the priest, and he and his entire family were baptized. He told the priest much of his former life and of the "penances" the devil extracted from him in return for extraordinary powers: he could speak in foreign languages, predict the future and read minds. All of this had been done through the power of Satan.

Wandering yogis, or sannyasi, of whom India has untold numbers, are greatly feared by village people, due to the powers they possess. Anything they ask of the people is given to them, for fear of the yogi's curse, which, they believe, can bring untold misfortune down on their heads. The people even believe that these yogis can change themselves into animals, by the power of the devil.

CHAPTER 25

The Song of Lord Krishna

A phone call at the convent one morning, while I was having breakfast there, informed me that Mrs. Ghose had invited me to come to her house for a private performance of dance. I was delighted, and on the appointed day, arrived at her lovely home on the side of the hill, descended the stone stairway into her garden, and was admitted by the butler. She greeted me in the living room, which had been transformed into a little theatre. It was divided into two portions—stage and audience—by a small raised barrier covered with Tibetan striped cloth and lit by a brass oil lamp. The "stage" portion had been darkened by the heavy curtains over the windows and was now lit by the little spotlights suspended near the ceiling.

Roshan Jajifdar Ghose is a very beautiful woman, one of the most beautiful I have ever seen. Her quality lies in the inner spirit, which radiates from her wonderful eyes and animates her lovely face as she speaks. She has a beautiful, lithe figure, which might be expected in a great dancer; today it was swathed in a sari of peacock blue, green, edged in purple and girdled at the waist by a festoon of silver. Her long black hair was worn in a chignon fastened by a silver ornament, and her ears and throat were also adorned in silver. Beneath the beautifully draped sari, worn short for this dance, she wore skin-colored tight leggings, the anklets of which were covered in rows of little silver bells, which made a pleasant jingling sound when she moved. Her feet were bare.

Tea was served to me, in my lone audience chair, as she prepared the tape recorder that would accompany her dance. She would do "The Song of Lord Krishna" for me: her own composition, based on the Bharata Natyam dance style but using her own interpretative innovations. The accompaniment had been recorded for her in Bombay, under studio conditions, and was a combination of magnificent music and an English-speaking voice describing the tale as it was unfolded in dance.

The story of Krishna and Radha, which appears at first glance a rather profane tale of love among the cowherds, was revealed as far more than that through the dance that followed. Krishna, whom devout Hindus worship as a god, had an earthly incarnation long ago, and having been saved from death at the hands of a tyrant, much as Jesus had been during the slaughter of the innocents, was reared in the pastoral setting of a shepherd's home. In his youth, the story goes, he lingered amorously among the cowherd girls—gopis—and though he preferred the lovely Radha, he extended his attentions to a wide number of these sprites. The "Gita-Govinda" is Radha's story as she passes through several stages of jealousy, anticipation, recollection, anger, frustration, despair and final fulfillment.

The first scene depicts Radha in a mood of jealousy, as her friend tells her how Krishna is dallying with the cowherds and leaving her thus abandoned in her love. The scene that follows depicts the painful situation she was compelled to endure. Her friend goes to Krishna to plead for her; he tells her he awaits her, but when they finally meet again, she is overcome with hatred for his infidelity to her, and sends him away again. In the end, she masters her pride and ego, and Krishna himself pleads with her. They are finally united in an ecstasy of love.

As danced by Roshan Ghose, the tale takes on a dimension of new meaning and mystery. It is the search of the soul for God, so well known in the writings of the saints. One can discern, in the passionate, wonderfully expressive face of the dancer, the longing of the soul for union with its Creator. It marvelously depicts the Dark Night of the Soul of John of the Cross and the more modern Hound of Heaven of Francis Thompson. And out of the sorrow, suffering, agony of separation, and despair, emerges the glory of final fulfillment.

The performance took one and one half hours, and such was the quality and sustained enthrallment, I was surprised, when it was ended, that so much time had elapsed. It was an experience I shall always remember.

Over lunch, we spoke of her professional career. She received her first training as a dancer under the guidance of her sister Shirin

Vajifder. She learned Bharata Natyam under Guru Mahalimgam Pillai. In 1954 she won the Government of India Scholarship for advanced studies and research in Bharata Natyam and went to the South to specialize under two well-known masters of the Pandanallur School, Sri Chokkalingam Pillai and Sri Kittappa Pillai. In 1956 and 1957 she gave a number of highly successful performances throughout India and was widely acclaimed as an outstanding exponent of this dance form.

She toured Russia and Germany during 1958, giving Bharata Natyam recitals in public and at the universities. She returned to Europe in 1959 on a lecture-demonstration tour. In 1960 she visited Russia and Mongolia as a member of the cultural delegation sent by the Government of India.

From 1960, she began a spiritual evolution, which was reflected in her dance. She taught dance to the students in Sri Aurobindo Ashram, Pondicherry, and fell under the influence of divine grace. Her "Pilgrimage of the Soul," another dance recital, reflects this experience and transformation. She promised me to dance this program at a later date.

We discussed the possibility of a visit to America to give recitals there. But the difficulty of this plan seems to be that India does not permit anyone to leave the country with more than ten dollars. So any plan for recitals has to be arranged for in advance, with the transportation, living arrangements, and possible concert dates set up already. As an artist, she shrinks from this kind of involvement, and has no agent.

"Besides," she said to me, her beautiful eyes wide and sincere, "I believe that if God wants me to do that, He will make it possible. The fact that it does not happen indicates to me that He wants me to remain here, and help my husband with his plan." I couldn't argue with that, though I am a firm believer in aiding Providence wherever possible with a well-organized plan. God expects us to use the brains He gave us, or He would not have created so complex a system as the human mind.

CHAPTER 26

Mari

Near the lake is a grassy area where large, friendly trees shade sojourners. Most of the time, these are coolies resting from the run down the hill with their bundles of wood. One day however, a beggar woman whom I knew came up with the pitiful whine and outstretched hand. I had no money with me, except a hundred-rupee note, which I intended to change when I bought some tea. I indicated "no" and was going on my way when she began pointing to a small bundle on the ground near the water. It was a child, very young. A man was passing at the moment, so I stopped him and asked him to inquire what was wrong. He did so, and after an agitated period of hand waving and rapid Tamil, he told me the baby was very sick, and needed injections. She wanted me to give money for these.

"What's wrong with the baby?" I asked through the bored interpreter.

"Fever and vomiting," was the reply.

"Can't she take it to the hospital?" I asked then.

"The hospital wants money for the injections," he translated.

The old woman was shaking her head vigorously, and still held out her hand. I knew by now, however, that this story was not necessarily true, and since I had a little time to do so, decided to try to get the baby some of the medical help I knew was available.

At this point Mrs. Tubro's car pulled up.

"Want a lift?" she asked me through the open window.

I explained the situation briefly and told her I was going to try to help.

"But why doesn't that man help?" she asked, not unreasonably.

I didn't know the answer to that one, however.

"They're funny people," she said from her 45 years' experience. "They never help their own." She had errands to do, and departed.

At Spencer's, I inquired how to contact Corsock, the social agency Father d'Silva worked with.

"Try Mrs. Henderson or Mrs. de Jonge," I was told. This wouldn't work, since they lived clear over on the other side of town and would be in their homes by now, since it was the supper hour. Nevertheless, I hiked up the road toward town, in the hope that a better solution would materialize.

At the Kodai School Dispensary, I found the lady doctor and her assistant, and told the tale again.

"Sounds like one of those cases who prey on the sympathy of visitors," the doctor said. "She can take the baby to the government hospital. There is no charge for treatment there."

"Where is the government hospital?"

"Take the road down at the corner, pass Corsock's place, and it's the next building farther down." I thanked her, and hiked off again.

At the government hospital I found a group of men outside the Labor Department (the OB ward!) and inquired where I might find the doctor. He was in the darkened ward, a nice-looking young man in a yellow sleeveless pullover, with a stethoscope around his neck. I related the story again, and received his assurance that if I brought the child to the hospital it would be admitted immediately. There would be no charge. They had no facilities for getting her there, however; that would be my department.

On the road outside, I found Raja, who had a fare to take to Mungigal but would come immediately to the place near the lake and meet me there. I hurried back to the lake. The place was deserted.

At the tea stall nearby, I asked who spoke English. A man came out, listened to my description, and said he knew where the old woman was. Motioning me to wait, he hurried off, his sandals clicking on the roadway. Raja drove up, and we waited together. Raja, however, hearing the tale, was somewhat skeptical. His doubts increased as he saw the tea-stall man running back, followed by the old lady in dirty pink rags, with a small boy with her. "This lady is a beggar, madam. She lives like that all the time." This was not news, since she had regularly nicked me in the bazaar, but the baby was a different matter.

They came up, breathless, from the long run. Raja questioned the

lady. The baby was in the hospital, she said. I asked where its
mother was. The mother, one of the wood-bearing coolies, had taken
it there. She held out her hand again, and pointed to the small boy,
whose legs were covered with sores, and who had had a perpetual
running nose for the three months I had seen him scrounging in the
bazaar.

"Ask her why she doesn't take the boy to the crèche," I told Raja.
I knew that Mrs. Henderson operated a crèche for the children of
working mothers, where they were bathed, clothed and fed daily,
free of charge. A long palaver followed, the gist of which was that
they already had two other children in this crèche. I didn't think
that would matter; the needs of this small boy were painfully obvious, and the fact that he had brothers and sisters would not matter
to Mrs. Henderson. I told Raja to tell her to take the boy to the
crèche tomorrow, and started back to the car. She followed, with
the same whine, running along behind me to keep up. The boy followed. Through the car window, I gave her five rupees, and told Raja
to instruct her that the boy must be taken to the crèche. She grasped
the money and agreed.

It was two days before I could return to the government hospital
to check on the baby, Mari. On the afternoon of the second day, as I
returned from an engagement, I found the old woman on my front
lawn, with the baby and the little boy. All were in the same state of
shambles, except the boy, whose sores had been picked open and
looked much worse. The child Mari was filthy dirty, wrapped in a
black sack. Regina came out, and so was able to interpret.

"Why isn't this child in the hospital?" I asked through Regina.

"Two injections, madam. All well now." I looked at Mari, whose
sad, bright eyes peered out from a tangle of hair. I felt its forehead.
There was no fever.

"Why isn't the boy at the crèche?" I asked hopelessly.

"Crèche chases him out," Regina said with no conviction.

"And Corsock? Why doesn't she ask help from Corsock?"

This source of aid, also, was apparently closed to this pathetic
crew. The hand was out again. I put five rupees in it and turned to
go into the house. It was obvious that the old woman was not going
to turn the children over to a place where they would be given food
and care, because she was using them for her begging act. The little
baby might be saved if rescued in time, but the boy was already an

accomplished beggar, and I doubted whether anything could now change his fate. Life on the streets was more attractive to him than life in the crèche, playing games on a mat with other children.

Two days later, at the height of the monsoon rain, the old woman was back at my door again, with the baby wrapped in a rag. There was no way I could talk to her without an interpreter, and I sent them away. The following day, as I went into the bazaar, there she was again, accompanied by the baby, the small boy, and an alert-looking little girl who also begged there and whom I had not realized belonged to this family. Fortunately, at the same time, I spotted Elisabeth Rani and the Swiss nun, and was able to enlist them as interpreters. We stood in the blazing sun, in front of the bank, and tried to work out the questions and answers.

"Why isn't the baby at the crèche?"

"They won't take the baby there. They say no."

"Where is the mother?"

"She is at home now."

"Why don't you go to Corsock?"

"Corsock chased us away. No help."

The old woman held out her hand, but the Swiss nun told her, "Madam has already helped you. You must not keep begging like this. It is not right." The hand was withdrawn and the sari moved to reveal the dirty, naked breasts underneath. I had errands at the bank and decided to get on with them. The old woman took up a post outside, waiting for me to emerge. As I was conducting the waiting game in the bank, the Presentation driver came in. I knew he knew all the people in the bazaar, and drew him aside. "See that woman there, Nathan, the one with the two children?"

"Yes."

"She keeps asking me for money. Shouldn't she be able to put that baby in the crèche? It would be fed and cared for there, instead of being dragged around like that."

Nathan smiled and shrugged his shoulders. "She doesn't want to give up the baby every day. Foreigners will give money when they see the baby."

"You tell her this: At two o'clock she must come to Corsock. I will meet her there, and we'll see what can be done."

Nathan told her this and drove off.

At two P.M. it was pouring rain, and I really didn't feel much like going for a mile hike in it, but neither did I want to fail them. So I took my umbrella and told Regina I was going out. She was amazed, but by now ready to accept any peculiarities of madam's. Anyone who typed or read all day was slightly strange anyway.

At Corsock I found Mrs. de Jonge and explained the tale. She thought she knew the family I meant. If it was the same one, she said the mother was a prostitute who stood all day at the bus stand, soliciting. This shook me a bit, but nevertheless I was determined that the children be helped, in spite of the mother's failings. At length, the eight-year-old girl came along, with the poor baby, Mari, riding on her hip, and a blind girl of about twenty hobbling along behind them. The three of them were drenched, their rags flopping around their legs, and I knew the baby would soon have that mysterious "fever" again. It was really a miracle it was still alive.

The little girl was questioned, and said the crèche wouldn't take the baby; they had tried. We asked when they had tried, since Mrs. Henderson, who aided the crèche, was there at Corsock and had never seen this set of kids. "Two or three years ago" was the answer. Since the baby was about six months old, I realized she must be talking about an experience with another child, perhaps the little boy.

Mrs. de Jonge spoke through an interpreter to the child, and told her to go and get her mother. The girl bounced the baby down in the arms of the blind girl and took off, her tangled hair bouncing as she ran. The people at Corsock all got interested in the little drama by this time, and I asked one of them to inquire of the blind girl who she was. The answer was that she was no relative; they had taken her in because she had no father and no mother, and nowhere to live.

This was a startling revelation to me, which I pointed out to Mrs. de Jonge; here was a family so poor they had to beg, yet they had shared their living space with a total stranger who was blind. In my mind, at least, it pointed to a charity among them that was greater than the small one I was attempting.

When the baby's mother arrived, everyone in the shop gave a little sigh. It was indeed the prostitute they all knew about. She was hardly the type to drive men wild. She had no front teeth at all and was in a state of such dirty dishabille it was difficult to imagine her as successful in her chosen profession. There was a pitiful simplicity in her humble stance as she tried to ward off the fire of questions that tore away her pretense. She claimed to be a wood coolie. Mrs. de Jonge asked her why she was not now carrying wood. The baby was sick. Yet the baby was out in the rain. Nothing made much sense, and I soon realized that this turn of questioning would not be productive. I dragged the conversation back to the question of care for the baby in the crèche.

Mrs. Henderson said the crèche would not take the baby unless the mother was working.

"This mother is working," I said firmly. "She carries wood." Mrs. Henderson looked at me with her kind eyes. Then she added, "The crèche will not take a child unless it is brought daily. I recall this family. Her sisters also brought children, once, or twice a week, and remained away for a week, and then would come again. We can't run the crèche like that. It must be on a regular, daily basis." I told her I would try to make it regular. Finally I asked if she would write a note to the crèche that we could take to the authorities there, and see about the matter. She did so. The mother took the note, and was instructed to bring me to the crèche. We set off down the road, and were joined by a pretty girl, also in rags, who looked about twelve years old. The woman said this was her eldest daughter. She had five children.

We walked a very long way, and I was beginning to tire. The crèche was in the next village, Mungigal. We passed well-dressed people who were obviously curious about my involvement with these ragamuffins, but I ignored them. Some small boys hooted at us as we passed, and the little girl tossed her head. We finally came to a set of buildings.

"Crèche" the woman said. We went in. There was quite a flurry of excitement among the neatly dressed matrons who ran the crèche, and I was ushered in with a low namaste. They tried to bar the family from entering, but I motioned them in with me. We gave the note to the person in charge. She read it, and spoke in Tamil to the woman. It developed that she was fed up with the family, due to their slovenly ways, and she was sure they would not bring the baby on a regular daily basis to the crèche. I assured her that they would, though on what authority I don't know. When that matter was settled, with the mother agreeing to show up at eight each morning with the child and to pick it up at five in the afternoon, I turned my attention to the two girls. I used the crèche lady as interpreter.

"Tell the mother that these two girls must go to the nonformal school." There was a great agreement among the matrons, and lots of heads nodding. They had been trying for a long time to get them into schools.

"Tell them they must go each day. They must wash and keep clean. If they do this, I will pay them thirty rupees each week for rice. If they stop school, the rupees also stop." I really don't know where this idea came from. It just seemed like the way to handle it at the time. It would accomplish several things. With a specific sum of money a guaranteed fact each week, the mother could perhaps give up her bus-stop activity and just carry wood. The girls, who could neither read nor write, would learn something and be able to escape the mother's fate. Thirty rupees per week was a very small sum, but it would buy the requisite food.

The mother then raised the skirt of the twelve-year-old girl and pointed to an angry burn scar. She told the crèche lady that this girl needed injections, and they had no money. I could see that the scar was healed, but something kept me from pointing this out. I questioned a bit further and was told there was another sore "higher up," and it was this that needed medication. We all trooped over to the dispensary next door.

There I found a capable Belgian I.C.M. sister, Sister Angell, who took us all in because I was there, and listened to our story. I told her I would like to help the family but thought the begging pattern had to be broken. I planned to ask her to dispense money to the family each week, on condition that the two girls remained in school. She glanced at the girls. Then she looked at me intently and said, "I've seen this larger girl before. She has syphilis!"

I must have showed my shock and alarm. She told me to come into the examining room with the girl and she would show me. The girl got up on the table, and the nun donned plastic gloves. The sore, angry and festering on the black skin was a sight I would like to forget but never shall.

"My God, Sister, this is a little child. How could she get this?"

The nun was quite matter-of-fact. "It is terrible when you think of it, no? But it is very infectious. She could have picked it up by some contact in the village, squatting in a dirty place. Maybe from the mother herself." The nun seemed to know all about the mother. I insisted that the entire family be examined, including the baby. They were free of the disease. Only the twelve-year-old girl had it. What could be done?

"She needs a series of injections, ten at least, of penicillin. I can give them, but it would cost fourteen rupees." I handed over the miserable sum—about two dollars—that stood between the child and health. The first of the ten injections was administered on the spot. The nun told her to come back each Monday until all had been given, and she was sure that this would cure the disease. She also cautioned the others to avoid contact with her until she was well, though this seemed a futile precaution.

We got back to the school plan. The nonformal school had no objection to admitting the children, since treatment had begun. Sister Paula, who was in charge of the school, agreed to be the dispenser of the thirty rupees per week.

"Please explain to the mother that the money stops if the children stop going to school," I cautioned the nun. I knew how frequently children are taken from school to mind children or do small jobs about the house. Sister promised she would explain all of this thoroughly to them. I looked at the little family clustered around me. I started out the door.

Sister Angell called me, "But why don't you tell them yourself about the money? They would wish to thank you."

"Tell them to thank God," I told her, and added, "Tell them to pray to Our Lord, Jesus Christ." She said she would, and I walked back to Snyder "B." The money I had promised to pay weekly was not my money but Ted Huebsch's, and I knew that this arrangement would please his charitable heart very much.

Three hours later, the old woman was at my door again, with the small boy. She said, through Regina, that she wanted money. I explained, also through Regina, what had been done for her daughter and the children. It somehow eluded her. The whine continued. I knew then there would be no end to this project until I had finally left town. The habit of begging was so deeply ingrained in this poor soul that even with her larder filled, she would continue the habit.

I waited two days, and then went to Mungigal to see if the baby had been brought to the crèche. Raja pulled up outside, and about forty-five or fifty small kids, milling about in the compound, ran over to namaste to me. The lady in charge told me they had indeed brought the baby, but that Sister Angell had made an examination and found it ill and was treating it before it would be placed near the other babies in the crèche. At least, I thought, they had begun to follow through. My next stop was at St. John's nonformal school. The two girls had been there the day before, as I had asked. Arul, their teacher, listened carefully as I explained my little plot to her, and agreed to keep a watch over the family since they lived not far from her. She, too, began to tell me of the mother's "profession," but I waved it aside. And I could see by the sincere, intelligent face before me, that if the girls continued under her care, they would progress. It would be impossible not to.

The nonformal school is open daily from 3:30 to 5 P.M., three days a week, and from 5 to 7 P.M. on the other two. Most of the students are wood coolies, and they come there after carrying their loads down from the hills. Courses are offered in hygiene, history of India, and various social disciplines, and the children are thus broadened a bit beyond their normal benighted state. After several years in this school, it is often possible for the children to move to more productive work, and better pay.

The family are Hindu, but I begged a lovely picture of Christ the Good Shepherd from the nuns at Holy Cross and gave it to Sister Paula to give to the family. I thought they might like to have a picture of their Benefactor in the house. Ted had supplied the money, but only because of the very real love he and Mary have for Jesus Christ.

CHAPTER 27

Festival

Meenakshi, meaning "she who has fish eyes," is the goddess of Madurai. According to the "Vileiyadal," she was incarnated under the name of Thadadagei (the invincible), daughter of Maleyattavasa Pandiyen, to whom she succeeded for want of a male heir. She was married to Siva, who came to reign in Madurai under the name of Chockanathen, or Sunderesvaram. Meenakshi was the mother of Subramaniam, who was incarnated under the name of Oukrama Pandiyam. Her marriage is celebrated every year just before the full moon of the month of Sittirai: April–May.

I was very eager to go down to the temple city to witness this, since part of the festival consists of the drawing of a very heavy, towering cart through the streets. As many as two thousand persons are harnessed to accomplish this feat. The nuns were not enthusiastic.

"You'll die of the heat," said Sister Ethna.

"The crowds will be too great," said Sister Xavier.

"But I need to see this festival," I protested, smiling. "Think of my art!"

"I hope you'll come back with your art intact," said Sister Ethna.

I knew, however, that if I allowed this opportunity to see a genuine Hindu festival slip past me, I would kick myself later. I arranged to go. Sister Ethna gave me a medal of St. Benedict to keep me safe.

The mythology of the feast has Meenakshi planning to be married. Siva, her bridegroom, comes from a distance to the wedding. But, at the crucial moment, when the wedding is to be celebrated, a Brahmin priest sneezes, and the whole thing is postponed for another year. In addition, Meenakshi has a brother, Alahur, who has been invited to the wedding. But en route he stops to visit his lover,

Islam, who lives outside Madurai, and lingers there so long that he comes late for the wedding. As a punishment, when his image is carried back the six miles to his temple, on the backs of the Kallers, whose god he is, Alahur is not taken inside but left out in the weather for six months. This soap opera is enacted each year in the month of Sittirai.

And so cleverly is it contrived that not only the Hindu population but also the Muslim population are involved in the preparation for the festival, since Islam is a Muslim. The Kallers are drawn into it by reason of the fact that their patron, Alahur, is the tardy brother. I expected to see millions involved in this affair, and hoped the nuns of St. Joseph Convent would be able to arrange a safe place from which I could see at least some of the festival.

Once again, then, I boarded a bus for Madurai. This time, the ride held few terrors for me. I was beginning to feel a seasoned traveler. I arrived early, found a seat near the front of the bus with only one empty next to me. Outside, the bazaar was coming to life for the new day, though it was only 7 A.M. A large group of dogs came down the road, lacking only attaché cases to complete the illusion of businessmen on errands both urgent and important. They trotted through an open gate with a sense of high purpose. Three minutes afterward, a small brown latecomer came racing down the road, looking around in distraction as though wondering which gate the meeting was being held at and nearly biting his nails in anxiety. Meantime the thumping on the roof of the bus told me that sacks of potatoes were going to ride down to Madurai with us. Seven small girls in half saris boarded, and clambered up to the front of the bus, where they crowded into the seats opposite me and piled battered suitcases in the aisle. They all carried lunches. The Eucalyptus Oil Company (Branch ⚬3) gave off a pleasantly medicinal odor, which wafted through the open windows of the bus, and the fruit stands farther down opened their metal shutters; their owners began hanging bunches of bananas from the twine overhead. The tardy dog, weary of his fruitless search for the big conference, curled up on the road in front of the bus and went to sleep. Several benign cows sauntered past, barely missing the dog. Young men with oiled heads, wearing very clean dhotis and wristwatches, waited for the coffee stand to open and, chatting genially with one another, pausing to spit from time to time, caught up on the gossip.

The bus lumbered away, finally, and the seat next to me was empty. But at Mungigal a young woman boarded, carrying a small baby. She sat down next to me, dug her elbow companionably into my ribs, and finding a firm support there, transferred the baby to that arm. Thus I rode to Madurai with the burden of mother and child in my rib cage. She went to sleep and did not awaken until Uttu, where she leaned across me to purchase jackfruit from the vendor. I tried shifting my weight from time to time, to assert my right to half the seat, but she was quite pliant and ready to adjust to whatever position I assumed. Once I stopped squirming, she found her elbow rest once more and again went to sleep.

The convent at St. Joseph's kindly sent a man to the bus stop to find me. Again, the advantage of the only white skin on the bus came home to me; he found me at once, and asked if I were Mrs. Anton. Thus assured, he took my bag and we trotted off together in the blazing sunlight of Madurai. We found a small conveyance, which was actually a motorcycle with three wheels, surrounded by a kind of metal covering. The driver proved maniacal, whether drunk, on drugs, crazy, or all three, I could not tell. It may have been the frenzy induced by the sight of a foreign woman, though my gray hair and venerable years have surely buried whatever fatal charm I might have once possessed. At any rate, we flew in and out of bullock carts, large automobiles, goats, children and locals with such horrifyingly close encounters that I found myself, teeth chattering, praying madly. Several times, we were brought to a halt, pinched between taxis, with their drivers and our madman shouting at one another in Tamil. I begged my guide to tell this creature to go slowly, but the admonition only increased his desire to break the sound barrier. Zipping at last through large iron gates at the convent, he propelled me into the charitable arms of the Sisters of St. Joseph. I paid him off, and hoped never to see him again. It was some time before I regained my equilibrium and was able to recognize the terrific force of the April heat. Nearing noon, Madurai was a closed-in steam bath. The nuns gave me their guest room, showed me the eighteenth-century sanitary facilities, and left me to rest a bit before lunch.

At lunch I met the community. They are a venerable order, having been founded at Lyons by a Jesuit priest during the seventeenth century. The foreign sisters (French) have all departed for France now, save one or two too old to travel. Their sad leave-taking was still a matter of great discussion; most of the French nuns had been in India so long they were more Indian than French, and the decision to recall them caused great heartache. The members of the congregation are now Indians at Madurai. Very capable and devout religious, they will undoubtedly carry on with the work of the congregation as did the French before them. The work will now be completely Indian. They have four thousand children in school at Madurai.

In order to make it possible for me to learn about the festival, they had asked one of their teachers, a young Brahmin lady, to accompany me by cab to a site where I might see at least some of the festivities. She was A. Verkalakshmi, a neatly made, tiny little woman, wearing a cotton sari. She was a linguist who spoke four languages, including English, and proved a most willing and informative guide.

We engaged a cab to take us to a place near the Vaigai River, where Alahur's statue would be coming down from his shrine, carried on the shoulders of the Kallers. All along the road as we headed to the river, I could see shrines decorated to the rafters. Verkalakshmi told me that the god would be visiting each of these shrines, and had, indeed, been en route from his temple shrine for the past ten hours or so. The crowds grew denser as we progressed, and finally, though we still had about one and one half blocks to go, the driver was forced to halt the cab and park. He told us he would remain there and we could proceed through the sea of humanity on foot.

We alighted, and though I was carrying my umbrella, the blast of the sun penetrated its thin cloth and found my head. I was quickly drenched in perspiration. As the only foreigner in town, it appeared, I became almost as much a focal point for spectators as the god himself, and the effort to walk was hampered by a cordon of small boys and girls who surrounded me tightly. Verkalakshmi cautioned me to close the top of my camera bag and hold it close to me. She herself carried no purse, I noted. It took us more than half an hour to go the block and a half. By this time my legs had turned to jelly and my eyes smarted from the salt perspiration I was spouting from my hair. I was holding an umbrella with one hand, and the heavy, totally useless movie camera with the other, and was thus powerless to do more than wipe my brow with my cotton sleeve. At length we came to the shrine where the god was pausing on his journey. There was a large colored canopy of reeds and cloth at the entrance, and though it was tightly packed with the faithful, I thought it would be better there than in the sun. I was wrong. In that crush there was no air at all. By sheer will power I stayed there for about ten minutes, while my eyes searched the dim interior for a glimpse of the god. But I knew I had to breathe again, so I suggested we go out to the road in the sun again.

The god would soon be coming out now, Verkalakshmi told me, and I looked down at her serene face, showing no hint of difficulty with the intense heat. She smiled up at me. "We are used to the sun," she told me, adding, "but it must be terrible for you, after Kodai."

I thought to myself, she doesn't know the half of it. Verkalakshmi began relating again the tale of the festival, adding many little points of interest, while the crowd surged forward again, pressing hard around us, the small kids fighting to get close enough to gaze up into my white (but probably now red) face. The scene took on a strange unreality. The sun blazed down unmercifully on my umbrella. And suddenly the ground seemed to give way under my feet. I realized I was about to fall. Something in my brain, far, far back, said to me, "If you fall now, you'll never get up again. You'll be trampled to death here on this road." I remembered the medal of St. Benedict and, with my umbrella still in the same hand, I caught hold of it. "St. Benedict," I prayed silently, "please take care of me." I turned to Verkalakshmi and placed my hand on her shoulder for support. "I'll have to get out of this sun," I told her. One look at my face must have convinced her, too. We turned and began fighting our way through the crowd, which was now moving forward toward the shrine. I really don't know how we got back to the cab. I only know that when we did and I was finally sitting in that oven and my eyes began to focus again and I was certain that I was going to live, I closed my eyes and thanked God for my deliverance.

Meanwhile, several persons wearing false faces and plumes danced down the road in front of the cab, while drums beat and the crowd cheered. These were clowns, and they amused the children and capered in the dust with great energy. Finally the procession came past, Alahur carrying a staff, which marked him as one of the robber caste. He turned out to be a rather small statue, riding on a strange

litter with curved handles and much tasseled decoration. We left the
scene and drove off to the Temple of Meenakshi.

Verkalakshmi reminded me that I could not enter the temple
wearing my shoes, and I had no intention of walking around on that
damp, filthy floor in my nylons. I told her I must buy white sox. At a
shop nearby we found a pair, and I purchased them. We walked to
the temple entrance, left our shoes, and I donned the sox. Entering
the temple I remembered the last time I had seen it: with Bert
Nevett, in 1971. Now it was jammed with people. Once past the
porticos, lined with strange and ancient carved figures, we entered an
area where every kind of shop had been set up to enable the pilgrim
to combine business with devotion. There were vendors of flowers
and of bangles, food and drink stands, souvenir shops and jewelry
stalls, all doing a lively business. An elephant patiently stood in the
center, bored out of his mind, he seemed, while screaming children
were lifted to his back for good luck and their parents gave rupees to
the attendant, which constituted *his* good luck. The only light
within this bazaar was the dim skylight above and the neon of the
garish shops.

We left this arena and sought the inner reaches of the temple.
We passed through a *mundabum* (pillared courtyard), where hundreds of families had taken possession of small areas under the pillars
and had set up housekeeping. These had come from all over India,
according to my guide, and would remain here for several days, making *puja* to their favorite gods and joining in the annual joy of Sittirai. Copper pots, stainless-steel buckets and hampers of fruit, rice
and curry ranged around the straw mats, where many children already dozed amid the flies and smells of cooking.

The temple tank, dark brown waters lapping around the legs of
devotees, one of whom was actually drinking it in his cupped hands,
was open to the sunlight. Ranged around this tank were more porticos, where shade could be found. I stepped across banana peelings,
decaying flowers and damp rocks where germs had been congregating
for some one thousand two hundred years, according to Verkalakshmi. I was happy about the sox, though I knew they would never
be usable again.

The temple is an architectural wonder, no question about it. Once
the eyes are lifted above the ground, there are carved stone statues
that are marvels to behold. Shrines to every god in the pantheon

seem to be here. One such station held court for the gods of the planets, and as this was Saturday, Saturn was doing a big business. A Brahmin stood at the open gateway before the statue of the god and offered little lamps purchased at a nearby stall by the pilgrims. At another shrine, whose entrance was decorated by a mammoth statue of a dragon subduing an elephant, a very old woman in a purple sari prostrated herself on the stairs in front of the shrine. Hanuman, the monkey god, was accepting offerings of food baskets, and I noticed that many of the pilgrims carried these: they contained coconut, flowers and bananas. My guide told me that many would take these to the Brahmin for blessing. The priest would split the coconut and return half to the pilgrim, retaining the other half as an offering.

Entering another hall, we found Ganesh, the elephant-headed god, serenely seated with a white sheet over his huge legs, while many lamps of devotion burned on the greasy stand before him. But the shrine where Meenakshi reposed was off limits for me; we could not enter there. Instead, the dainty Verkalakshmi prostrated herself on a large design on the floor, which seemed to contain the Star of David but probably meant something else. To my horror, this exquisite little woman placed her forehead and hands on that floor, the filth of which I shall never get out of my white sox. I admired not only her devotion but her courage.

She was quite willing to continue the tour through the dim caverns of this great temple, where thousands of Hindus swarmed through the pillars and squatted on the stones. I felt, however, that I had seen enough of this aspect of the festival, and asked about the lovely palace I remembered from a former visit.

Outside, we found our shoes and our cab and set off for the palace of the Madurai kings of the seventeenth century. It is called Thirumaldi Naiker Mahal, and it is a magnificent architectural gem. I had seen it in 1971, when there were a series of dreary offices set up between the lovely pillars, where law courts conducted their business. I had been distressed to see the electrical wires running all over the pillars and walls, in a primitive attempt to bring a crude illumination to the vast structure. Now all the naked wiring was gone, and I was delighted to see that the pillars were being restored and the neglected ceilings and fluted archways were beginning to show the hand of intelligent restoration.

The palace must have been a glory in its day. A vast open courtyard is surrounded by pillared verandas of enormous depth and size, but the harmony and symmetry of the structure are very pleasing. I searched in vain for the enormous stone horses I remembered from my previous visit; they must be in a museum now. We wandered around for a while and found a marvelous hall with three levels to the floor and with incredibly beautiful stone carvings high up on the walls, interspersed with wonderfully shaped windows. This was the hall where the kings of Madurai were entertained by dancing girls, and it was easy to reconstruct the scene. Lit by torches, in vast sconces on the pillars, the hall must have been something out of *The Arabian Nights*. One could almost hear the music of the tabla and veena and the whine of the sitar still echoing in that haunted hall. Walking through this pleasure dome brought home the spell of Madurai's former glory. The palace, the temple, the shrines now crumbling on the outskirts of the city—these must have been important centers for the people of South India long ago. There was nothing remotely as grand in present-day Madurai.

And then we drove to the famous tank, now filled with water only for the feast: Teppakulam. This covers about two square blocks and is surrounded by a low white-and-red wall. I asked Verkalakshmi about the red and white stripes, used on many temple walls. It is a decoration meant to bring good fortune, she told me. On an island in the center of this tank is a pleasant little temple surrounded by greenery. One could take a small boat and venture there for the day, bringing lunch. Many did this during festival time. And on the roadway all around the tank, the brown rice was spread out, awaiting the wheels of carts, trucks, cabs and rickshaws to aid in the removal of the husks. Several women bent from the waist and stroked it into shape with the short Indian whisk.

Back at the convent, I dined with the sisters, chatted awhile at recreation, and then excused myself early. I was quite exhausted. The festivities in the morning would include the coming of Alahur to the Vaigai River, where his toe would be permitted to touch the water, and thereafter he would be conveyed back to his temple again, to fulfill his punishment of outdoor living for the next six months. But the event was planned for 6 A.M. The hour was certainly wise from the standpoint of weather, I thought, but when I sought a cab to take me to the river, I was told it would be impossible for a car to get through the mob. One had to walk. I thought of the crowded scene of that afternoon, and knowing that the river was a full four miles from the convent, decided to forget about seeing Alahur dip his toe in the Vaigai. Instead, I dipped my toe into a small bucket in the guest washroom and had a "teacup bath."

Sleep that night was an adventure. The guest room was next to the road, about one block from the nuns' quarters, probably because their guests would be priests giving retreats, and these would require privacy, away from the convent. Whitewashed and very clean, the walls ascended to the regulation twenty feet, unrelieved by any decoration save a crucifix and a small wall lizard. After two and one half months in India, I knew what degree of comfort might be expected from nuns' mattresses, and was not disappointed. It was like a rock; a narrow one. I inched myself onto it and found that the electric fan, thoughtfully provided, was so placed that it blew a tornado at my head, and though it felt good, I knew I would have a cold by morning. I got up and arranged the bedspread over the high netting post, to divert the gale. I now had a sail on my bed, with a breeze blowing all along the edges of it. It worked fine. Thus launched, I fell asleep.

At about 2 A.M. Alahur and his army of devotees came roaring down the road past my room. The din was terrific, and at first I was bewildered, thinking a riot had broken out. Then I remembered the festival and lay there while the crowd shouted, whistled, sang, drummed and stamped past, their footsteps finally becoming fainter in the distance. I wished the footsore Hindus Godspeed, suddenly aware that the phrase had seldom been more appropriate, and went back to sleep.

CHAPTER 28

Farewell to Kodai

The time of my stay in Kodai was drawing to a close. I would leave some things there in a trunk, and put it in the keeping of the sisters at Presentation Convent. If God willed it, I planned to return as soon as possible to those beautiful hills.

But now my thoughts were turned northward, toward another hill station, Darjeeling, in the Himalayas, two thousand miles north. Father Nevett was there, at St. Joseph's College, and I had planned to spend ten days there, to report my conclusions on the experiment, to discuss the children on the Nevett Fund with him, and to enjoy again the warm and delightful friendship that was ours.

"I've been made cricket coach for the big tournament," he wrote me. "Cricket is a mystery to Americans, and a religion to the English, Australians and West Indians. You're invited to the match."

I wrote back that I would come only if there was a coach's uniform, preferably with a little cap.

Bert Nevett has been in Darjeeling now for many years. Some years ago, he had been president of St. Joseph's College and then had been transferred South. Now he had returned there, where his health was always better than anywhere else, probably due to the cooler climate of those hills. I had twice before visited Darjeeling and knew many of the people there. The culture of the North was entirely different, of course. In Darjeeling the people are Nepalese, Sherpas, Tibetans, or Bengalis. Their dress, language, mental processes, work habits and religion are quite distinct from those of the people of Tamil Nadu, and I looked forward to another glimpse of this fascinating culture.

Leaving Snyder "B" for Darjeeling required intense consideration of my luggage, which, like Gaul, was divided into three parts. The steel trunk, containing kitchen utensils, sleeping bag, typewriter, lamps and miscellaneous household chattels, would remain at Kodai with the Presentation Sisters, pending my return. They had instructions on further disposal in case of my death: send it to Father Nevett or, failing that, back home to Oak Park. A second contingent, of two suitcases, would be shipped from Madras via Air India as unaccompanied luggage; the third, of one suitcase, one bag of fragile souvenirs and a small overnight case, would accompany me to Darjeeling.

Raja would drive me to Madurai for the early flight to Madras; he would come to the house at 3 A.M. The previous day would be spent paying Mohan Lal, retracing the inventory with Job, bringing the trunk to Presentation Convent, and saying good-bye to all my friends in Kodai. I would also go to Shembag to return the bed linen, thank the Jesuits, and take from there any material the archives would release for Father Nevett's book on St. John de Britto. Regina would also be taken home, paid, thanked and bidden good-bye.

The route to Darjeeling would take me to Madras again, for an entire day. I needed this to arrange shipment of my bags back to America. Then I'd fly from Madras to Calcutta, where I would remain for what I hoped would be a less dreadful night and at noon on April 30 fly to Bagdogra, where Father Nevett would meet me with a car for the ride up the mountain road to Darjeeling.

It seemed wise, after packing, to rest as much as possible before the strenuous two-day journey through the heat. I would be leaving 75 degrees, descending into 105+ for two days, and returning to the 70s again.

Walking down my garden path, under a deep blue sky where white cumulus clouds billowed up giving a hint of the rain that might come two hours later, I rejoiced in the lovely results of Muthusamy's care. There were geraniums, impatiens, cactuses, several marvelous climbing pink roses, violets, chrysanthemums, begonia bushes five feet high, marigolds, alyssums, daisies in several colors, a stand or two of sweet peas, many poppies in various shades, Canterbury bells, buttercups, phlox, and three or four varieties I did not know. All of this bordered by a gray-green low herb. Only in mid-July, at home, in very special gardens would this kind of heavenly scented beauty be possible. I would miss my garden. Muthusamy asked me to give him a letter of recommendation, for what mystic purpose I could not guess, but I gave him a glowing one, together with some money.

Two days before I was to leave, Father John Clayton came unexpectedly to Kodai. During my previous visits, I had hoped to meet this Jesuit missionary who cared for many of our children in the deep South, but he had always been too far away from our route. Now, by the grace of God, here he was. We spent a fine morning together. From him I learned the distilled wisdom of fifty-two years on the mission station. And listening to him, I knew the truth of Father Nevett's frequently stated belief that here was a living saint. He spoke of his life with great simplicity, pausing often to praise God for the loving Providence that had given him so many opportunities to serve Him. There was so much hardship evident in the shadowed eyes and the halting gait, that I was overcome with admiration at his spirit and his complete devotion to the cause of Christ. But conversions? There had been very few. Not even that consolation had been given to this holy man. Only the joy of service, unremitting sacrifice, day in and day out, as he went to his twenty-seven villages to offer Mass and bring the people the sacraments. We spoke of our children on the fund, and from him I learned of the new lives possible only because of the educations we were providing through our members in the States. He thanked them all, through me. And as I watched him leave and walk down my garden path, I thought that if all we had done in our lives was to somehow bring a measure of comfort by our support of such a man, all our efforts were worthwhile. Father Clayton has been a channel of hope and grace to countless people.

Leave-taking was even more difficult than I had thought: in two and one half months I had found so many friends; and though I was leaving my trunk behind as a tenuous thread designed to pull me back to Kodai, the future lay hidden; and only God knew if and when I might return. I bade the nuns at Presentation good-bye, totally failing in my emotion to convey adequately what their friendship and love had meant to me; Father Montaud gave me his blessing in a graceful little farewell that only a Frenchman could have devised; the Tubros gave me a lovely luncheon, and we spoke of next year in a hopeful manner. The Jesuits at Shembag were away at meetings, but I had said good-bye to them a few weeks previously.

Raja arrived at 3 A.M. to drive me to the airport at Madurai. We dropped Regina at her home. Her family came pouring out of the little hut to wave, and Regina wept. The car drifted through the night mists down the ghat road; there was less traffic at that hour, though about seven lorries lumbered past us on the dark path. I dozed a bit, and thought of the American school, High Clerc, and the teachers there who had been so kind to me: Miss Dennison, who taught the primary grades and lived in a charming cottage on campus, where I had gone for lunch one day. Her golden room was lit in the noon sun, which glinted off the bell collection at one window, and the friendly hearth. A deep red carpet provided space for about seven or eight small children, who played with her games pulled from a cupboard kept especially for this use. She and I had lunch at a table near the wall. Occasionally the games would become noisy, and her gentle voice would rebuke them with the reminder that she had a guest and they must keep their voices lower, while I wondered silently if the parents of these small children knew what a haven their exiled babies had found under that hospitable roof. The High Clerc Library had provided me with books to read in the lonely evenings, and Mrs. Mary Moon, the librarian, had also entertained me in her chic and spotless cottage near the bazaar. It almost seemed to me that traveling alone provided a wonderful benefit in that it made it necessary to leave a natural reserve behind and go out to meet the world in which I had found myself, and thus to discover so many interesting and wonderful people. Traveling with a friend would have restricted this opportunity; I had observed many travelers in pairs who, having a companion already, did not venture forth alone or chance conversations with local people. It was reassuring to discover again what I had always known: the world is filled with interesting and worthwhile people, and one has only to be open and willingly take the small risk necessary to find them. In spite of the dictum my mother had always preached: "Never speak to strangers," which I had faithfully passed on in the training of my own children, I found that really one never speaks to strangers: the vast majority of people one encounters are not strangers, but friends one has not yet had the opportunity to meet.

CHAPTER 29

Darjeeling

The journey north from Kodaikanal was broken in Madras. Three of my suitcases containing heavier clothing could now be shipped home, reversing the process by which they had arrived in India. Because of the miserable performance of Pan Am, I decided to place this task in the hands of Air India, and accordingly, upon arrival at Madras, I found a cab, loaded my luggage aboard, and asked the driver to take me to the Air India cargo section, and wait for me. It proved to be as mysterious and prolonged a wait as that for the Second Coming.

I found a man at the cargo desk who told me to put my luggage in a corner of his office and go to get the papers processed. This should have warned me I was in for another Indian jigsaw, the essential pieces missing, but it didn't. I calmly directed the cab driver to place my luggage in a remote corner of the room and then to wait for me in the parking lot. Meandering around, I found a man with a cloth bag around his neck, who understood what I needed and drew a packet of forms from the bag. Together we found a solid ledge where he could write, and began the process with great courtesy and high hope. An electric fan in the ceiling kept ruffling the multiform, so that he was continually delayed while he straightened out the carbon again. The form was 15 by 24 and seemed to require many carbons, so this shuffling consumed a great deal of time. Finally he found a brick and placed it on the airborne edge and continued recording the details of my shipment.

Completing this process, which had been interrupted by the casual visit of a relative or friend, during which the amenities were exchanged in leisurely fashion while he placed a protecting arm over the massive form to prevent it from taking off in the breeze, the little man turned to me and said, "Now, madam, you must take this form to the desk over there and have it signed by an officer."

I thanked him, and made my way to the counter, pondering the time already consumed on the ticking meter of my waiting cab. The officer whose signature was required was not available.

"Where is he?" I queried, beads of perspiration forming on my brow.

"He's just taking his tea," said the desk clerk, smiling. "Just sit down, he should be here in about fifteen minutes."

"But I have a cab waiting," I said. "Can't someone else sign this paper?"

The clerk acknowledged with a secret smile this obviously foreign notion of customer service. "No, madam," he said gently, "only he can sign the form."

I sat down and waited.

When the tea-refreshed officer appeared, it was to direct me to another building.

"But this is the cargo section," I stated firmly. "I was directed here."

"Madam, we have three cargo buildings," he said. "The one you want is just down the road."

I gathered up my purse and documents, took a firm hold on my temper, and went out to the blinding sun and the 100+ temperature to find my driver. He was asleep behind the wheel. I explained where we were to go next and leaned gingerly back against the sticky imitation leather. We wound our way past the security station and drove down the sandy road to a stucco building behind a fence. The officer in this building was on the second floor. I used the elevator.

There I found the same crew I had encountered some three months before, when I had tried to find my luggage. They were busy, but eventually someone noticed me dripping near the counter and asked what I wanted. I produced the documents for signature. They pondered them for a while, conferring with one another in Tamil, and told me that the cargo office I needed was the one in the airport. I descended via the elevator again and found my cab. The airport was two blocks away. There I entered the cargo section by dint of physically thrusting myself through a thick crowd of passengers, and tried to gain the attention of the clerk. A flight was either just coming or just leaving, and he was disinclined to enter negotiations with me.

"Come back in half an hour, madam," he said. "I'm very busy just now." Mopping my brow with a damp handkerchief, I persisted. Finally I found a man who looked official (he wore shoes) and asked if he could sign the papers.

"You want the other cargo room. It's upstairs," he said. About one hour had now elapsed. I pushed my way through the listless passengers again and climbed the stairs. There a man deigned to sign the papers, and then spoiled it by telling me I must take them back to the cargo section down the road. Only they could arrange for payment.

The cab driver seemed glad to see me again. He found the process an interesting diversion in an otherwise dull existence. We drove back to Base #2. Payment would be two hundred dollars. Cash, please. The American Express card was totally useless. But I was wary now, recalling that my previous misadventure with Pan Am had been prepaid. "I prefer to pay on arrival," I said, thinking that this would at least ensure that the costly bags would finally arrive, if only to collect on them.

"That is impossible, madam," he said. But by now I was wearing combat boots.

"Where is the manager of this section?" I yelped. "I want to speak to him." This was magical. I was ushered into a large office that was delightfully cool, and upon stating my wishes, was immediately granted permission to do it my way. Only the underlings are difficult, I decided. The Men in Command are usually gracious and helpful. Perhaps the air-conditioned office had something to do with it. I should, of course, have told him of my difficulties with the blasted paperwork, but I refrained in the ignorant belief that my business was concluded, shipment arranged, and I was prepared to leave. But it was not to be.

"What is the weight of your luggage?" the counterman wanted to know.

"I don't know," I confessed. "It's all over in the other cargo building."

"Then, you will return there, have them weighed, and bring me that information." I thought of the white heat outside, the ticking meter, and the distinct impression of quicksand around my ankles. I returned to Cargo Section ⅓1, found coolies to carry the luggage to a scale, waited for a series of mysterious adjustments and several other weighings, and then had my stuff weighed. I brought this information back to Cargo Section ⅓2, hanging on to the desk for support. When still another signature was required, I began to crack. It meant another trip back to the airport. There I must have seemed on the verge of fainting, because the man at the cargo window took pity on me as he pointed out that I was at a wrong station. He gave me a hand-picked guide to bring me to the "proper authority." The guide wore a mustard-colored jacket over his dhoti, and no shoes. We wound our way to another office. The "proper authority" examined the papers as though they were moon rocks. He knew nothing whatever of the nature of his function with regard to them, nor anything at all about where to sign them. I staggered out of the office followed by my perspiring guide. In the corridor I encountered what looked like an admiral, complete with golden epaulets on his shoulders and a yachting cap.

"Sir," I began slowly, "if you do not help me this instant I intend to stage a spectacular nervous breakdown immediately."

"What is the nature of your difficulty, madam?" he said kindly, sensing its urgency.

This compassion had a strange effect. My lips began to tremble, and my eyes filled with tears. "I have been wandering around this damned cargo area for the past two and one half hours, trying to ship my luggage to America. It's hot, and I'm going to be sick. Do you understand anything at all about these papers?" I thrust the pile of documents at his chest.

He glanced through them casually.

"But you're in the wrong building," he said.

"Look," I said, trembling unaccountably. "They gave me this guide to find the right office, and even he can't find it."

The splendid one glanced at the guide. "How could he know? He's a waiter from the dining room!" I must have begun to sway. He pointed me into a chair and disappeared with the papers. Within seconds he was back again, and they had been signed. By whom, I will never know. I should have been grateful, I suppose. His next words, however, forever removed that impulse.

"But you should have come to me immediately, you know," he chided. "You could have saved yourself a lot of trouble." Beyond the fact that no one in cargo seemed to know of this man's existence, nor of his mysterious power of obtaining signatures (could he have been Michael the Archangel?), the tremendous illogicality of this statement all but finished me. I had, of course, then to return to Cargo Base #1 and get my luggage cleared through customs.

My advice to travelers to India: carry with you only one change of clothing, strap it to your back. Have nothing whatever to do with shipments, baggage rooms or cargo sections, and enter not the maze of bureaucracy that envelops the airlines of India. That way madness lies. My chief regret was in having finally to surrender that document. I had been considering an ornate frame for it.

The cab driver was beginning to awaken after his long siesta, and had ground into low gear to begin the trip to the hotel, when the first cargo man, the one with the bag of forms around his neck, came padding out in his bare feet, waving his arms at me. I feared that there must be more signatures required. He wanted five rupees for the forms.

At Calcutta I rented a room at the airport, where I could escape the airless, hot waiting room, and shower before my Bagdogra flight. But I was unable to resist the impulse to have one look at the ghoulish city. I engaged a cab to drive me to the Grand Hotel, where I remembered a good gift shop that had tiny porcelain elephants. I reasoned it would be worth the cab fare. It was. Calcutta had improved since 1971. It was still a spectacularly ugly city but seemed to have cleaned up its act somewhat. Though black smoke left a pall over the dingy buildings and ragged trees, I saw few bodies on the sidewalks, and almost no beggars. It was the hour when office workers and business people were going home, and the buses were packed inside and out with lethargic lean Indians, who seemed, however, somewhat better garbed than previously. Many wore shoes. Perhaps Indira's regime had accomplished this? I didn't know. But I was happy that there was a noticeable improvement. I found the gift shop, the tiny elephants, and a camel as well. Tucking these in my purse as gifts, I returned to my airport room, where I showered and rested until flight time.

At Bagdogra I found Bert Nevett beaming a welcome. He looked well and greeted me warmly. Then he turned me over to Father Tony Milledge, because he wanted to talk about a cricket match with one of the tea planters. Father Milledge was charming, as always, and invited me to come to his new mission station for tea. When all the formalities with my passport and luggage had been accomplished by Father Milledge, we three drove to the mission station in the Jesuit jeep. Father Milledge had just completed sixteen years at Bhimbar, where he built a school and beautiful new church. Now that it was finished and functioning, the Jesuits had transferred him to a raw mission, with directions to do it all over again. He seemed to thrive on challenge. His people are, once again, aboriginals, in need of everything from a school to a dispensary and chapel, so the next fifteen years will not be idle for him.

Bert and I climbed back into the jeep with my bags and began the ascent into the Himalayas. The scenery was beautiful, more wild than gentle Kodai. Mongolian faces reminded me of the tribal differences here. The air was crisp and cool, and I was happy I had put a sweater in my shoulder bag. As we bumped up the road, glimpses of the tiny train appeared, and the rubble from recent landslides everywhere gave evidence of the dangers of these mountains. The air got colder as we ascended. About three hours later, we were at the terrace below the Windamere Hotel in Darjeeling.

Rugged little Tibetan coolies slid my luggage to their heads and preceded us up the steep path. The hotel had reserved a little room for me. I had been assigned the same one before, in 1971, but had quickly changed to a larger one then. Now I was weary of changes and decided to keep it for the duration of my short stay. It was very small and cramped, but it would do. There were hot water and a bathtub, which seemed like rare luxury after my bathroom at Kodai.

The Windamere is one of the great hotels of India. It is small—only twenty-six rooms—which perhaps accounts for the good service and quiet atmosphere. It is situated high on a hill, and from its two terraces, on either side, can be seen some of the world's best scenery. On good days, while reclining on the terrace, sipping tea, Kanchenjunga, the queen peak, can be seen, lifting her white tent into the azure sky and inspiring prayer. Behind the hotel a little Buddhist temple hides amid towering pines, its fluttering prayer flags waving like God's laundry in the brisk breeze. Devout Tibetans climb up daily for prayer and almsgiving to the ragged beggars who line the steep pathway. The dining room of the Windamere is family style, presided over by Mr. and Mrs. Tendaf La, the owners. She wears the *bukkhu*, the Tibetan dress with the striped apron. Any visitor is quickly assimilated into the friendly hotel life. I met two young men from Seattle the first day, and we were friends from the start. Having been in Darj twice before, I was able to give them some tips on what to see there, and put them in touch with Father Richard Mac-Donald, S.J., of Hayden Hall, who has a reliable tourist agency called Summit Tours. Thus they arranged to trek to Sun Duk Phu, and visited the Mountaineering Institute. They were disappointed that the great Tenzing Norgay, Sir Edmund Hillary's guide in the conquest of Everest, was out of town; but they enjoyed their visit tremendously. An urbane and highly intelligent priest from America, Father George McLean, professor of philosophy at Catholic University in Washington, ate at my table and made for lively and delightful conversation daily during my stay. He had been studying Hindu philosophy in Madras for many months previously, and so we had experiences to share. Meals were thus pleasant and friendly. When the Seattle men and I in turn came down with the usual tourist complaint, we exchanged remedies, medicines, books and sympathy until we all recovered.

I knew Bert would be busy with his office work at St. Joseph's College, though he came to the hotel almost daily to visit with me and to work on the fund. As newly appointed cricket coach, he also had to give most of his free time to the team, and for several days was tied up completely. I found my way to the cricket field to watch the practice before the big match with the local planters, and confirmed what he had previously told me: cricket is a religion to the English and Indians, and a mystery to Americans. Having sat through a portion of one match, which began at 9 A.M. and at 6 P.M. was still not resolved, I knew what the mystery was: why anyone in his right mind would devote so much time to this endlessly boring activity. But Bert was intrigued with it. So were the Indian spectators, who sat on hard folding chairs in the Victorian viewing stand and shouted such approved accolades as "Good show" and "Well done" at appropriate intervals. Frequently the little red ball would disappear over the high fence and bound down two thousand feet into a wooded ravine, and the game would halt while someone climbed down to find it. In this way a great deal of free time was provided, during which philosophical commentary could be exchanged by players and spectators, and energies be renewed by short naps. I realized then that the object of cricket was not to complete the game, but to strive, with amazing patience and British fortitude, to prevent its completion. No wonder it's popular in India. For this is the ultimate rationale behind every activity in the subcontinent. Prolongation, not completion, is the name of the game.

Perhaps they have something, after all. It's not whether you win or lose, but how you play the game. Americans are geared for completion. In India, playing the game, or cutting wood, or buying a ticket, or shipping luggage, or purchasing a pound of cheese is geared not to the eventual conclusion but to finding new and more interesting ways to delay for as long as possible the final (and boring) outcome. The more time elapsed, the more complex and tortuous the game plan, the greater the laurels of the combatant. In a country that has nothing but time, it makes a crazy sense to invent ways of wasting, extending and providing time with a mask of activity, profitless though it be. When a task is completed, what will then take up the slack? How to distract the mind during the aching, long, boring hours ahead? The human mind craves something to chew on. Efficiency is thus the enemy. Why finish a task in half an hour when with the slightest ingenuity one can not only make it last for a day but involve fifteen or twenty people in it as well? Time is not money in India, it's monotony.

But India is a splendid country in which to relax. Things get done eventually, though it is far better to turn the gaze away from the process, to prevent strokes and high blood pressure. Sometimes the tourist learns patience. Cricket, which was invented in a more leisurely era of history, is greatly admired by Indians, who are, perhaps, the only race left on earth who have the time to wait for the game to be concluded. When Bert told me at 6 P.M. (I had long since left the field to rest in one of the college rooms), that the game had not been completed but would be continued the next day, I was no longer shocked or surprised. It was quite in keeping with every other function in this strange and fascinating land.

The snows of Darjeeling were hidden by mist and fog for the first four days, and in between visits to Hayden Hall and chats with my friends at the hotel, I managed to read six books from cover to cover. I investigated the eye clinic at Hayden Hall, where an Indian doctor had successfully removed sixty-one cataracts from the same number of patients during a marathon of free operations and where these patients were now bedded down on the floor of the Jesuits' auditorium,

with expert care provided by a staff of volunteers. I visited the Horti-
cultural Gardens with Bert, and sheltered in a little garden house
while the premonsoon pelted the flowers into the mud. I attended a
fine dinner party at St. Joseph's College and met delightful Father
Stanford again, whom I had last seen in Trivandrum in 1975. He is
now rector at St. Joseph's.

Bert said Mass just for me in a tiny chapel atop St. Joseph's College, and together we prayed for the success of our work and for the
intentions of all our members in America and Canada. We worked
out some procedures for the fund and discussed the more difficult
cases.

One such case, that of tiny Rupa and her impoverished family,
was particularly absorbing. Bert told me to go to the bazaar and
purchase some sweaters, hair ribbons, hair oil (!) and toothpaste for
the family. He was involved with cricket practice. The following day,
we went to visit Rupa's family. The hut they inhabited was below
the road, down about three hundred feet, and could be reached only
by means of narrow and difficult ledges of rock. I managed to make
it, though my hose were ripped in many places by the time I had
clambered down with the parcels and camera. Descending past many
huts where poor families were cramped, I had an opportunity to observe Bert with these children. All the ragged kids knew him and
came running out of the hovels to greet him. He was obviously a
highly valued visitor, who had the foresight to stash candy in his
pockets whenever he appeared among them. They played games to
ease the candy out of its hiding place, and then permitted us to
climb down still farther, through the litter of chickens and offal, to
Rupa's house. A small boy with the perennial running nose ran out
to climb up Bert's leg; I knew this must be the little brother. Rupa
was on crutches.

Some years before, when Bert first found Rupa crawling on the
road, he had arranged an operation in Calcutta so that with a leg
brace she could stand and learn to walk upright. Now the brace was
broken (probably on those rock ledges), and she would have to
return for another fitting. This was only one of the problems. The
thin, bedraggled mother was inside the house, a long and narrow
shelter of mismatched old boards shaped like a railway car and just
as dark inside. Only one small window gave any light to the dank

and rotting hovel, though one could see sky through the open places in the roof. The floor was dirt, and in one corner I could make out the pile of stones where she cooked their meager meals. A long narrow bed was the only furniture. A small baby played on the dirt floor. The mother looked sallow and tired but happy to see Bert. He had brought the weekly supply of rice and vegetables, along with our clothing purchases and some bags of popcorn for the kids. These they ravenously tore into, smiling and chattering as we sat on the bed to visit. Something bit my ankle so badly it was swollen for two weeks afterward. The camera was of little use; there wasn't enough light for photos. In halting voices, Rupa's mother and Bert exchanged information and news. I don't understand Nepali, but it was clear that she was in need of other things, and he was assuring her he would try to bring them next time. I was happy to leave. I'm not good with spiders, or whatever those crawling bugs were.

The climb up was even more difficult, and both my knees were bruised on a rock when Bert dragged me up across its sharp edge. We were very quiet on the walk back to the hotel. I was shocked by the condition of the family. We both agreed there was only one thing to do: try to move them out of there as quickly as possible. Bert had investigated, and found that new quarters for them would cost thirteen hundred dollars. I told him I would try to raise the money in America. The holes in that rotting roof would be no protection whatever when the monsoon began in earnest. Meantime, he planned to try to get Rupa to Calcutta to fit her with a new leg brace.

The cricket match was on again the morning I was to leave Darjeeling, so Bert could not come to see me off. I had the Tibetan coolies take my luggage down to the bus stop and load them aboard. I descended from the mountains again. The snows were beautiful. I had now come three times to Darjeeling. Something told me I would not return there again.

Bagdogra, Calcutta, Delhi, and then the flight home. New York was crisp and clean. The passage through customs presented no horrors. They didn't even open my luggage. I found the United flight to Chicago, and when I alighted from it, discovered my beautiful family all there waiting to greet me with loud cheers and fond kisses.

Oak Park, even lit by streetlights, was unbelievably clean, the wide lawns clipped and green, the homes spacious and neat, and the streets free of litter. My own home was more lovely than a palace. The two dogs were at the door, yapping a frantic welcome. It was like entering paradise.

CHAPTER 30

Home

June is lovely in the north woods. The winter had been fierce, according to my Wisconsin neighbors. But, in the fields around the cabin, daffodils, columbine and fuchsia were timidly dotting the green shadows under our pines. Birds sang in the birches, and their song floated over the sapphire-blue waters of Garth like a benediction. As I removed plastic covers and reconnected lamps, I thought about my Indian experience, and its meaning for my future.

Obviously, I had now to return to work and earn money. My real estate license had been reactivated, and the W. R. James Realtors firm, in Oak Park, was glad to have me come back, and so I entered a time of reorientation to a field I had always enjoyed. I attended several real estate institutes, to catch up on recent legislation and to hone my skills a bit before entering the market to list and to sell property.

Inspecting the houses of Oak Park and River Forest and measuring the spacious rooms, noting the efficient conveniences built into them by careful builders and thoughtful owners, I became once more skilled in the art of market evaluation of property. I learned again where to check on the amps and voltage entering the houses, where to find the value of the land, and how to draw up comparative studies of similar houses in the area. It was all absorbing and interesting, and this, and the business itself, kept me very busy for six months.

Prolonged reflection on my Indian experience proved very difficult. The phones, always efficient, rang constantly. TV, newly interesting after the three-month absence, began to project a materialistic and slightly annoying tendency to devote more ingenuity to the ads than to the programming. Despairing of the latest films, I found a movie theatre showing Indian films, and went several times, reveling in the scenes of train journeys and reliving the discomfort, the smells, the strange sights and towns, with what seemed like nostalgia. One of these films, about Akbar, the great Mogul ruler of the North, had been filmed in an impossibly ornate palace, with hundreds of gorgeously clad servants, luxurious settings and furnishings. During the intermission (there is always an intermission in Hindu films) I waited in the lobby along with the twelve or fourteen Indians who had gathered in the darkness with me to watch this epic. One of them, gathering courage, came over and said, "What do you think of this film, madam?"

"It's very interesting," I told him. "I'm enjoying it very much."

He smiled knowingly. "You are surprised to see how beautiful is India, aren't you?"

"It's only a film," I told him.

"A film done on the spot, madam. You can see the gorgeous palace, the wonderfully rich furnishings—the wealth and beauty of India."

"I have just come from India," I told him. His face dropped, in silent acknowledgment that the reality of India today had spoiled this dream spun by the filmmakers, which he was striving with all his lonely heart to believe. We chatted for a while about his town there, a pitiful little place I had visited, and then he rejoined his wife and friends.

Throughout a busy summer, I worked, phoning clients, driving prospective customers to possible homes, discussing financial arrangements, attending closings at title companies, and going to the post office to redeem parcels from India. Each time I opened one of these, containing cashmere shawls, or old brass lamps, a whiff of India reached my brain via my nose and called me back to that land of exquisite inefficiency and the beautiful, dream-walking people.

The words of Father Pedro Arrupe, superior general of the Jesuits, came back to haunt me: "Instead of feeling obliged to possess as many things as our friends, we should abstain from certain luxuries that have become necessities in our social circle and which the greatest part of humanity must do without. We must recognize 'enough is enough' and having more than this 'enough' poses a substantial question. This 'enough' must be measured not by our own social condition, nor by a social condition higher than ours, but by what we see among the real poor and the marginal people of our society and the Third World."

"Enough" for Regina had been a dark hovel, with clothing hanging on the walls, and a humble hearth where the cooking was done. The fireplace in her home was not the luxury we advertised in real estate, but the center of its warmth and meals. "Enough" for the men like Father Montaud, Father Clayton and Brother James meant an extra cassock, enough gas for an ancient motorbike, and a handful of rice and vegetables once or twice a day. "Enough" for Father Nevett was the bare high-ceilinged room where he dispensed the scholarships we provided and where he bundled into his coat and sweater to work at his desk in the winter months. "Enough" for the nuns at Presentation Convent meant a clean place to rest and a beautiful chapel for Mass each day and the rows of shining black heads to teach. All of these have the One Essential. All have Christ within them. They neither pine for, nor do they need, much else.

In Spokane, where Bishop Topel lives in a small four-room house, having sold the bishop's mansion, his cross and possessions and having given the proceeds to the poor, his "enough" consists of a ragged garden where he grows his own food and prepares it himself after a day of administration.

And so I wonder what is "enough" for me. At what point do I have "enough"? Where are my real treasures? Counting downwards, I find that my beloved children and grandchildren come first. After that, my friends. Then the health God blessed me with, and the capacity to dream. Finally, the house and its "things," the most valuable of which are two small dogs.

Calculating the time it takes to maintain my home, to say nothing of the cabin in the north woods, it is obvious that there is too much stuff to dust, store, maintain, repair and use. I can only sleep in one bedroom. Three are extraneous. The only reason to keep large stocks of silverware and china is to entertain the family at occasional dinners. There are eight chairs in my dining room, and four in my breakfast nook, and only one I. The living room contains a piano I do not play. The basement storerooms bulge with the memorabilia of thirty-six years, including shelves filled with appliances no longer in use, phonograph records no longer played, tennis rackets, bats, movie cameras, boxes of slides and films, and even, so help me, my

satin wedding gown and the beautiful veil and crown. These last
were kept for daughters' use, but as two married, they preferred their
own, and the youngest one will be gloriously too small to wear it.
Yet I keep it. There are two granddaughters who may one day consider using an ivory satin and lace gown, empire style, with a four-
foot train. The rest can go.

Autumn is here again. It is just one year since I began to plan my
sojourn in India. Once again I went to the cabin to tighten it up
against the coming wintry winds. And once again my heart turns to
that far-off, impossibly inconvenient land, so rich in mystery and
beauty and so poor in everything else. On the cabin porch, looking
out at the pines and graying sky, I found the time to ponder on the
years left to me. The soothsayer at Kulithalai said I would live until
eighty-three. I've had a look at the very old in nursing homes, and do
not cheerfully anticipate that age. The Chinese used to honor the
sage, who was old and wise.

Perhaps it was only that the sage was also a very rare bird. I have
known only about three people in my entire life in whom I glimpsed
a wisdom worthy of the name.

And it is obvious to me that my life has been neatly divided into
two parts: the early one, in which I married and had five happy children, and the present time, in which I have eight grandchildren and
a family thankfully independent and capable of making their way
in life without my constant supervision. In the first part I was
needed, and under contract. This time I am not needed, and free.
What shall I do with this freedom in the years left to me?

I have always known, yet (in the words of Phyllis McGinley) not
till now known that I have known, that life is given to us in order to
know God. He took on the personage of Christ to give us that
chance. And we find Christ today in His poor. Thousands of people
the world over realize this, and have cheerfully handed over their
youth, freedom, and will to the service of Christ. I, on the other
hand, have only taken from Him the immeasurable gifts He gave:
my children, my husband, the happy home, the good health, and the
yearning for heaven. Now, at last, I have the opportunity to share
what He gave with others.

Does this mean I must give up my family? I doubt it. Since He
gave them to me, I believe He will be more glorified if I retain this
relationship. What if I remain here six months out of the year, work-

ing, and seeing my beloved ones; and six months in India living among the poor, and sharing their life?

Certainly there must be places in India where a six-month volunteer would be useful. But the life there must be a sharing of the lot of the poor; not living in a fine house, with a servant. Charity dispensed at the doorway remains sterile. I must share the daily work and bread of the poor. There are countless poor convents where I might live with the nuns, sharing their toil and their rice. From the far North, in Nepal, to the southernmost tip of India, there are hundreds of poor convents where I might be useful. But I suspect that when my place is finally found, it will not be a convent. I am probably too independent now to try to live by a set of rules. They would be good for me, doubtless, but I would spend all my time trying to follow the rules, rather than getting down to the work of serving the poor.

I have thus commissioned one Jesuit friend, who is going to India soon, to try to find me a place where my half-year service might be useful. At fifty-eight, I still have some time to share, preferring by far to wear out rather than to rust.

I shall return to India with one suitcase. At Kodai I have a sleeping bag and a typewriter, and some kitchen pots. Please God, I'll find the place He is most neglected and unknown. And if it please Him, I'll find at least one small child and teach him of the love and the presence of Christ.